First Edition

POLITICS IN ACTION

CASES FROM THE FRONTLINES
OF AMERICAN GOVERNMENT

Gary Wasserman

Georgetown University

PEARSON

Boston   Columbus   Indianapolis   New York   San Francisco   Upper Saddle River
Amsterdam   Cape Town   Dubai   London   Madrid   Milan   Munich   Paris
Montreal   Toronto   Delhi   Mexico City   Sao Paulo   Sydney   Hong Kong
Seoul   Singapore   Taipei   Tokyo

Executive Editor: Reid Hester
Senior Marketing Manager: Lindsay Prudhomme
Project Coordination, Text Design, and Electronic Page Makeup: Abinaya Rajendran,
    Integra Software Services
Production Manager: Fran Russello
Cover Manager: Jayne Conte
Cover Designer: Suzanne Duda
Printer and Binder: King Printing Co., Inc.

Library of Congress Cataloging-in-Publication Data
Wasserman, Gary
    Politics in action : cases from the frontlines of American government/Gary Wasserman. — 1st ed.
    p. cm.
    ISBN-13: 978-0-205-21049-7 (alk. paper)
    ISBN-10: 0-205-21049-X (alk. paper)
    1. United States—Politics and government—1989——Case studies.   I. Title.
    JK275.W37 2012
    320.473—dc22

                                                                                    2011016890

3 4 5 6 7 8 9 10—V0CR—14 13 12

ISBN-13: 978-0-205-21049-7
ISBN-10:   0-205-21049-X

BRIEF CONTENTS

CONTENTS

Contrary to popular myth, America's founding fathers were pragmatic politicians. Chapter 1 chronicles how three founders—James Madison, Thomas Jefferson, and Alexander Hamilton—came to a historic agreement in the early days of the republic while dining at Jefferson's home. In exchange for Madison's support for having the new federal government assume all state debts, Hamilton agreed to allow the national capital to be built along the Potomac River, bordering Madison and Jefferson's home state of Virginia. The story is a powerful example of the North–South split in the early years of the United States, as well as the compromises which preserved the new republic.

The federal nature of the U.S. political system assures a struggle for power between national, state, and local governments. This tension is apparent in current education policy. While states and localities have traditionally taken the lead in education, the federal government has become a central player. This chapter focuses on the interaction between states and the national government from President Bush's 2001 No Child Left Behind Act to President Obama's "Race to the Top." It discusses the motives and impact of these initiatives as examples of coercive federalism, where the federal government offers money to states in exchange for reaching national goals—in this instance, reforming their education systems.

Affirmative action has long been a highly charged civil rights issue. Here the focus is on the attempts of the Supreme Court to find a balance in applying civil rights principles to conflicts among groups. In a pair of legal cases regarding the admissions policy at the

University of Michigan, the Court in landmark decisions ruled that race may be a factor in university admissions, but cannot be the *only* factor. The court issued several additional rulings in the years that followed—each time ruling against expanding affirmative action, yet retaining the principle. Mirroring the Court, President Obama has argued that affirmative action is useful, though only a partial answer to the country's divisions of race and class.

Chapter 4 CIVIL LIBERTIES—FREEDOM OF SPEECH ON CAMPUS: THE FIGHT OVER FIGHTING WORDS 42

Free speech is a treasured American value, embodied in the First Amendment. This right becomes complicated, however, when applied to speech that hurts others because of their race, gender, or sexual preference. Over the years, universities have limited speech through campus speech codes, as well as administrators' actions, justified as protecting students from discrimination. Defenders of free speech, including the courts, worry that university restrictions are vague and ultimately silence those engaged in legitimate political expression. The chapter chronicles the current controversy through real-life conflicts taken from American campuses.

Part II The Public 53

Chapter 5 PUBLIC OPINION—ABORTION AND THE PUBLIC: A SURPRISING STABILITY 54

Over the past several decades, no issue has dominated the culture war's "values" debate more than abortion. It caught fire with the 1973 Supreme Court ruling of *Roe v. Wade*, which legalized abortion nationwide. Since then public opinion has remained remarkably stable with a majority supporting legal abortion in limited circumstances. The chapter details intense groups on both sides framing the debate to win public support—whether by focusing on parental permission or the privacy of doctor–patient relations. This has ensured that it stays a volatile part of national political campaigns and Washington governing, most recently in health-care reform. Yet the American public remains balanced, moderate, and unchanged on the issue.

Chapter 6 CAMPAIGNS—HILLARY CLINTON AND SARAH PALIN: SEXISM IN THE 2008 PRESIDENTIAL RACE 66

The 2008 presidential campaign was historic in the roles played by two women. Hillary Clinton came closer than any female to capturing the nomination of a major party; Sarah Palin was only the second woman nominated for vice president. Though representing opposing parties and ideologies, they shared a political frame in which their qualifications for office were often skeptically viewed through their gender. Clinton, as part of an older generation of professional women was criticized for a lack of feminine empathy— a cold-hearted intellectual badly dressed in pantsuits. Palin was an underqualified naïf, overwhelmed by family responsibilities, and prone to showing more leg than brains. Both, in turn, used their gender in creatively different ways to market themselves to voters. That both lost leaves the question of whether women can succeed in running for the White House unanswered.

Through an in-depth interview with a congressional campaign manager, Chapter 7 highlights the realities of modern political elections—or how incumbents reduce the competitiveness of most congressional races. The manager frankly discusses the advantages of incumbency, the influence of the redistricting process, and the critical role of staff. He presents an insider's views of putting together a political campaign, including imperfect attempts to encourage voter participation. Finally, he explains the vices and virtues, for both citizens and candidates, of today's "normal" business of elections.

Political parties want to win elections. They are therefore interested in the tools of the trade that can help them. Each of the two major parties has adopted modern technologies to mobilize voters. Parties have long targeted voters with messages that they believe will generate support, as shown in a Republican campaign in 1980s Colorado. But in recent years, microtargeting has allowed campaigns to collect personal information about individuals— voting history, demographics, and consumer habits—and send them personal messages. A second example, the 2008 Obama campaign, features their microtargeting efforts and comments on its consequences for democracy.

The Clinton administration's campaign for health-care reform ironically demonstrated the successful influence and tactics of its adversaries: health-care interest groups. The industry spent millions of dollars to turn public opinion against reform. It followed a strategy of "going public" by running television ads (including the celebrity fictional couple Harry & Louise), organizing grassroots campaigns in key congressional districts, and aligning with the antigovernment message of the ascending Republican party. The interest groups' efforts worked as reformers lost control of the message and Congress lost its stomach for reform.

Early in 2010, President Obama signed a comprehensive health-care reform bill into law. He succeeded where the Clintons had failed. This chapter focuses on a key strategy toward interest groups that led to victory. Obama recognized early on that for reform to pass Congress, the health-care industry would need to be an ally, not an opponent. By first agreeing to deals with hospitals, drugmakers, and insurance companies, Obama crafted a bill that they accepted. Though the insurance industry and Obama ended up at odds, other interest groups signed on and ran ads supporting reform. Bringing these stakeholders into an issue network helped pass health care. It also may have produced a less comprehensive law with higher costs and lower popularity.

In his second term President Bill Clinton faced public scrutiny over an extramarital affair he had with a White House intern, Monica Lewinsky. This chapter dissects the media's involvement in the scandal. It touches on how the media used their power of "agenda-setting" and framed the revelation as an important issue of governing. The coverage reflected a media shaped by competition, the rise of inexpensive cable 24/7 news, Internet blogs, and the need to keep their audiences entertained with the news. The mainstream media got caught in a feeding frenzy of adversarial journalism that served the goals of White House opponents and raised questions about the role of a free press.

Policymaking requires representatives reaching agreements with each other on issues that affect the nation. But immediate interests intensely held by influential regional and industry groups often overwhelm long-term national goals, especially for elected policymakers depending on voters for their jobs. This "tragedy of the commons" emerges in Congress's compromises and ultimate rejection of climate change legislation in 2010. The House patched together "cap and trade" reforms to balance local economic interests with scientific evidence of global warming. But the more decentralized Senate reflecting weak party leadership and regional objections failed to follow even these modest steps. Climate

PREFACE

Like many political scientists, I got into the discipline because I thought politics was exciting and important. After working for a number of years in Washington, I returned to teaching hoping to communicate the excitement and importance of American politics to college students. There were frustrations.

With some exceptions my students didn't feel the same interest in the subject as their teacher. There were many reasons for this indifference, beyond the quality of the instruction. I wanted them to be familiar with the contemporary history that formed the setting and language of our class discussions; they needed cases with a point that could compete with the more entertaining distractions in their lives.

The fifteen cases that follow are a step in reengaging students. They present brief histories of important events in modern American politics and tie these events to the chapters of an introductory course. As snapshots of politicians and reporters, parties and bureaucracies, presidents and lobbyists, the cases allow teachers to extend textbook concepts. In short, these are stories of how the game of American politics is played.

GOALS OF THE TEXT

They have three objectives.

The first is to show contemporary politics in action; to offer students a revealing look at our country's political institutions and actors. Gender stereotypes provide obstacles for both Hillary Clinton and Sarah Palin in the 2008 election; President Obama avoids the fate of the Clinton health reforms by networking industry lobbyists into helping pass his reforms. A young campaign manager explains how his congressman plays the "redistricting racket" to ensure reelection to a 'safe seat'. On campus a loud debate tests the boundaries between free speech and harassment. And we look over the shoulders of the founding fathers as they sit down to dinner to reach a secret bargain to relocate the nation's capital.

The cases are organized to parallel the chapters in an introductory American government textbook, from the framers of the Constitution to civil liberties, from public opinion to media, from Congress to the judiciary. Yet the political actors in these cases cannot be contained in one chapter in a text, any more than they can be confined in real life. Their multiple appearances enrich these stories for teaching. For example, media appears in its designated chapter on the Lewinsky scandal (Chapter 11). But media puts in an appearance in other chapters as well: It figures into the campaign for health-care reform (Chapter 9), into the circulation of gender stereotypes during the 2008 presidential campaign (Chapter 6), and in uncovering the Watergate scandal (Chapter 15). Even media's absence in the reelection campaign of a House incumbent (Chapter 7) has something to teach.

The second goal is to illustrate political science concepts. These focus our thinking about the behavior of government institutions and political actors. The concepts help explain the cases. Most chapters have one major focus—groupthink in the bureaucracy behind the shuttle disasters (Chapter 14), or "going public" in examining interest groups' responses to President Clinton's health-care reform (Chapter 9), and the concept of "issue networks" in organizing President Obama's strategy for health reforms some years later. Many cases spill over conceptual confines to teach other lessons as well. One brief chapter on abortion (Chapter 5) touches on the social revolution of the sixties, the impact of the women's movement, pro- and antiabortion groups efforts to frame the issue, the two-way influence of government leaders and public opinion, and the rationality of popular opinion. Similarly overlapping themes of other chapters can be uncovered in class discussions.

The third goal is to bring American political history alive. Materials used in introductory classes often premise a background that many students don't have. Assuming that most know about the events surrounding Clinton's impeachment or Watergate or even the 9/11 attacks (when our students were in elementary school) is a mistake often discovered too late in a course. Modern history is the laboratory where political scientists observe, compare and collect information. Students may know something about these events; they seldom know enough. They also don't know the language of political practice with terms like "downsizing," "fighting words," "voter targeting," "leaks," "grassroots tactics," "sound bites," and "feeding frenzy." The cases show these phrases in their real-world settings.

ORGANIZATION

Divided into three sections, the fifteen case stories follow the order of an introductory American government course. The first section covers the foundations of American politics: the constitutional period, federalism, civil rights, and civil liberties. Next is the public, the groups and structures that link citizens with the policy process: public opinion, campaigns, elections, political parties, interest groups, and media. The final section is the institutions of the national government: Congress, the presidency, the bureaucracy, and the judiciary. The cases extend the general discussions of a textbook to the political activities of these institutions and groups.

In addition, there are organizational aids for students. An introduction at the beginning of each chapter briefly establishes a connection to the concepts discussed in class and frames the issues presented in the case study. A "Concepts to Consider" feature directly following the case introduction helps students read for the key ideas presented in the case.

ACKNOWLEDGMENTS

This is a collection written by the author but dependent on the work of others. The first is Elliott Fullmer who provided excellent research and valuable insights even as he finished his PhD at Georgetown. There are many scholars cited in the notes on whose original works these cases rest. I hope this volume pays adequate respect to them and motivates the reader to delve deeper into the subjects. The edition was written while I taught at Georgetown University's innovative School of Foreign Service in Doha, Qatar, and supported by a Faculty Research Grant. My colleagues helped with their valuable comments. An earlier edition of this work was written for Houghton Mifflin. After that distinguished press sold their textbook business, Cengage was professional and thoughtful in returning the copyright to the author. Reid Hester, Rona Tuccillo and Fran Russello at Pearson contributed advice and guidance. I would also like to thank Abinaya Rajendran and her team in Integra Software Services, for effectively turning drafts into a finished book.

Others who helped include my family, notably brother Ed, son Daniel, daughter Laura, and wife Ann, all of whom grounded me in the thinking of readers.

Any mistakes are mine, and despite this help.

Gary Wasserman
Doha, Qatar

For Ann

CREDITS

THE FOUNDATIONS

1 | THE CONSTITUTION

THE MEAL DEAL

The Bargain of 1790 That Established Washington, DC

Many Americans picture the founding fathers as a heavenly choir, harmonizing a constitutional hymn to the republic. Not quite. While both the breadth of their vision and the height of their accomplishments deserve our respect, a closer look reveals politicians going about the messy business of creating a nation.

These men are not diminished by being called politicians. They were practical people who were not about to loosen their grip on the daily tasks of governing, or pursuing their own interests, in a period of great change. Throughout the early years of the republic, these leaders had to both represent their regions and compromise to shape a lasting Union.

The story that follows embodies some of the conflicts, compromises, and personalities of the period immediately following the adoption of the U.S. Constitution. It tells the story of what a historian called "one of the most complex, fascinating, and controversial political deals in American history."[1] The Compromise of 1790 established the site of the nation's capital on the banks of the Potomac River while securing the financial stability of the new government. It was a trade done on behalf of conflicting regional and economic interests. Both sides gained, and the infant republic survived. So if we don't find angels singing on cue, then the drumbeat of a politician's victory march will have to do.

Much of what follows came from a dinner at Thomas Jefferson's house. Dining with him on that warm June night in 1790 were Alexander Hamilton and James Madison.

CONCEPTS TO CONSIDER _____

1. The **North–South regional conflict** looms over this bargain. Are there hints of irreconcilable differences between the regions that would later surface in a civil war? Was this a reasonable compromise, or was Jefferson correct in saying that his side had lost?
2. Often their **states' interests predominated** in these men's calculations. To what extent were the key figures representing their states' narrow interests, and to what extent were they speaking of their own conflicting visions for the new republic?

3. **International weakness and domestic turmoil** loomed as great threats to all the founders, encouraging them toward compromise. Which side in this conflict seems most threatened by the prospect of the Union dissolving? Is Hamilton a "nationalist," while Jefferson is for states' rights?

4. Much of what the framers accomplished could be described as **a marriage of interest and principle**. President Washington's lobbying to locate the capital near his lands on the Potomac River reveals the blend of ideals and self-interest that motivated him. At that time, did this reflect a conflict of interest between Washington's public role and his private wealth? Would it be seen differently today? Are all the parties violating their democratic principles by not having the compromise publicly debated?

According to Thomas Jefferson, he got involved in the issue through a chance encounter: He bumped into Alexander Hamilton on the street. Actually, Jefferson was waiting outside George Washington's presidential office on Broadway in New York City, where in June 1790 the Constitution's first administration was based. The two did not know each other well, even though Jefferson was secretary of state and Hamilton was secretary of the treasury.

Neither was in the best of spirits. Jefferson was just recovering from one of his frequent migraine headaches, this one lasting over a month. Hamilton, who was usually well dressed and confident, appeared disheveled and depressed. Jefferson described him as a beaten man—"somber, haggard, and dejected beyond comparison." Hamilton declared he was prepared to resign from the cabinet and feared the Union was coming apart.

What had upset Hamilton was the stalemate in Congress over whether the new government would take responsibility for state debts. This was a key part of Hamilton's grand plan to firmly establish the public credit of the United States as a reliable borrower among the nations of the world. It was being blocked by a group of southern congressmen led by James Madison, Jefferson's friend and protégé. Jefferson who claimed ignorance of the matter—having recently returned from his post as U.S. minister in Paris—offered to host a dinner at his house for the two rivals. It would be a private affair, where, over wine and good food, the three of them could have, in Jefferson's words, "a friendly discussion of the subject."

In writing his account of the evening two years later, Jefferson soft-pedaled what one historian called "the most meaningful dinner party in American history."[2] Probably held on Sunday, June 20, the meal deal would pave the way for Hamilton's centralizing financial plan and establish the seat of government (only to be more grandly referred to as "the nation's capital" in the mid-nineteenth century) that was sandwiched between two southern states. Jefferson brokered a political bargain that would mediate differences between state and national loyalties, between agrarian and urban interests, and between those wanting a feeble federal government and a strong one. The simmering North–South conflict would be deferred that night, only to surface again for resolution in future compromises and a later generation's civil war.

GUESS WHO'S COMING TO DINNER

Accounts of the day give a clear picture of the diners. Hamilton, thirty-five years old at the time, was an administrative and financial genius—bold, disciplined, and confident—determined to establish a strong central government supported by a ruling class based on industry and finance. He had the energy of his decisive convictions and a bulldog tendency to charge straight at an issue. In contrast to Jefferson's blue blood and inherited estate, Hamilton had been born in the West Indies, the illegitimate son in a broken home of an unsuccessful Scottish businessman and an independent-minded, frequently disgraced French woman. He had come to America poor. A compact figure at 5 feet 6 inches, with a crisp military bearing, he had risen to a position of equality among the wealthy, urban commercial classes he so ably represented.[3]

Madison was Hamilton's age but even shorter, described as "no bigger than half a piece of soap." He was frail in appearance, easily mistaken for a shy librarian. But his gentle manner was deceptive. It concealed a stealth that disarmed opponents with the simple brilliance of his thoughts. In the two years since he had collaborated with Hamilton on the *The Federalist Papers*, his nationalist loyalties had returned home to Virginia, which elected him to Congress. He now opposed Hamilton, speaking for the interests of his state's planter class, who feared a central government that would threaten their power, their rights, and their slaves.

Madison was Jefferson's loyal lieutenant, the detail man—a collaboration being renewed after Jefferson's five years in France. At forty-seven Jefferson was older than both Hamilton and Madison and, standing 6 feet 2 inches, reinforced his position as the senior member at dinner. He could not stand personal conflict and had been glad to miss the rough politics surrounding the adoption of the Constitution. He seemed happier reading the classics, usually in Greek and Latin, and avoided public debates. At the time of the dinner Jefferson was not widely known to have penned the Declaration of Independence. With untidy clothes and rambling sentences he looked the part of an absentminded professor.

The contrast with his rival Hamilton was unmistakable. Jefferson was the idealistic dreamer, an aristocrat who was ever hopeful of democracy's potential. Hamilton was a pessimist about human nature, putting his faith in a structured social order ruled by an elite of merit and money. Hamilton radiated intensity; Jefferson had a laid-back carelessness about him. Hamilton spoke for six hours in his initial "remarks" to the Constitutional Convention. John Adams reported that he couldn't recall Jefferson uttering more than two or three sentences, even in committee, when he was in the Continental Congress. On a personal level, "women found [Hamilton] irresistible, but they did not care much for Jefferson."[4]

WASHINGTON AND HIS CABINET.

Washington's first cabinet. From left to right: President Washington, Secretary of War Henry Knox, Secretary of the Treasury Alexander Hamilton (standing), Secretary of State Thomas Jefferson, and Attorney General Edmund Randolph.

Jefferson was a lukewarm supporter of the Constitution and had only reluctantly returned from Europe to join Washington's administration and the political infighting that both his guests had perfected. But Jefferson was well aware of the present danger challenging the fragile republic. In a letter to another future president, James Monroe, Jefferson wrote that he felt a compromise on debt payment was necessary "for the sake of union, and to save us from the greatest of all calamities, the total extinction of our credit in Europe." Jefferson warned, "If this plan of compromise does not take place, I fear one infinitely worse."[5] Indeed, what had led up to the dinner made his worries seem well-founded.

BACKGROUND TO THE COMPROMISE

The issue of paying off state debts, called assumption, was tying up Congress in knots. It had overwhelmed all other debates, including where to locate the new nation's capital. Hamilton asked Congress in January 1790 to refund at face value all the paper money and certificates that had been used to pay soldiers and suppliers during the Revolutionary War. For Hamilton, assuming

A young James Madison, described at the time as "no bigger than half a piece of soap."

the war debt of the states with new federal bonds paying interest was a blessing in disguise. It would cement the Union, revitalize the country's lagging economic growth, tie wealthy creditors' interests to the success of the Union, and enable the new republic to take its place in the ranks of nations honoring their war debts.

What seemed eminently fair on the surface, however, launched bitter opposition. Many soldiers who had been paid in seemingly worthless currency had over the years sold this paper to speculators at considerably less than face value. Now it would not be the veterans who profited from their military service but the speculators. Also, raising the fury of opponents were the stories that associates of Hamilton had leaked details of his plan before they were released to the public. They and congressmen from New England and New York promptly sent agents into the countryside, notably North Carolina, to buy up notes from the unknowing. At a quarter on the dollar, it was a dream scam for political insiders.[6]

Like most of the major controversies of these early years, this conflict rumbled along regional fault lines. Massachusetts held a large part of the debt, while Virginia's remaining debt was small. As the most populous state, Virginia would pay the heaviest taxes to fund this new national debt while already having paid off much of its own. Virginia led the fight against assumption, which quickly took on a North–South dimension—even though South Carolina held the largest per capita debt it opposed assumption. With one-fifth the nation's population, one-third its commerce, and an elite that felt it had practically won the Revolution alone, Virginia (where "all Geese are Swans," declared John Adams) was not about to surrender to a federal government run by northern financiers.

Southern representatives defeated Hamilton's proposal for assumption in the House. Madison's counterproposal to discriminate between original and present holders of the securities was dismissed by Hamilton as naive and unrealistic. (How could these multiple transactions ever be sorted out?) Hamilton responded that there would be no repayment of loans to Holland and France, whose money had been critical to winning the war. The new government could not pay its overseas creditors—or New York speculators for that matter. The stalemate over assumption caused Congress to grind to a halt. Would the Union survive?[7]

FIGHTING THEIR WAY TO THE CAPITAL

The fight over locating the new nation's capital had been simmering for as long as the debt issue. This generation of leaders had fought over the locations of county seats and state capitals, and they knew the practical benefits associated with capital cities. Property values near these sites would skyrocket, thus enriching large landowners. Access to government offices benefited the well placed in the form of legislation, contracts, and jobs. The entire local economy would get a boost from a government providing improved transportation and military protection.[8]

Questions of regional influence were never far below the surface. Power and prestige would come to the region closest to the capital. As usual the great North–South division loomed over the issue. The South, already sensitive to being a minority within the Union, felt it needed leverage to be heard in national forums on the divisive issue of slavery. The West, too, where the country's future expansion lay, wanted a voice in the decision. On the positive side, a capital properly located could knit together the competing regions and ensure the survival of the Union. The geography underlying this goal narrowed the possibilities to locations accessible to both the West and the Atlantic Ocean and near the country's center.

Alas, definitions of "center" varied. The North argued that it should be based on population and found that to be close to Philadelphia. The South made the point that territory was more important, insisting that the future westward growth of the Union should be taken into account. The South's argument was bolstered by the knowledge that the geographic midpoint between the northern and southern boundaries of the United States (northern Maine and southern Georgia) was on the Potomac River, near Georgetown. And with spiritual overtones, the spot pointed to was literally next door to the home of the nation's leading citizen, the first president of the United States and owner of Mount Vernon, Virginia.

By 1790, the political debate over the site of the new capital had narrowed. The great mid-coastal rivers and the cities on them competed to become the main avenue for economic development of the expanding American empire. In these pre-railroad years, major rivers were the interstate highways to the wealth of the interior—the Hudson ending in New York City's harbor, the Delaware River championed by Philadelphia, the Susquehanna emptying into Chesapeake Bay above Baltimore, or the Potomac linked to the Ohio River and promoted by Virginians. Although each side made the case in terms of the benefits to the new Union, all pushed their own interests. As one observer said at the time, "It...amuses me to see the arguments our grave politicians bring forward when I know it will be determined by local Interests."[9] The debate swirled among interests representing three cities: New York, where in 1790 Congress was meeting; Philadelphia, the traditional home of Congress during the Revolution; and the not-yet-built city on the Potomac.

Working behind the scenes to powerfully promote the Potomac location was George Washington. He envisioned the metropolis of America on the banks of the river, enriching his nation, his state, and himself.[10] A landowner and explorer of the region, Washington had long sought navigation improvements to the Potomac based on the misconception that it offered a direct link between the American interior and Chesapeake Bay. On leaving command of the army in 1783, he declared that only one public project interested him: opening up the Potomac above Georgetown. He became president of the Potomac Company, which aimed to do exactly that. As a young man, Washington had fallen victim to "Potomac Fever" and held on to this lifelong obsession for making the river the gateway to the future wealth of the West.

In Washington's era, political leaders saw little conflict between their public goals and their private interests. Mount Vernon's ten miles of Potomac River frontage, next to the federal district he selected, was only the beginning of Washington's lands. Of the other 60,000 acres he owned throughout the country, some two-thirds of it was along the Potomac–Ohio river system, which would benefit from improved navigation. When he asked Congress to expand the federal district to Alexandria—risking the greatest public criticism of his presidency—it meant including 1,200 acres of woodland he owned as well as his wife's family's 950-acre plantation that would later become Arlington National Cemetery.[11] Nor was the increased land wealth in the new capital a small matter. John Adams somewhat sourly thought Washington's choice of a capital had raised the value of his properties by 1,000 percent. Adams wasn't far off the mark. In October 1791, after the district had been selected, the price for a lot averaged around $265. A few years earlier, a good price for one acre containing eleven lots was $50—when you could sell them at all.[12]

Washington's motives were not only land speculation. Creating a federal city that would be the equal to any in Europe was a "key component" of his nationalist vision.[13] While masking his own role, he had worked with Jefferson and Madison for seven years to place the capital on the Potomac. Now the moment had arrived.

THE COMPROMISE OF 1790

The two great questions of funding the debt and fixing the seat of government have been agitated, as was natural, with a good deal of warmth as well as ability. . . . They were more in danger of having convulsed the government itself than any other points.

George Washington, August 10, 1790

The bargaining surrounding the compromise was a complex chess game. It involved a three-dimensional conflict of regional, economic, and national interests. The states alone represented a wide variety of concerns—wider than found in modern politics. An elected official from Virginia or Pennsylvania might be representing multiple interests that today would speak through lobbyists, trade associations, political parties, media, and government agencies. This less-specialized political system channeled the economic, political, and regional forces through a small number of leaders. This meant that a leader like Jefferson could be speaking for slaveholding plantations, rural debtors, small farmers, the state of Virginia, the entire southern region, or his own populist ideology.

The meal deal cut by Jefferson, Hamilton, and Madison during their June 20 dinner had several moving parts. One element was to locate the capital in Philadelphia for ten years. The Pennsylvanians thought that getting the temporary capital out of New York would be good enough, somewhat smugly concluding that no city would ever be built on the Potomac that could lure Congress away from the bright lights of Philadelphia. Their brief alliance with the Virginians was based on this miscalculation.

While the friends of New York wanted Congress to stay next to Wall Street, there was something closer to the bottom line, more dear to them than location. Many New Yorkers had a direct financial interest in the repayment of state debts, which they were owed. The Virginians, who were blocking assumption, were in a position to help. At the Jefferson dinner, Madison agreed that although he could not himself vote for the bitterly opposed assumption, he would stop organizing against it and "leave it to its fate." This was provided, of course, that Hamilton could offer assistance on that other issue of moving the capital. Jefferson put it this way.

> It was observed, I forget by which one of them, that as the pill would be a bitter one to Southern States, something should be done to soothe them, that the removal of the seat of Government to the Patowmac was a just measure, & would probably be a popular one with them and would be a proper one to follow assumption.[14]

IMPLEMENTING THE BARGAIN

Carrying out the compromise involved the sort of wheeling and dealing familiar to modern students of Congress. Madison secured votes for assumption from four congressmen whose districts either bordered on or had an interest in the Potomac. One was assured that if Georgetown was given the capital, his town of Alexandria would be included in the federal district. Two members of the Carroll family of Maryland who were serving in Congress signed on as supporters of assumption. Part of the price of their agreement was that all the public buildings in the capital would be restricted to the Maryland side of the Potomac. The Carroll family's holdings of tens of thousands of acres in the area of the future capital did not go unnoticed.

New England supporters of assumption kept their part of the bargain. They backed the core agreement for moving the temporary capital from New York to Philadelphia followed by the establishment of a permanent one on the Potomac. Hamilton cemented Virginia's agreement to assumption by reworking the numbers of its financial obligations. In the revised version, Virginia's assumed debt and its federal taxes owed turned out "rather miraculously" to be the same: $3.5 million. Assumption became a wash for Virginia. Adding in the rewards from locating the new capital on its northern border (estimated by Jefferson at half a million a year), Virginia came out the clear financial winner.[15]

Soon after the dinner, the House passed the seat of government bill on July 9. By July 16, 1790, President Washington had signed it. Within days, the funding bill, including assumption, passed the House. On July 21, it passed the Senate by one vote. The link between the two issues was kept secret but was widely suspected.

Both sides of the bargain had public opponents. Southern newspapers carried letters that called for dissolving the Union rather than accepting assumption. In Virginia, under the leadership of anti-federalists like Patrick Henry, the legislature adopted a resolution denouncing assumption as "fatal to the existence of American liberty." Hamilton, smelling the threat of secession, warned that this was "the first symptom of a spirit which must either be killed or will kill the constitution of the United States." Moving the capital in exchange for assumption was called a bribe by a New York editor "to the lasting disgrace of the majority in both houses." The first cartoon attacking a president of the United States accused Washington of signing the seat of government bill for "self-gratification." New England journals ridiculed placing the seat of empire on a creek on the "wild and savage" Potomac. Most in Congress doubted they would ever relocate to a "wigwam place" more suited for hunters and hermits.[16]

Like political deals, then and now, the focus now moved to whether it could be implemented. Washington's strategy, pursued by Jefferson and Madison, was to prevent the issue of the capital's location from ever coming before Congress again. This meant appropriating once, in 1790, all the money that would be needed to move the capital. The decisions about the size, location, and shape of the new federal city would rest solely with the president. Congress had in its bill authorized Washington to place the capital anywhere along 110 miles of the Potomac. To avoid returning to Congress for money, Washington negotiated with landholders to donate land for the capital that the government could then sell to raise funds for construction. Landholders would exchange parcels of land with the understanding that their remaining holdings would appreciate handsomely. Before finalizing the location, Washington encouraged offers all along the river, shrewdly getting rival bids to keep land prices low for the government.

His decision to locate the capital to the east of Georgetown was announced in January 1791. By March, Washington had negotiated Congress's approval for adding his hometown of Alexandria to the federal district, a controversy that brought down rare public criticism on the president. Jefferson urged that construction begin as soon as possible. This savvy tactic (often used by modern bureaucrats) aimed to physically commit the government to its existing policy and to undermine Philadelphia's hopes of extending its hold on the seat of government. By the time Washington retired to Mount Vernon in 1797, the only opposition to the 1800 move to the Potomac existed in Philadelphia. A large majority of Americans favored it. To refuse such a move would, an English visitor wrote at the time, destroy the harmony of the Union, if not the Union itself.[17]

AFTER DINNER

The three diners continued their distinguished careers, some with differing views of the evening's handiwork. Two years after the historic meal, Jefferson told Washington (for whom he may have been informally acting by holding the dinner) that the bargain was the greatest political mistake of his life. He believed Hamilton had "duped" him and that assumption had given eastern financial interests the power to control the government's finances. The location of the capital seemed of little importance by comparison. In terms of the Constitution, Jefferson saw, correctly as it turned out, that Congress's use of implied powers to enact Hamilton's plans paved the way for a federal government that would grow in power at the expense of the states.

The dinner marked a new flowering of Jefferson's collaboration with Madison. Their partnership propelled both to the presidency. Jefferson would assume that office because of the political organizing, the party building, and the strategies carried out by Madison. Madison was Jefferson's political Go-To Guy, the chief manager and operative who established the Republican-Democratic party and utterly destroyed the opposition Federalists. Madison's final act to save the 1790 Compromise came in 1814, when as president during the War of 1812 he fled the British burning of the Capitol and the White House. Afterward, pressure in Congress mounted for removing the capital from its precarious perch. Madison let it be known that he would veto such a measure. He reminded citizens of General Washington's commitment to the Potomac, and he labeled any move as a cowardly response to the English assault. When this crisis passed, the capital's site, despite several attempts to move it over the next half century, was largely secure.[18]

For Hamilton, assumption had been only one part of his plans for the nation's finances. As the nation's first secretary of the treasury, his goal was to shape a unified government to stand as the equal of the great powers of Europe. To do this he proposed a program of taxes, mostly on trade, the encouragement of manufacturing, and the creation of a national bank. Establishing the credit of the United States was essential for gaining the confidence of foreign and domestic lenders and allowing the government to borrow in the future. Hamilton's economic vision would become the financial base for the growth of a powerful federal government. Understandably, Hamilton's statue stands alone today at the entrance of the U.S. Treasury Department.

Hamilton's plans for a strong government ran directly into Jefferson's dream of a decentralized agrarian republic. As political enemies, their arguments defined the first decade of the Constitution. Washington's support for Hamilton's program led to Jefferson leaving the cabinet in 1792. Despite the depth of their rivalry, it was ironically Hamilton's respect for Jefferson that eventually led to the younger man's death. When the presidential election of 1800 was thrown into the House of Representatives because both Jefferson and his running mate, Aaron Burr, got the same number of electoral college votes—a constitutional oversight corrected by the Twelfth Amendment—it was up to the opposing Federalist party to decide who should be president. By strongly endorsing Jefferson as a man of character, Hamilton helped resolve the deadlock and gave Jefferson the presidency. This cemented Hamilton and Burr as implacable enemies, a bitterness that ended on the morning of July 11, 1804, with a duel between the two and the death of Alexander Hamilton.

Washington remained deeply attached to the "federal city" that was named after him in 1791. He devoted his energies to the details, including appointing the commissioners who would manage the district and personally resolving most of the crises that arose. He selected, worked with, and defended the young French-born planner P. Charles L'Enfant in mapping out the broad avenues and landscapes of the city. Political compromises were hardwired into the capital. The long distance between the White House and the Capitol building came from the need to reconcile competing groups of landowners by using land in each of their territories. Naming the central street that linked both branches of government, "Pennsylvania Avenue" was a gesture meant to appease opponents in Philadelphia. Even locating the public buildings in the flat river plains of the Potomac rather than the hills above Georgetown reflected the General's bow to republican principles rather than monarchical heights. Jefferson's refusal to bury Washington in his capital had similar motives.[19]

Curiously, both Washington and Jefferson got the nation's capital wrong: Washington misstated its importance; Jefferson understated it.

Washington was the rare American leader of that time who had never been to Europe. This reflected his core belief that America's future lay in the other direction, to the west. Yet, he was wrong that the main route to this expanding American empire was through a navigable Potomac. By 1828, ground was broken for a railroad from Baltimore into the Ohio Valley to link the mid-Atlantic with the interior. The completion of the Erie Canal in New York three years earlier had connected the upper Midwest to the coast, elevating the port of New York and further dimming the attraction of the Potomac route. The economic vitality of Washington, DC, would have to wait for another century. And even then, this prosperity would have little to do with access to the West and more to do with Hamilton's financial vision.

As the first president to serve his full term in the new capital, Jefferson helped realize his predecessor's dreams for the city. Yet, by viewing the Compromise of 1790 as a defeat, he seems to have understood the centralizing impact of Hamilton's financial measures but not that placing the capital on the Potomac achieved the opposite. Unlike the major capitals of Europe, from London to Rome, the economic and political centers of the new republic were separated from each other. The forces of decentralization, which sought to keep political power out of the hands of the moneymen while elevating the values of agrarian democracy, won a significant victory. The small new capital symbolized that this was not a grandiose government next door to, and presumably corrupted by, Wall Street. The isolation and size of the capital reflected the republican creed behind it. And in the coming century, when visitors asked for the location of the nation's capital—only to be informed that they were in the middle of it—that, too, was reassurance that this was not an overpowering central government that might strip away the rights and powers that the Constitution insisted were reserved to the states and the people.

Notes

1. Forrest McDonald, *Alexander Hamilton* (New York: W. W. Norton & Company, 1979), 181.
2. This account benefited from the very fine chapter "The Dinner," from Joseph J. Ellis, *Founding Brothers* (New York: Vintage Books, 2000).
3. See Ron Chernow, *Alexander Hamilton* (New York: The Penguin Press, 2004).
4. Samuel Eliot Morison and Henry Steele Commager, *The Growth of the American Republic* 1 (New York: Oxford University Press, 1962), 332.
5. McDonald, 184.
6. Bob Arnebeck, *Through a Fiery Trial, Building Washington, 1790–1800* (New York: Madison Books, 1991), 20–24.

7. See Charlene Bangs Bickford and Kenneth R. Bowling, *Birth of the Nation: The First Federal Congress, 1789–1791* (Washington, DC: The First Federal Congress Project, 1989), Chapter IX, "Funding the Revolutionary War Debt."

8. For a comprehensive and lively treatment of the debates over locating the capital, see Kenneth R. Bowling, *The Creation of Washington, DC: The Idea and Location of the American Capital* (Fairfax, VA: George Mason University Press, 1991), Introduction.

9. Ellis, 70.

10. James Thomas Flexner, *Washington: The Indispensable Man* (Boston: Little, Brown and Company, 1974), 237.

11. Bowling, *The Creation of Washington, DC*, 110–111.

12. Bob Arnebeck, "Tracking the Speculators," *Washington History* 3, no. 1 (Spring/Summer 1991): 113–125.

13. C. M. Harris, "Washington's Gamble, L'Enfant's Dream: Politics, Design and the Founding of the National Capital," *William & Mary Quarterly*, 3rd Series, LVI, no. 3 (July 1999): 527.

14. Ellis, 49.

15. Ibid., 73–74.

16. Ibid., 76–77; Bowling, *The Creation of Washington, DC*, 201.

17. Bowling, *The Creation of Washington, DC*, 233.

18. Ulysses S. Grant was the president who firmly established the national capital's permanence. See Kenneth R. Bowling, "From 'Federal Town' to 'National Capital,' " *Washington History* 14, no. 1 (Spring/Summer 2002): 8–25.

19. Bowling, *The Creation of Washington, DC*, 224.

2 | FEDERALISM

THE POLITICS OF EDUCATIONAL FEDERALISM
A Race to Washington

When it came to accepting federalism, the framers of the Constitution didn't have much choice. Some division of powers between the central and state governments was a given. In the framers' view, the decentralized confederation of states hadn't worked out very well, and it would have been politically unthinkable to ignore the states they represented to form a unified government. What emerged was a distribution of responsibilities, with those for the federal government written into the Constitution and the far more numerous ones remaining with the states, as stated clearly in the Tenth Amendment.

Federalism has evolved quite a bit from the vision of the framers. In the last fifty years, Congress and the president have attempted to accomplish national goals through creative uses of the federal system. What evolved has been called **cooperative federalism**, in which the federal government provided funds to the states for accomplishing policies set by Congress. In these supportive relations, Washington, although reluctant to directly command the states, used the money as a carrot (some called it a bribe) to meet national standards or fulfill policy goals. The states, for their part, maneuvered to get the national funds without having to follow the restraints found in federal rules, formulas, or grant proposals.[1]

More recently, the federal government has increased activities that have a centralizing impact on the federal system. Setting national priorities and then putting money behind them have aimed at forcing changes in state and local policies. Whether these are direct orders imposed on state and local governments or indirect actions that resulted in higher costs on localities, they reflected a more insistent role by the federal government. These measures have been called **coercive federalism**. Such policies reflected a widespread public and political consensus that important national objectives were not being accomplished in the blurry set of relations undertaken in the federal framework. Nowhere was this more true than in public education.[2]

Education has been traditionally overseen and funded on the local level with support from the states. The federal government has gotten increasingly involved in schools since Lyndon Johnson's "War on Poverty" programs of the 1960s. The 2002 No Child Left Behind law marked a significant change in federal involvement by setting standards for regular testing and qualified teachers in every classroom. The Race to the Top program begun in 2009 continued to strengthen Washington's role. The Race set up a competitive grant program where states that demonstrated a commitment to reform, including evaluating teachers based on student test results, could be awarded federal money.

The failure of past efforts to improve public education had led to this increased federal role. Whether current programs would work, would adapt to regional differences, and would overcome state and local resistance remained debatable. In short, federalism remained alive and well, and central to whether No Child Left Behind and Race to the Top actually improved America's public schools.

CONCEPTS TO CONSIDER _____

1. Federalism sets the boundaries of a **struggle for power** among national, state, and local governments. This case of education reform spotlights the history of the politics between the different levels of government. What advantages does each side have in influencing education policies? How do state and local officials limit federal involvement in education?

2. **Cooperative federalism** is the use of funds by the federal government to encourage (rather than command) states and localities to pursue national goals. How has the federal government used its money to gain state and local agreement for education changes in the past and present? Considering that it contributes less than 10 percent of education monies, how successful has the federal government been?

3. Despite referring to recent reforms as **coercive federalism**, the blurred lines between the various levels of government—federal, state, and local—remained. In both passing and implementing Race to the Top and No Child Left Behind, issues like test standards and teaching accountability were interpreted differently in various public school systems. Note the examples of these differences and argue whether they are obstacles to reform or necessary local adaptations. Are they inevitable in any national program?

4. The argument for **local control over education** has both history and educational arguments behind it. How would you make the case that less federal involvement and more community input would improve public education? Who makes this argument in the battleground of federalism, and why? Is federal involvement incomplete: setting out requirements for the states without providing enough money to cover the costs of the programs?

Secretary of Education Arne Duncan was speaking about how badly America was doing in educating its young.

> One-quarter of U.S high school students drop out or fail to graduate on time. Almost 1 million students leave our schools for the streets each year . . . 75 percent of young Americans, between the ages of 17 to 24, are unable to enlist in the military today because they have failed to graduate from high school, have a criminal record or are physically unfit. . . .We've got to be much more ambitious. We've got to be disruptive. You can't keep doing the same stuff and expect different results.[3]

The Secretary was not only criticizing public education, he was also justifying the Obama administration's Race to the Top competitive grant program. When Congress passed the $787 billion economic stimulus in 2009, the administration had set aside $4.35 billion to be distributed on the basis of merit rather than the usual automatic formulas—where most federal education money continued to go. "Merit" for the administration meant a commitment to reform, such as paying teachers based on their ability to raise student achievement, or establishing high-quality charter schools or developing plans for turning around failing schools. States would be awarded grants as they demonstrated a commitment to reform. Some thirty states changed their education policies in hopes of winning federal grants.

In this first round twelve states won grants. More importantly, the federal government had pressured states into reform before actually spending any of the money. States had adopted reforms including evaluating teachers based on student test performance, and simplifying their systems for firing ineffective teachers. One of Obama's education advisors declared, "It's been one of the most important seasons for education reform in American history."[4]

This reform was the latest effort by the federal government to speak to a central dilemma of American education: a country that spends more per pupil than any other has a student performance that ranks in the bottom third of developed nations. Recent education reforms had shifted the focus of federal aid from the lack of resources to the lack of accountability. This insistence by Washington on testing, on academic standards, and on holding teachers responsible for test results had been key to the No Child Left Behind legislation passed under George W. Bush in 2002. Both Obama's "Race" and Bush's "No Child" were federal government attempts to overcome the shortcomings in America's locally run public schools.

Yet at the beginning of the twenty-first century, there remained widespread signs of failure in K–12 schooling (kindergarten through twelfth grade). Despite a national average of $8,000 per child spent annually, two-thirds of fourth graders could not read at grade level, while 88 percent of African American students and 85 percent of Hispanic students could not read proficiently. Even where the money seemed adequate, the results did not match up. In Congress's backyard, Washington, DC, spent more than

$13,000 per child but consistently ranked among the lowest in national scores in student achievement.

The federal government remained a secondary player in public education, compared to state and local governments. Even after considerable increases in spending, Washington was providing less than 10 percent of funding: aid of some $47 billion for school systems that spent some $580 billion a year. The federal portion of education spending had more than tripled since 1970, but reading and math scores had remained flat. This inability to improve education resulted in popular pressure for greater involvement of the federal government. And yet there was hesitation; lurking behind the scenes was the historically unsteady embrace of federalism and education.

A PRIMER ON FEDERALISM AND EDUCATION

A reporter's visit in 2010 to a single building in the Harlem neighborhood of New York City illustrates the argument that the quality of teachers and principals can make a difference in students' education. On one side of the building, separated by a fire door is an independently run public charter school for elementary students; on the other side is a regular public school, pre-K to 8th grade—same building, same-size classes, same community, sometimes even the same parents.

On the charter side, the children are quiet, dressed in uniform and hard at work for a longer school day. They are typically performing at or above grade level, with their progress regularly tracked and teachers held accountable. The teachers work more hours than in public schools, are paid better, and must be available for parent consultations and after-hour group meetings. With reduced pensions and fringe benefits the charter's per-student costs are lower than in the public school.

On the public school side, the reporter found a hundred children at 9:00 a.m. watching a video in an auditorium, with others wandering the halls. Teachers were not obligated to receive phone calls from students or parents at home. Nor were they required to attend after-school meetings. If they did, they got extra pay. The reporter found that while 51 percent of the third-grade students were reading at grade level, 49 percent were below, and none were reading above. The charter school's third graders showed 72 percent were at grade, 5 percent were below, and 23 percent were above.

In conclusion, the reporter quoted an education researcher: "The effect of increases in teacher quality swamps the impact of any other educational investment, such as reductions in class size."[5]

Issues of federalism—primarily the powers of state and local authorities versus those of the federal government—have surfaced throughout the national government's involvement in education. Five decades of Washington's expansion into this arena led to President Obama's proposed reforms, building on efforts dating back to Democratic President Lyndon Johnson and continuing through the No Child Left Behind law crafted by Republican George W. Bush.

Under President Lyndon Johnson, the 1965 Elementary and Secondary Education Act appropriated $2 billion to the states to improve education for the poor. This first major step in Washington's support for education was narrowly targeted to disadvantaged students, and focused on adding resources to schools in neglected areas. There were few federal requirements or standards in the programs. This assistance to the states continued and increased over the next fifteen years. But control of public education remained, as it had since the nation's beginnings, in the hands of state and local governments.

Then, in 1980, Republican Ronald Reagan took office opposed to Washington's role in education. Federal funding for education declined by 21 percent in the first five years of his administration. More positively, this conservative administration found that the education system was producing mediocre results and that higher academic standards needed to be established. But this was left to the states. The result was that the states began implementing a variety of reforms that defined a core curriculum and the basic knowledge that students were expected to achieve at certain grade levels, called standards-based accountability. Some states also saw this as an unfunded mandate, with the federal government urging standards without providing the resources for achieving them.

Both of Reagan's successors, George H. W. Bush and Bill Clinton, provided federal funding to support state and local standards. The first President Bush set national education goals for the year 2000, including raising the high school graduation rate to 90 percent, requiring students to demonstrate competency in core disciplines, and making U.S. students the first in the world in science and math. President Clinton built on these policies wanting the federal government

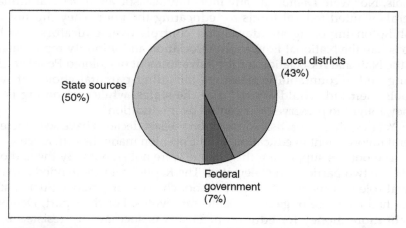

FIGURE 2.1   Education Spending: Federal, State, and Local Governments

to approve or reject states' standards. Republicans, who took over Congress in 1994, strongly opposed this increased federal role. Clinton later dropped it.[6]

Despite this setback for federal oversight, the 1994 reauthorization of the Elementary and Secondary Education Act established standards-based reform and holding the states accountable. The idea of "adequate yearly progress" was adopted, requiring the states to make progress toward goals of academic achievement for all students. However, neither deadlines nor penalties were put in place. Federal grants underlined this cooperative federalism by helping the states develop their own standards and tests. The 1994 reauthorization was important in developing standards and tests in most states. Equally important was that seven years later, only one-third of the states were complying with its requirements. This slow response would frustrate Washington political leaders and lead to the bipartisan consensus behind No Child Left Behind.

THE POLITICS OF EDUCATIONAL FEDERALISM

These reforms reflected the growth of federal responsibility for education. While the bulk of the funding and the daily administration of schools remain with state and local governments, policy for public education has been nationalized. In the last two decades, a political consensus has emerged supporting increased federal direction of education. What is curious about this national consensus is that it took place despite strong opposition from both Republicans and Democrats.[7]

Republican conservatives have traditionally fought federal involvement in education. Under Ronald Reagan, this reached the point of seeking to abolish the Department of Education. States' rights advocates, joining religious and antigovernment conservatives, from the Christian Coalition to the Heritage Foundation, bitterly resented the feds expanding into local schools. Nor were Democrats any more enthusiastic about federal influence. Liberals wanted federal funds for educating the poor. They did not want Washington imposing standards and controls over educators. Teachers' unions like the National Education Association and minority representatives like the National Association for the Advancement of Colored People resisted testing and accountability measures including parental choice of which schools their kids could attend. And the states, while welcoming federal money, fought to preserve their control over education.

Yet despite this partisan opposition the last decades have seen increased federal involvement in education. Public opinion made the difference.

The politics supporting this change were not smooth. By the end of the 1980s, the two parties had stalemated. The Republicans demanded a reduced federal role and increased private school choices for parents. Such a stance never had a chance of gaining Democratic votes. For their part, Democrats sought more money for education. This was successfully resisted by the GOP's philosophical objections and their squeeze on federal spending. George H. W. Bush's attempt to be "the education president" in 1990 meant switching the focus from inputs (funding) to outputs (achievement). It failed as both sides opposed this attempt at moderate reform. President Clinton expanded on these policies by seeking to increase federal funding *and* accountability. These efforts suffered defeat at the hands of a conservative backlash when Republicans took over Congress in 1994.

Despite these failures, Republican and Democratic presidents were responding to popular pressure. The view spread that schools were in decline. Voters increasingly declared improving education to be one of their highest priorities. Politicians reacted by giving speeches on the issue when campaigning and paying attention to it when they took office. The debate between the two parties by the end of the 1990s was no longer whether there should be a federal role, but what kind of role it should be. In this search for public support, the leaders of both parties were willing to ignore key supporters. As one scholar concluded, "In each case, party leaders opted to go against powerful but narrow constituent groups in the pursuit of political gain among the broader electorate."[8]

George W. Bush's embrace of No Child Left Behind after his 2000 election illustrates this evolution. Public opinion polls showed that education was the top issue that voters wanted addressed and, further, they saw increased government funding as the way to improve education.[9] Bush understood that his Republican party was badly positioned on education, pushing for unpopular cuts in spending while Democrats advocated more funds for schools. Running as a "compassionate conservative," Bush had expressed sympathy for minority students trapped by "the soft bigotry of low expectations." His support for a strong federal role put him at odds with conservative Republicans. His business model of reform with tests and standards was an attempt to reach party moderates. Bush's political flexibility was shown in the very title of the legislation, taken from the liberal Children's Defense Fund, whose mission was "to leave no child behind."[10]

GEORGE W. BUSH LEAVES A FEW CHILDREN BEHIND

Kodiak Island in the Gulf of Alaska serves nearly 3,000 students most of whom are Alaska Natives and Pacific Islanders. Many are English language learners, making it difficult for Kodiak to meet annual yearly progress levels in English and math as called for in No Child Left Behind. The harshness and loneliness of long winters makes it hard for the rural district to keep qualified teachers—sometimes the turnover is 50 percent a year. This leaves the schools depending on paraprofessionals most of whom do not meet the NCLB definition of "highly qualified." A typical village school may have one teacher and a paraprofessional teaching twenty students in all twelve grades. How can one teacher meet standards for every subject he or she is teaching?

The Alaskan environment undermines solutions. Instructors trying to upgrade their skills often can't do it in the short summer when they hunt for deer and fish to feed their families during the winter. The economic downturn has caused state budget cuts and hindered efforts to develop an Internet learning program. Even the NCLB provisions that require offering students another choice when their local school fails to meet standards is difficult to carry out in Alaska. Students cannot just be put on a bus to another school. In Kodiak they have to be flown by plane.[11]

In 2001, the new Republican president announced that education would be his number one domestic priority. Beyond the partisan calculations, there was George W. Bush's experience as governor of Texas where he supported annual testing and state ratings of schools. Borrowing from Clinton administration education plans, Bush introduced a thirty-page general blueprint for reform. Learning from Clinton's massive, and unsuccessful, 1993 health-care reform bill, the GOP White House tried not to get bogged down in details. It didn't quite work out.

Federalism played a role in passing the bill on Capitol Hill. The states, represented by their governors, wanted restraints on the federal government. They pressured the White House to weaken the bill's requirement that states must make adequate yearly progress in teaching various groups of students. The fear was that many of their schools would be identified as failing, and penalized for that. They also tried to weaken the tests. In one compromise favorable to the states, school districts were allowed to average test results over three years and penalties for states with low test scores were eliminated.

"Accountability" was the vague term unifying support in Congress for No Child Left Behind. For Democrats, it justified increased spending for education. For Republicans, it echoed a businesslike approach to investments in education. For the states, "accountability" wasn't all bad. It meant "no national tests" and no binding enforcement by the federal government. There were no penalties for states not achieving adequate yearly progress. Each state could define student achievement through its own tests, leaving open the real possibility that the states could then lower standards. The blurred responsibility in the law left the fate of reform in different local, state, and federal hands.[12]

And yet NCLB marked an unprecedented expansion of federal authority over the 50 states, 15,000 school districts, and their 80,000 public schools. It established some federal accountability, requiring states to develop standards in reading and math, and then testing students on those standards. The law required states to raise the qualifications for new teachers and certify the qualifications of current ones in the subjects they taught. The reform pushed more testing and more concentration on basics such as reading and math. If they qualified, lower-income school districts would receive additional federal funding.

Whatever the lure of more federal dollars, anxiety was a common response among education officials across the country. The actual consequences of these muddy political compromises would be determined by how they were implemented.[13]

IMPLEMENTATION

Despite the bipartisan backing that NCLB enjoyed when signed into law in 2002, it soon lost that support. By 2007, when it was supposed to be reauthorized, it couldn't gain enough momentum in either party, in either house, to pass Congress. The law was generally praised for exposing the wide gaps between white students and minorities, and for identifying low-performing schools. But the law was criticized for harming the education the schools actually provided. Because it provided no federal standards at each grade level for what students should be learning, the states could "dumb down" their tests to meet the law's requirements. As Obama's Secretary of Education Arne Duncan said, "The biggest problem with NCLB is that it doesn't encourage high learning standards."[14]

The law tried to square the circle of federalism. It imposed strict exam requirements, unrealistic goals of 100 percent "proficient" by 2014 and then harsh penalties for schools not reaching these goals. Yet the law only required states to set "challenging academic standards" to receive federal money for poor students. In a bow to federalism, the law let each state define "challenging." Not surprisingly given the penalties attached to poor test results, many states set the bar too low. At the same time, the schools weren't given enough federal resources for the support needed to raise students to any common standard. As a result, rarely were students actually prepared for college or careers, no matter what the tests said.

States and localities found ways to get around the requirements. In Baltimore some 30,000 students were in failing schools, but only 194 slots were opened for transfers. Michigan, with relatively high standards, had the highest number of failing schools, more than 1,500. Arkansas, with very weak standards, had none. Michigan's response to its embarrassment was to lower standards.[15] Holding states accountable was not the same as equipping schools with the tools to improve.

OBAMA'S RACE TO THE TOP

When Michelle Rhee took over as head of the Washington, DC, school system in 2007, it was the most dysfunctional school district in the nation, despite receiving the most funding per pupil. Only 8 percent of eighth graders were at grade level in math, and only 9 percent of ninth graders could be expected to finish high school and college. At the same time, 95 percent of the teachers were rated as excellent, and no teachers were fired for ineffectiveness in 2006. Declaring that the children could not afford gradual change, the thirty-seven-year-old reformer swiftly shut down underperforming schools, and fired unproductive teachers and principals. Her major proposal was to tie teacher pay to student performance. Flying in the teeth of teachers' union opposition, she wanted to get rid of tenure for teachers in exchange for more generous pay. Rather than have mediocre teachers paid mediocre salaries, she envisioned excellent teachers rewarded with excellent pay.

Rhee had success, for a while. Student test scores rose and the teacher's union signed a contract incorporating many of Rhee's reforms. DC schools won $75 million of Race to the Top money in 2010. The achievement gap between white and black students closed from 70 percent to 50 percent, a difference between the races that Rhee declared was still unacceptable. In the fall of 2010, she terminated 241 teachers for poor performance. Shortly afterward, the mayor who had appointed her was defeated for reelection. Having lost her political backer and support in much of Washington's black community, Rhee resigned.[16]

During his campaign, President Obama had supported the goals of No Child Left Behind but criticized its lack of funding and flexibility for the states, both popular positions. He called the law "one of the emptiest slogans in the history of American politics." His administration's Race to the Top contest came to be seen as "a dry run" for the next version of NCLB. This meant making future educational money conditional on school districts' taking action to improve schools. Rather than having the money sent out based on formulas, such as the district's population of poor children, states would have to take the pledge to reform before they got the money. This focused attention on the 30,000 schools that NCLB had labeled as "in need of improvement," which meant they were failing. Little had been done to change them. Now the question was whether competition could be used to either close these failing schools or reward schools that were overcoming achievement gaps.[17]

What mattered most in the Race to the Top was good teachers. This meant making teachers accountable for what their students learned each year as demonstrated by exams. The political sticking point to holding teachers responsible has been the power of their unions. The 4.6 million members of the two national unions were important supporters of the Democratic party, supplying it with volunteers, tens of millions of campaign dollars, and 10 percent of the delegates to the 2008 Democratic National Convention. Their organizing over the years had elevated a poorly paid profession and helped negotiate contracts that protected teachers from dismissal. These contracts now stood in the way, reformers claimed, of rewarding competent teachers, and removing incompetent ones. For example, most of the states had signed labor agreements with their teachers that called for any layoffs caused by budget reductions to take place on the basis of seniority: that is, the newest teachers would be removed first, no matter how effective they were. The results were an educational system that wasn't educating. As Michelle Rhee, the reform Washington schools' superintendent, said, "When I came here all the [teachers] were fine; they all had satisfactory ratings. But only 8 percent of eighth graders were on grade level for math. How's that for an accountable system that puts the children first?"[18]

Once again a political party ignored a key interest group; this time Democrat Obama overruled objections by the teachers' unions. The multi billion dollar economic stimulus package passed by Congress in 2009 offered, in

Education Secretary Duncan's words, "the chance of a lifetime" to change this. Some of the billions in federal aid that flowed to states according to population formulas could now be based on Race-like competitions designed to encourage reform. And the federal contest seemed to work. Reformers in over 30 states passed legislation in hopes of getting some of the money. The feds money motivated states to embrace reform. Washington was energizing—or coercing—states and local communities.

For example, Colorado passed a law aimed at increasing the state's chances in the grant competition. It required school principals to evaluate teachers' classroom effectiveness each year; half of their overall rating was tied to student achievement. Tenured teachers performing poorly for two years in a row could be fired. The two Colorado teachers' unions split over the bill with one opposing it and one negotiating amendments that led to their endorsing the bill. Most Democrats in the state legislature voted against the reform.

In order to avoid the political favoritism which had shaped federal educational funds in the past, the judges of the applications for Race to the Top were independent educational experts with no political involvement. Five reviewers read each state's proposal and the average of the five scores was the final grade. The problem was that a number of states including Rhode Island, Louisiana, and Massachusetts passed reform legislation in an effort to gain federal funds—and then didn't get them. Colorado which hoped to get $377 million ended up out of the money. This led the governor to criticize the anonymous evaluators. "It was like the Olympic Games, and we were an American skater with a Soviet judge from the 1980s."

Whether Washington could gain the needed leverage over public education that under federalism remained a local and state responsibility was as uncertain under Obama as it had been under past administrations. The feds were still "a bit player" when it came to financing education. Between 1970 and 2004, per-pupil education spending more than doubled, and the federal portion of that spending nearly tripled. And yet reading scores on national standardized test have remained flat. There continued to be a wide gap between black and Hispanic students and whites in the same grade. Could these new approaches from the federal government make a difference?

EDUCATIONAL FEDERALISM: NO EASY WAY AHEAD

Adapting reasonable federal standards to local circumstances remains a problem. The New York Times *reported in 2010 that a popular and effective principal of an elementary school in Burlington, Vermont, was being removed. Joyce Irvine's school had very low test scores and in order for the district to qualify for $3 million in federal money the district was faced with some uncomfortable choices. They could close down; they could be replaced by a charter (Vermont doesn't have charter schools); or they could remove the principal and transform the school. It didn't* *matter that Ms. Irvine had developed a new arts curriculum, created partnerships with local theater groups, rented vans for teachers to visit other schools, and attracted an influx of students to her school. Her firing was the least disruptive option.*

The problem of bad test scores, however, didn't rest with the principal. Burlington was a major resettlement area for African refugees whose children were expected to take the standardized tests, even if they had just arrived. Which is more or less what happened when 28 students from Africa entered the school system in September; they took a standardized test in October. One Somali student struggled through a passage on Neil Armstrong landing his Eagle spacecraft on the moon. When asked whether the passage was fact or fiction, the student responded that no man could go on the back of an eagle to the moon. He missed the five follow-up questions.

Despite Principal Irvine's 80-hour workweeks, her innovative programs, and the warm comments of parents and positive evaluations by her superiors, she lost her job. Burlington's school superintendent concluded, "What's happened to her is not at all connected to reality."[19]

Nine times nine is the same in any state.

Paul O'Neill

The federal government's modern role in public education began with a concern for those in greatest need. Federal dollars became "leadership dollars," with the goal of reforming education by closing the achievement gap between students of different races and developing programs based on scientific research. Although less than a dime for every dollar spent on K–12 education, federal money became a vital ingredient in motivating change in the system.

The incentives in a federal system work against the hopes of national education reformers. Determining whether students are learning and how well teachers are teaching is hard enough. But when independent layers of political control are added to the mix, the problems multiply. The Obama administration insists it will not bow to political pressure in handing out funds to states. Educational standards will determine which states are most likely to succeed, and which will get more funds. Yet states with poor reform records continue to lobby for making exceptions from the tests of No Child Left Behind and the contests of Race to the Top. Would they succeed? Would other federal needs, like reducing the deficit, squash these attempts at local reforms? These were not just education questions, but political challenges as well.

Federalism has historically allowed local dominance in public education. It has not provided a coherent system of high standards, regular assessments of students and teachers, and accountability to the citizens paying the bills. Local control has been an effective rallying cry to limit changes to America's public schools. Whether it has produced world-quality education for the nation is another question entirely.

Notes

1. Martin Grodzins called cooperative federalism a "marble cake" because of its overlapping local, state, and federal involvements unlike the divisions in a layer cake. Morton Grodzins, "The Federal System," *Goals for Americans* (Englewood Cliffs, NJ: Prentice-Hall, 1960).

2. For a brief description of coercive federalism, see Paul Posner, "The Politics of Coercive Federalism in the Bush Era," in David T. Canon, et al., ed. *The Enduring Debate*, 5th ed. (New York: W.W. Norton & Company, 2008), 108–117.

3. As quoted by Thomas Friedman, "Teaching for America," *The New York Times*, November 20, 2010.

4. Sam Dillon, "States Create Flood of Education Bills," *The New York Times*, May 31, 2010.

5. Steven Brill, "The Teachers' Unions' Last Stand," *The New York Times Magazine*, May 17, 2010.

6. Christopher T. Cross, *Political Education* (New York: Teachers College Press, 2004). Also see "History of the Federal Role in Education," www.educationnext.org

7. This discussion owes much to the fine study by Patrick J. McGuinn, *No Child Left Behind and the Transformation of Federal Education Policy, 1965–2005* (Lawrence, KS: University of Kansas Press, 2006).

8. McQuinn, 208.

9. Kathleen Frankovic and Monika McDermott, "Public Opinion in the 2000 Election: The Ambivalent Electorate," in Gerald M. Pomper, ed. *The Election of 2000* (New York: Chatham House, 2001), 77.

10. For a conservative critique of President Bush's educational reforms, see Neal P. McCluskey, *Feds in the Classroom* (Lanham, MD: Rowman & Littlefield, 2007).

11. Center on Education Policy, *Case Studies of Local Implementation of the No Child Left Behind Act* (Alaska: Kodiak Island Borough School District, October 7, 2003). See the center's website: www.cep-dc.org

12. Brian Friel, "Damage Control for 'No Child Left Behind,' " *National Journal*, June 5, 2004, 1786.

13. Andrew Rudalevige, "The Politics of No Child Left Behind," in Paul E. Peterson and Martin R. West, eds. *No Child Left Behind? The Politics and Practice of Accountability* (Washington, DC: The Brookings Institution Press, 2004).

14. Zach Miners, "The Challenge to Find a New Standard," *U.S. News & World Report*, January 2010.

15. McCluskey, 89–90.

16. Lauren Smith, "Reformer Ruffles Feathers in D.C.," *U.S. News & World Report*, January 2010.

17. Sam Dillon, "Obama to Seek Sweeping Change in 'No Child' Law," *The New York Times*, February 1, 2010.

18. From Brill, "The Teachers' Union."

19. Michael Winerip, "A Highly Regarded Principal. Wounded by Government's Good Intentions," *The New York Times*, July 19, 2010.

3 | CIVIL RIGHTS

AFFIRMATIVE ACTION

The University Admissions Debate and Beyond

One of the easiest arguments to start in American politics is over affirmative action. These civil rights programs are designed to compensate for past discrimination and encourage future diversity. Although sometimes applied to various ethnic groups and women, they originally focused on the rights of black Americans. The programs' goals are to overcome injustices, but they often cause resentment between those favored and those left out.

The institutions of government, while seldom neutral, attempt to maintain a balance among these competing claims. The courts are at the forefront in interpreting and applying policies in this arena of civil rights. They do so within the framework of the Constitution, relevant laws, and their own previous decisions. (And, as often noted, the justices read not only the Constitution but the newspaper as well.) The courts' historical record of reaching compromises without inciting violence among these conflicting "politics of rights" is a tribute both to the judges and to the groups' understanding that even the most cherished rights cannot be absolute.

In the cases covering admission to the college and law school of the University of Michigan, the Supreme Court and other policymakers struggled to find a balance. The two Michigan cases involved similar lawsuits filed by rejected white applicants. In one, *Gratz v. Bollinger,* the Court was asked to judge an admissions policy at the college that awarded bonus points for race. In the other, *Grutter v. Bollinger,* the Court reviewed the law school admissions policy that considered race in promoting educational diversity. The Court had to determine whether race-conscious admission was a constitutional way to promote diversity and whether the Michigan programs were a limited means to do it. Since the Court's landmark decisions, political views and practices prevailing in the country have evolved. Universities have shied away from explicit affirmative action policies, while government and business have more readily embraced them. And just as race is not likely to disappear from the nation's political landscape, neither are programs speaking to the issue or the arguments about them.

CONCEPTS TO CONSIDER _____

1. **Equal opportunity versus equal outcome** sums up the conflicting positions toward affirmative action. The first stresses the historic tradition that individuals should be given the same chance to get ahead, whereas the second seeks some share of benefits for a disadvantaged group. Does equality of outcome mean restricting the free competition—in hiring, for example—that lies behind equality of opportunity? Should some people be treated differently _now_—say, in admissions—to be treated equally in the future—for example, in grades?
2. Those objecting to the Michigan program contend that it results in **reverse discrimination**: that members of the majority do not get the same benefits—in this case admission to the university—that minority students do. Were the two women bringing the case the victims of reverse discrimination? Were they also harmed by university policies favoring athletes and children of alumni?
3. **Preference policies** began as temporary measures, and one justice voiced the hope that affirmative action would not be needed in twenty-five years. These programs, however, have inevitably included formerly unprotected groups (such as women and people with disabilities) and encouraged politicians to expand the benefits. Do these policies promote group privileges and divisions? Can they be expected to disappear as prejudice declines?
4. The Court's decisions are examples of **judicial activism** that vigorously shape government policies over conflicted civil rights. Notice how the justices acted as policymakers, balancing objections to the programs while stressing the gains for society from affirmative action. Show how the Court acted as a politically sensitive representative body, rather than simply judges interpreting the law?
5. The debate remains whether **unofficial affirmative action** policies aim to help the targeted minorities or to enhance the reputation of the institution using them. Are such quiet programs now undertaken in many universities likely to be tolerated by the public or the courts? Will they work better than the past programs? Why do government and business appear to be more favorable toward affirmative action?

MAKING THE CASE

60 Minutes correspondent Ed Bradley was interviewing a young blonde woman about how affirmative action had changed her life. Jennifer Gratz, who had brought a suit against the University of Michigan, described growing up in a Detroit suburb with dreams of attending college in Ann Arbor. She had a 3.8 grade point average, scored in the top 20 percent on her SATs, was a National Honor Society member, vice president of the student council, and a

Jennifer Gratz (l) and Barbara Grutter (r), the two plaintiffs in the University of Michigan affirmative action cases

senior citizen helper. "But," concluded Bradley, "for the University of Michigan, it wasn't enough. She was rejected." Gratz told of her reaction to the news.

> I remember the day like it was yesterday. I came home from practice, cheerleading practice, and grabbed the mail. And it was a thin envelope. And then I opened it, and I-I—I read probably the first three lines at that point and started crying. . . .

Gratz blamed affirmative action. A university spokesman denied that these policies led to her rejection, pointing out that many factors figured into every decision. Admissions awarded applicants points for various criteria. For example, a perfect GPA got 80 points, an alumni parent was worth 4 points, athletes were given 20 points, an outstanding essay merited 1, and being a minority was 20. A skeptical Bradley asked, "Is being a minority twenty times more important than writing an outstanding essay?"

Later in the show, Bradley talked with Tom Turner, a black student who grew up in poverty and had a difficult home life but managed to graduate high school with a mediocre record.

I was a mid-C student at best. But the fact of the matter is, that since I've arrived at the University of Michigan, I've done far better than my GPA or my SAT scores would have implied. . . . I'm a 3.9, Phi Beta Kappa, honor student in American culture now. Nobody could have possibly predicted that based on my high school scores or anything that came from high school.[1]

When asked about Gratz, Turner agreed that the process had not been fair to her.

60 Minutes reported that the Center for Individual Rights had brought Gratz's suit against the undergraduate college as well as a parallel lawsuit for Barbara Grutter, who was rejected by the law school. CIR charged the university with violating both women's rights to equal treatment by giving unlawful preference to minorities in admissions. Funded by conservative foundations, CIR was a public interest law firm assisted by lawyers from established private firms who donated their services pro bono (at no charge). CIR had won significant victories against affirmative action in California and Washington State. In selecting attractive test cases, the center had not just stumbled upon Gratz by chance, as this account from the *Washington Post* makes clear.

When the group decided to sue, staffers pored over resumes and biographies of about 100 potential plaintiffs, information sent to them by sympathetic state legislators in Michigan. . . . The group's search for a camera-ready lead plaintiff ended when Gratz, a blonde homecoming queen from a blue-collar family, walked in the door. She had stellar grades, no apparent political leanings, and good looks to boot. CIR staffers tipped off the New York *Times* about her suit, and soon a long line of print and television journalists formed.[2]

Both *Gratz v. Bollinger* and *Grutter v. Bollinger* gave the Supreme Court an opportunity to deliver landmark decisions on affirmative action.

AFFIRMATIVE ACTION: THE DEBATE

The seeds of affirmative action lay in the civil rights movement of the 1950s and the 1960s. The argument is heard that affirmative action reflects a change in the goals of the early movement—from equalizing opportunity by removing discrimination to overcoming the consequences of discrimination by using compensating remedies. A simpler way to say it might be *equal opportunities versus equal results*. But as early as 1965, President Lyndon Johnson directed government agencies to hire minorities and minority-run companies. These efforts to correct racial inequities spread to private employment and college admissions, and they were pushed by the government, including Republicans in the 1970s like Richard Nixon. Soon they also applied to women and disadvantaged ethnic groups not originally identified as benefiting from the programs. Quotas were used to guarantee these groups access to business, employment, and universities.

The rise of conservatives to national power in the 1980s accelerated opposition to affirmative action. Republicans took advantage of popular dissent toward the programs to shape a "wedge issue" that would divide black and white Democrats. Demands for a "color-blind society" were heard, often from the same voices that objected to this goal of equality when segregation was the law of the land. The political system, from state and local referendums to federal agency and court decisions, steadily chipped away at affirmative action. In response, advocates revamped the programs, following President Clinton's advice in his notable 1995 speech on the subject, "Mend It, Don't End It."[3] The debate, however, was far from ending.

On the pro side, supporters of affirmative action argue that programs are needed because simply removing barriers to advancement is not enough to help victims of historic discrimination. Equality in the law is a false promise for people who are unequal in education, income, and opportunities. Preference in hiring and education is needed until these groups achieve equality with the majority. Although opponents of affirmative action often quote Martin Luther King—"I have a dream that my four little children will one day live in a nation where they will not be judged by the color of their skin but by the content of their character"—King also said the following.

> It is impossible to create a formula for the future which does not take into account that our society has been doing something special against the Negro for hundreds of years. How then can he be absorbed into the mainstream of American life if we do not do something special for him now, in order to balance the equation and equip him to compete on a just and equal basis?[4]

In addition to a remedy for discrimination, there is another argument stressing diversity. We are a multiracial society, and our institutions, if they are to function effectively, must reflect that. Tolerance and a sense of community come from working, learning, and serving together. Minorities in leadership positions not only provide role models for others in these disadvantaged groups but also give the institutions a credibility they otherwise wouldn't have. As one dean at UCLA's law school said, "Do you think in this day and age we would be justified—legally or morally—if we had the only public law school in the country without any black students?"[5]

On the con side, critics charge that the programs violate a basic American principle: that people should be judged as individuals and not as members of a group. Whether it was discrimination *for* whites 100 years ago, or discrimination *for* blacks today, both policies look at race rather than individual talent. The argument that the law must be color conscious today so it may be color blind tomorrow suffers from the same flaw as foreign political leaders who "suspend" their constitution in order to "build" a stronger

Protestors outside the Supreme Court building with signs regarding the University of Michigan affirmative action case.

democracy. In fact, the opposite happens: Affirmative action inevitably promotes racial categories rather than diminishing them.[6]

Critics argue that these programs fail in practice as well as in theory. Their benefits inevitably go to those most able to take advantage of them. In higher education, this means the main beneficiaries are middle-class people of color, not the poor. Even those benefiting find themselves stigmatized as being incapable of "making it" on the basis of individual worth. By attempting to remedy past wrongs, the programs discriminate against those not belonging to the favored groups, increasing interracial tensions. Each side seeks selfish advantages in a game where one group's gain is another's loss. According to President Reagan's assistant attorney general for civil rights, William Bradford Reynolds, "What had started as a journey to reach the ideal of color blindness deteriorated into a nasty squabble among vying racial groups, each making stronger and stronger claims for its share of the affirmative action pie, not by reason of merit but solely on the grounds of racial or ethnic entitlement."[7]

Public opinion listened to the debate and showed both ambiguity and decreasing support for affirmative action. Two polls taken in 2003 illustrate the ambiguous part. A poll for the Pew Research Center showed support for affirmative action programs stood at 63 to 29 percent. That same year, Gallup took a poll showing that 69 percent of those asked thought that merit alone should be considered in college admissions. Part of the problem of polling on affirmative action is that responses often depend on how the question is framed. For example when speaking of minorities, if the phrase "preferential treatment" was used, opinion turned negative. Nonetheless, a chilling in attitudes toward these programs seems evident. A 2009 poll from Quinnipiac University reported that affirmative action is opposed by 61 to 33 percent, despite support from black and Hispanic voters.[8]

LEGAL PRINCIPLES AT MICHIGAN

> Scarcely any political question arises in the United States that is not resolved sooner or later into a judicial question.
>
> *Alexis de Tocqueville*

Given the disputes set off by affirmative action, it is no surprise that the courts soon got involved. In dealing with the issue of race in higher education, judges looked to the Constitution, specifically the Equal Protection Clause of the Fourteenth Amendment. It provides that "no state shall . . . deny to any person within its jurisdiction the equal protection of the laws." Ratified in 1868, three years after the Civil War ended, the Fourteenth Amendment's purpose was to protect newly freed slaves from southern governments. Since then, the principles underlying the amendment have taken on broader significance. For example, the Equal Protection Clause served as the legal foundation for desegregating public schools.

Equal protection is triggered when the government (including public universities) classifies individuals by race. The Court first evaluates the purposes of the classifications made by the law or regulation. In the case of race, the Court applies the highest, most skeptical level of review, which is called "strict scrutiny." Under strict scrutiny, the Court allows racial classifications only if they pass two criteria: (1) they are narrowly tailored, and (2) they further compelling government interests. Thus, race-conscious admissions programs that group applicants by race are subject to strict scrutiny. Although the Court will not automatically invalidate these racial classifications, any higher-education admissions must pass through the screens of being narrowly tailored and are needed to achieve a compelling interest. In the two cases before the Court, diversity in Michigan's student body had to be shown to be a sufficiently compelling interest. Would the university's policies fit?

The Court had its own precedents to follow in weighing the programs. Chief among them was the 1978 case *Regents of the University of California v. Allan Bakke*. Here, a state's medical school had rejected a white student at the same time it had reserved 16 of the 100 places in its entering class for members of minority groups. In its 5 to 4 decision, the Court rejected this system of admissions as a quota and ordered Bakke admitted. But the majority opinion written by Justice Lewis Powell endorsed the goal of student diversity in higher education as a compelling government interest. Powell's opinion in *Bakke* had kept affirmative action alive. Now, a generation later, the issue was whether the Court would prohibit or allow the continued widespread use of race in admissions.

Gratz and Grutter filed their lawsuits late in 1997, challenging race-based admissions. Both charged that preferences for black, Hispanic, and Native American applicants violated the Equal Protection Clause of the Fourteenth Amendment. For several years, the cases bounced around the federal court system—district courts as well as courts of appeal. In March 2001, a federal district court struck down the law school's race-based admissions system, finding that a diverse student body was *not* a compelling governmental interest. Further, the policy was not narrowly tailored to serve that interest because it was "indistinguishable from a straight quota system." The university appealed, and the Sixth Circuit Appeals Court agreed to hear both cases.

A deeply divided Sixth Circuit reversed the district judge's decision in May 2002. A 5 to 4 majority found that the law school's race-based admissions program *was* narrowly tailored to further a compelling governmental interest in diversity. No decision was issued in Gratz. The women's attorneys appealed, and in December 2002 the Supreme Court agreed to hear both Grutter and Gratz. The Court heard oral arguments in the two University of Michigan cases on April 1, 2003.

THE SUPREME COURT LISTENS

Outside groups made sure they were heard. A record number of briefs signed by organizations and individuals were filed: seventy-eight in support of affirmative action and nineteen opposed. Their significance went beyond mere numbers. An astute observer of the Court (Linda Greenhouse, reporter for *The New York Times*) noted, "What is most striking is the range and sheer weight of the establishment voices on the affirmative action side." This "establishment" meant the nation's leading law schools, including the alma maters of every member of the Court, dozens of Fortune 500 companies such as General Motors and Microsoft, and professional associations, including the American Bar Association. Unexpectedly important were twenty-one retired generals and admirals, including three former military academy superintendents. Their conclusion, mentioned later by several justices, stated, "At present, the military cannot achieve an officer corps that is both highly qualified and racially diverse" without affirmative action. That an integrated officer corps was deemed essential to national security could not be dismissed lightly in post-9/11 America.[9]

In their presentations both sides followed their well-honed arguments. The plaintiffs, Gratz and Grutter, challenged the university's affirmative action policy as unlawfully discriminating against them by taking race into account as a "plus" factor in admissions. The university maintained that the Constitution allowed it to use race and ethnicity to achieve the educational benefits of a diverse student body. Diversity was the "compelling governmental interest" justifying the use of racial categories in admissions. Then the justices began firing questions at the lawyers.

Justice Ruth Bader Ginsburg asked the university's opponents if the race preference programs at the military academies were illegal. The lawyer for the plaintiffs dodged: "We haven't examined that. . . . " Questioning the other side, Justice Antonin Scalia complained that Michigan had brought the problem on itself by creating an elite law school. They could achieve diversity by making the state school less "exclusive." "Why have a super-duper law school?" asked the justice, a graduate of Harvard Law School. The university's attorney replied, "I don't think there's anything in this court's cases that suggests that the law school has to make an election between academic excellence and racial diversity." Justice Sandra Day O'Connor, expected to be the crucial swing vote, asked the womens' counsel whether he was saying that race "can't be a factor at all." His response: "Race itself should not be a factor among others in choosing students, because of the Constitution." O'Connor's objection hinted at the decision that lay ahead: "You are speaking in absolutes, and it isn't quite that."[10]

THE COURT DECIDES

On June 23, 2003, the U.S. Supreme Court ruled on the cases. It permitted the law school's admissions challenged by Grutter, but ruled against the undergraduate system in the *Gratz* suit. In both cases, the Court found that diversity was a compelling interest in higher education that could justify race as a plus factor in admissions. The Court felt it should give some deference to universities when they made educational decisions on the benefits from diversity. In Grutter, the Court approved of the individualized review used by the law school in admissions, finding it was narrowly tailored to achieve diversity. Race could be one of several factors in evaluating each applicant. The law school's use of admissions to produce a critical mass of underrepresented minority students did not change a flexible program into a rigid quota. The vote by the Court was 5 to 4, with Justice O'Connor writing the Grutter opinion.

Michigan's undergraduate admissions did not do so well. In *Gratz* (a 6 to 3 decision, with Justice O'Connor again in the majority), Chief Justice Rehnquist held that the automatic distribution of twenty points to students from minority groups was not narrowly tailored. By not considering other individual merits in awarding the points, the system made race decisive for "virtually every minimally qualified underrepresented minority applicant." This had to change. Despite the administrative difficulties, admissions should provide an individualized review of what each applicant might contribute to the diversity of the entering class, including factors other than race. All candidates should compete against the entire pool, not just against members of the same race. Any system should impose the smallest possible burden on nonminority students.[11]

In its opinions, the Court provided a blueprint for considering race without violating the Constitution's guarantee of equal protection. The key issue was whether the programs were narrowly tailored: The college's twenty-point formula wasn't; the individualized law school process was. Flexibility was a theme in the Court's decisions. Both opinions indicated that race *can* be a factor, not that it *must* be. Programs that prohibited the use of race in states like California and Washington were allowed to continue.

The emotions and the divisions within the Court were strikingly captured by Justices Sandra Day O'Connor and Clarence Thomas. Writing for the majority in the *Grutter* case, Justice O'Connor saw a broad national consensus in favor of affirmative action in higher education. Clearly influenced by the many briefs from the country's leading institutions, she concluded that affirmative action's benefits were real, not theoretical, and were still needed in business, the military, and universities. The Court's job was reactive: to reflect and support this political consensus behind building a more equal society.

Justice Thomas's dissent was more personal. He criticized affirmative action as a "cruel farce of racial discrimination." The Court's lone African American justice and an accomplished graduate of Yale Law School, Thomas accused Michigan's law school of tantalizing unprepared students with the promise of a degree. Only later would they discover that they could not succeed against the competition. "The majority of blacks are admitted to the law school because of discrimination, and because of this policy all are tarred as undeserving." Who can tell who belongs and who does not? The question itself, Thomas concluded, stigmatizes black students as "otherwise unqualified."[12]

AFFIRMATIVE ACTION AFTER MICHIGAN

The initial reaction to the Court's decision was a sigh of relief from the civil rights communities that a conservative court had provided universities with a "green light" to pursue diversity. But in the years that followed programs to promote diversity have seen their public support diminish. The supposed gains from affirmative action programs have become a lot less clear. And this uncertainty has been reflected in the actions of national political leaders, the courts, and grassroots citizens groups.

The first beneficiary of these programs to sit in the White House sent mixed signals on affirmative action. When he was a candidate, Barack Obama emphasized helping disadvantaged people of all races. An ABC news reporter asked him whether his own daughters should benefit from affirmative action in college admissions and he replied that no, that they were pretty advantaged and that white students who had grown up in poverty would be a better target for such programs. Obama said that these programs were "not a long-term solution to the problems of race in America, because, frankly, if you've got 50 percent of African American or Latino kids dropping out of high school, it doesn't really matter what you do in terms of affirmative action. Those kids are not getting into college."[13]

Emphasizing class-based affirmative action was good politics for Obama. White voters were ambivalent about programs that directly favored minorities. But efforts that helped Americans from "low income brackets" to "get ahead" received overwhelming support in polls. As the nation's first black president, Obama operated under considerable constraints in dealing with race. Whether it was the controversy over his minister, Jeremiah Wright, or the arrest of a black Harvard professor by Boston police that he tried to mediate, Obama has recognized his vulnerability when issues of race arise, as illustrated by his ambivalent endorsement of affirmative action: "It hasn't been as potent a force for racial progress as advocates will claim and it hasn't been as bad on white students seeking admissions or seeking a job as its critics say."[14]

An increasingly conservative Supreme Court was more eager to whittle away at affirmative action. With John Roberts taking over as chief justice in 2005, the Court has been reluctant to approve programs aimed at promoting racial balance. In a 2007 case, the Court ruled that Seattle public schools had acted unconstitutionally by denying transfers of students that unbalanced black–white ratios in the classroom. (One of the cases was filed by a mother whose son was denied a transfer to another kindergarten because the school he wanted to leave needed its white students in order to stay within the program's racial guidelines.) Writing for a 5-4 majority the chief justice said such programs were aimed only at racial balance, a goal forbidden by the Fourteenth Amendment's guarantee of equal protection. In an oft-quoted line, Roberts declared, "The way to stop discrimination on the basis of race is to stop discriminating on the basis of race."[15]

In 2009, the Supreme Court restricted how far employers could go in considering race in hiring and promotion decisions. In the case of *Ricci v. DeStefano*, the Court ruled for white firefighters in New Haven, Connecticut, who said city officials had violated their rights by discarding the results of a promotion test on which few minorities did well. This case of "reverse discrimination" did not mean that race couldn't be considered in the makeup of workforces. It did mean that the results of a fair test equally applied couldn't be thrown out solely because they had an unequal impact on members of one group.

In a surprise to some who thought the president was moving away from affirmative action, the Obama administration in 2010 asked a federal appeals court to uphold a race-conscious admissions system at the University of Texas. The university was being sued by two white students who were rejected for admission. The university had a two-prong admission system. Three-quarters of their freshmen were admitted because they ranked in the top 10 percent of their graduating class. The rest were accepted through a "holistic" evaluation that included their family background, socioeconomic status, and racial or ethnic identity. This seemed to follow the guidelines from the Michigan case but that didn't stop the white students charging they had been discriminated against. While the lower courts and the Obama administration supported the Texas program, most observers thought the case would end up before the Supreme Court where the conservative majority was likely to reject Texas' race-specific program.[16]

Within the states, support for affirmative action eroded even faster. Following the University of Michigan decisions by the Court, the citizens there passed the "Michigan Civil Rights Initiative" amending their constitution to prohibit state agencies and institutions from operating affirmative action programs or granting preferences based on race, color, ethnicity, or gender. Jennifer Gratz, the plaintiff in the college case had graduated from Michigan's satellite campus in Dearborn, and went on to become executive director of the initiative. Winning 58 percent of the vote, it became law in December 2006.

California and Washington had passed similar laws a decade before. Florida banned affirmative action by an executive order of the governor, while Nebraska easily passed the ban by legislation prior to the 2008 elections. In November 2010, Arizona voters approved Proposition 107 preventing consideration of race, ethnicity, or gender by any part of state government including state universities.

In the face of declining public and political support, colleges and universities across the country have quietly backed away from affirmative action programs. Since the mid-1990s, the use of race and ethnicity in admissions has declined sharply. Public four-year colleges that admit to considering minority status in admissions have fallen from above 60 to 35 percent. Private institutions have shown less of a decline—57 to 45 percent—but the direction is the same. Facing the threat of lawsuits and the lack of political support, public universities have retreated from affirmative action faster than private universities.[17]

TO THE FUTURE

While the public's support for affirmative action has decreased in recent years, some of the bitterness from the debate may also have moderated. Curiously the benefits from such programs are more likely to be accepted in business and government than they are in education. These benefits, in line with the Court's decisions, largely focus on the institutions involved, ignoring whether they actually improve the education or status of minorities. And here the results are decidedly mixed. A 2004 Century Foundation study found that at the most selective 146 universities, only 3 percent of students are from the least advantaged socioeconomic quarter—meaning that one is 25 times as likely to run into rich kids as poor ones on the nation's selective campuses.[18]

Affirmative action's justification that programs encouraging diversity are needed in higher education may have been overtaken by time. The increased presence on campus of ethnic groups from Vietnamese to Iranians, Cubans to Chinese have made colleges more diverse, certainly less dominated by white students. The argument that these programs were aimed at the descendants of former slaves victimized by American racism is out of sync with the reality that the benefits are coming to black students from immigrant families. More than a quarter of the black students enrolled at selective American colleges are immigrants or the children of immigrants. In five Ivy League universities, no less than 40 percent of those admitted as "black" are of immigrant origin. They may bring diversity to campuses, but these are not the offspring of those who have suffered from a history of American racism.[19]

The most at-risk part of these minority populations continue to be underrepresented in higher education. While the proportion of black students in college has risen from 9 percent in 1976 to 13 percent in 2002, the proportion who were men was the same, 4.3 percent. Black women have continued to ascend, while black men have not. Black men have the lowest college graduation rate among all racial groups for both sexes. Many of the black male students at the leading universities (one in five) wouldn't be there if they weren't athletes. College sports may be black men's most important affirmative action program.

Affirmative action remains a widely accepted practice in large corporations and in much of the civil service, including the armed services. Where a minority presence is important to these leadership institutions, some form of affirmative action will be applied. In university admissions it now prevails in the nation's leading private institutions. Private colleges are not covered by the state bans on preferences and may, ironically, end up being more diverse in their student bodies than public colleges. In many public universities unofficial affirmative action efforts will likely be practiced in defiance of state law and public opinion. But here it will be carried out, in Justice Ruth Bader Ginsburg's disapproving words in her dissent in the *Gratz* case, "through winks, nods and disguises."

Notes

1. Both the Gratz and Turner quotes are from "Negative About Affirmative Action?" anchor Ed Bradley, *60 Minutes* (CBS News Broadcast, October 29, 2000).
2. *Washington Post,* February 20, 1998, quoted by Lee Cokorinos, *The Assault on Diversity* (New York: Rowman & Littlefield Publishers, 2003), 63–64. Sponsored by the Institute for Democracy Studies, this is a critical look at conservative legal attacks on affirmative action.
3. A copy of the speech can be found in George E. Curry, ed., *The Affirmative Action Debate* (Reading, MA: Addison-Wesley, 1996), 258–276.
4. As quoted by Christopher Edley, Jr., *Not All Black and White* (New York: Hill and Wang, 1996), 85.
5. As quoted by Christopher Shea, "Under UCLA's Elaborate System Race Makes a Big Difference," in Robert Emmet Long, ed., *Affirmative Action* (New York: H. W. Wilson Company, 1995), 89.
6. Carl Cohen, as quoted by Richard F. Tomasson et al., *Affirmative Action: The Pros and Cons of Policy and Practice* (Washington, DC: American University Press, 1996), 117.
7. William Bradford Reynolds, "An Experiment Gone Awry," in Curry, 133.
8. Poll information taken from Pew Research Center, "Conflicted Views of Affirmative Action," News Release, May 14, 2003; William M. Chace, "Affirmative Inaction," *The American Scholar,* Winter 2011, p 26.
9. Linda Greenhouse, "Affirmative Reaction: Can the Justices Buck What the Establishment Backs?" *New York Times,* Week in Review, March 30, 2003.

10. Linda Greenhouse, "Justices Look for Nuance in Race-Preference Case," *New York Times,* April 2, 2003.
11. Summaries of the court decisions can be found at www.umich.edu/~urel/admissions/overview/
12. Linda Greenhouse, "Justices Back Affirmative Action by 5 to 4, But Wider Vote Bans a Racial Point System," *New York Times,* June 24, 2003.
13. http://mije.org/richardprince/obama-mccain-split-affirmative-action (July 28, 2008).
14. As quoted by Kate Phillips, "Obama on the Economy, Affirmative Action and More," *The Caucus-Blog of the Times,* July 2, 2009.
15. *Parents Involved in Community Schools v. Seattle School District No. 1* (2007).
16. Richard D. Kahlenberg, "The Affirmative Action Trap," *The American Prospect,* April 2, 2010.
17. Chace, pp. 26–27.
18. Kahlenberg.
19. Chace, p. 27.

4

CIVIL LIBERTIES

FREEDOM OF SPEECH ON CAMPUS

The Fight Over Fighting Words

The right to speak one's mind is basic to democracy and to a university. Most of us would agree with that statement and generally endorse freedom of speech. Problems arise, however, when controversial ideas are expressed and people are offended. Further complicating the issue is that the courts have expanded the term "speech" to include symbolic actions like flag burning. Countering this trend is that some groups have embraced the concept of "fighting words," turning this form of speech into prohibited conduct verging on a physical attack. The division between words and actions summed up by the comment "Your right to swing your arm ends at the tip of my nose" does not distinguish words and actions as clearly today as it did when the Bill of Rights was first adopted. Some now believe that the tip of one's ego comes closer to defining the limit of a verbal assault.[1]

In a sense, on college campuses civil liberties have collided with civil rights. As universities have admitted more diverse student bodies, they have had to question many of their traditional ideas about education and speech allowed in the academic community. Feminists charge sexual harassment when a law professor lectures on how to question rape victims; gay rights groups are offended when a student describes homosexuality as a disease to be treated medically; and minorities protest when a DJ tells a racist joke on the college radio station. Can the principle of open discussions of controversial issues be maintained? Will diverse groups feel welcomed in the academic community? What will be the impact on a university's educational goals?

Speech codes (often appearing in "student conduct codes") have evolved as one answer. While paying homage to the principle of free speech, these codes attempt to discourage speech that could be considered offensive to a particular group. Whatever its good intentions, when a code disapproves of "sexual harassment" and then goes on to prohibit "remarks of a sexual nature" and "jesting" and "kidding" about sex or gender-specific traits, it invites problems of interpretation.[2] The vagueness of such codes and the awkwardness of their implementation have led some universities to adopt less ambitious, more traditional approaches. Many educators argue that speech is better governed by courts that are guided by legal precedents and the First Amendment. That, in turn, would allow universities to return to their educational mission of seeking knowledge through the widest possible discourse. This is not exactly a modest goal.

CONCEPTS TO CONSIDER

1. America's **marketplace of ideas** is a widely embraced value. Here opinions compete with one another to determine which will flourish and which will not. Although determined by the "hidden hand" of the market, the free expression that allows this competition merits legal protection. But how valid is this ideal? Does government intervention, opinion shaping by the media, and university guidelines make this hands-off ideal less than realistic? Therefore, shouldn't the consequences of speech be a reasonable way to judge the suitability of such expression on campus?

2. The Affirmative Action Donuts and Shippensburg examples illustrate attempts by universities to protect vulnerable students from harassment, even at the cost of limiting expression. The desire of some students for freedom clashes with that of others who want to be treated equally. Is this a case of **civil liberties versus civil rights?** Is this an unbridgeable division, or can the open exchange of ideas on a college campus be used to promote both?

3. **Fighting words** cause injury or incite an immediate breach of the peace. They are recognized by the courts and minority groups as different from ordinary speech. Without getting into the legal arguments, does such a concept make sense on college campuses? Should the affirmative action bake sales fall under this category and therefore be banned?

4. Do universities have **valid educational purposes** for limiting expression on campus? Should colleges meet a higher standard before being allowed to restrain expression? Or should this be part of the duties of a community of scholars policing ideas to weed out those with no redeeming intellectual value? And, of course, who should make these decisions?

5. How do universities, the government, and students **protect free speech**? The "heckler's veto" describes the intimidation that occurs when objections and intimidation by opponents keep certain speakers from voicing their views. This can be seen currently on issues such as abortion, religious dissent, Israel and gun control. How can citizens and democratic institutions encourage tolerance for unpopular opinions?

UNIVERSITIES AND SPEECH

If there is a bedrock principle underlying the First Amendment, it is that the Government may not prohibit the expression of an idea simply because society finds the idea itself offensive or disagreeable.

Justice William J. Brennan, Texas v. Johnson, 1989
(In decision upholding flag-burning protest)

MOHAMMED CARTOONS AND UNIVERSITY NEWSPAPERS

On February 9, 2006, the editor of the Daily Illini, *the student newspaper of the University of Illinois, wrote a column about a Danish newspaper's publication of editorial cartoons depicting the Muslim prophet Mohammed. Alongside the column, the editor printed six of the cartoons.*

The Danish newspaper's actions had led to widespread controversy, demonstrations, riots, and even murders. The Daily Illini *editor Acton Gorton felt that "a petrifying fear from news editors" was keeping them from discussing or showing the cartoons. He posed this question: "Does the value of letting my readers see the cartoons for themselves outweigh the negative consequences that might follow from my publishing them?"*

Not much of a public outcry followed publication of the cartoons. But there were objections from the newspaper's publisher and the staff. Some of the staff claimed that Gorton had put their lives at risk by publishing something offensive to Muslims. The board of directors suspended Gorton and his opinions editor. Next, they removed the cartoons and the editor's commentary from the Daily Illini *website. They asked Google to remove any related material from their records, and prohibited mentioning anything about the incident in their own newspaper. The* Daily Illini *ran a later story about college newspapers publishing the cartoons, but no mention was made of this incident. As the editor concluded, "It's a truly astonishing experience to be summarily fired from your job and then erased from the public's memory for trying to provide one's readers with information pertaining to one of the most newsworthy stories of the year."*

Student newspapers at the University of Wisconsin–Madison, Purdue University, the University of Arizona, and Harvard University printed some versions of the cartoons without official consequence.

In 2009, Yale University Press published a book about the controversy, The Cartoons That Shook the World. *The director of the academic press removed the cartoons from this book discussing censorship. He claimed that he feared violence, saying he didn't want "blood on my hands." The author, a Brandeis historian, remarked, "I became a chapter in my own book." The American Association of University Professors issued a statement denouncing Yale for censoring the cartoons.[3]*

The right to free speech would seem to be indispensable at a university. What is an ideal university if not a marketplace of ideas, allowing the most open free exchange of beliefs and opinions? Communicating knowledge, debating issues, and tolerating controversy, all to encourage learning, ought to demand unrestricted openness.

In practice, universities have widely accepted restraints on freedom of expression. In some instances, the campus is more restrictive than general society. Plagiarism is a striking example, reflecting the scholars' duty to credit others' research and ideas. The penalties for its violation are higher in academia than they are in the outside world, reflecting the university's special interest in the integrity of scholarship. Similarly, lying—a violation of many student honor codes—will mean sanctions from the university community, including expulsion, far harsher than anywhere else. These values and practices in defense of the university's mission are designed to produce standards of behavior applying to speech and expression higher than those of society at large.

A university's mission may also lead to greater protection for speech than found elsewhere in society. Academic freedom is the university's traditional safeguard for what professors, and others, say and write in the classroom and even outside class. Such speech goes to the heart of academia's pursuit of truth. Academic freedom is a unique protection offered at most campuses. It prohibits punishments, such as job loss, for expression at universities, and this heightened defense of speech has been recognized by the courts.

At American universities whether the institution is public or private affects the freedom of expression that's allowed. Private colleges and universities are generally freer to set their own limits on speech. For example, a church-affiliated school may set restrictions on student speech (e.g., blasphemy) that are stricter than what is acceptable in the off-campus world. Whereas the courts give private universities a bit more flexibility, public universities are directly answerable to the Constitution, and administrators at these tax-supported academies are treated as agents of the government and are restrained by the First Amendment in their ability to limit campus speech. This has led to their speech codes that restricted racist, sexist, or homophobic speech being consistently struck down by the courts as abridging constitutional freedoms. It happened a few years ago at a small state college in Pennsylvania.[4]

RESTRAINING SPEECH AND SPEECH CODES

Shippensburg University, a public college in central Pennsylvania, published a "Code of Conduct" similar to those of other universities. It gave each student a "primary" right to be free from harassment, intimidation, physical harm, or emotional abuse, and a "secondary" right to express personal beliefs in a manner that did not "provoke, harass, demean, intimidate, or harm" another. The university prohibited conduct that "annoys, threatens, or alarms a person or group" like sexual harassment, comments, insults, propositions, jokes about sex or gender-specific traits, and even "suggestive or insulting sounds," leering, whistling, or obscene gestures. Campus demonstrations and rallies were limited to two "speech zones."

Attorneys for a civil liberties nonprofit association, the Foundation for Individual Rights in Education (FIRE), filed a lawsuit against Shippensburg as part of its nationwide campaign against speech codes. FIRE charged that the code had a "chilling effect" on students' right to open discussions. The code made constitutionally protected free speech depend on the reaction of the most sensitive student. FIRE officials said that under this policy a student who accused Republicans of engaging in a racist war could be punished, as would a feminist who went to a rally with a sign reading "Keep your rosaries off my ovaries." The university responded that it "strongly and vigorously defends the right of free speech," adding that it expected students to "conduct themselves in a civil manner that allows them to express their opinions without interfering with the rights of others."

A U.S. district court judge issued a preliminary injunction ordering the university not to enforce its speech code. The judge concluded that the code was an attempt to achieve a "utopian community" but that good intentions did not justify censorship. Instructing students to apply the university's ideals of "racial tolerance, cultural diversity, and social justice" was found by the court to be clearly unconstitutional. Shippensburg agreed to rewrite its speech policies as an unenforceable university statement of values that did not restrict student expression in any way.[5]

The well-intended motives behind college speech codes are not questioned, even by opponents. In the late 1980s, the Carnegie Foundation surveyed university presidents and reported that more than half of them considered racial intimidation or harassment a serious problem on their campuses. The college heads could provide many examples of students fulfilling the comic Groucho Marx's goal for college: "We want to build a university our football team can be proud of."

- At the University of Wisconsin–Madison, a giant racist caricature announced an on-campus party.
- A college fraternity put on a skit featuring jokes that mocked gay and lesbian lifestyles.
- A University of Michigan student posted a story on the Internet about torturing his female classmate with a hot curling iron.
- Two women at a California junior college protested the sexist comments posted on a men-only campus computer bulletin board.

There are several arguments for speech codes. One is that simply condemning racist, sexist, and homophobic statements in these codes might reduce how often they occur. The codes serve as a symbol that the university will not tolerate such prejudice, thus providing a more comfortable environment for its students who might feel victimized. Banning offensive language is viewed as a way of preserving the best values of academic dialogue and preventing contamination from toxic comments with no redeeming social purpose. A constitutional scholar argued that concepts like genocide should not even be given the chance of acceptance in the market-place of ideas, since such evil thoughts could possibly be implemented in a democracy. Why wait to prevent them only when they begin to be acted on? "Where nothing is unspeakable, nothing is undoable."[6]

Few universities have worked to curb speech with any enthusiasm. Speech codes arose during a period of change when administrators were responding to troubling situations. Colleges were adapting to the admission of new ethnic and racial groups by changing a campus climate that was often exclusive and uncivil. Universities sought to protect and support the outraged victims of discrimination. Racist and abusive speech was seen as a pattern of behavior that interfered with learning and was contrary to the educational values of the university. The case for speech codes was put this way by one supporter: "What many speech code advocates are seeking is simple: a way of enlisting a whole community in creating an environment where people are not attacked and injured on the basis of their identity."[7]

BAKING BROWNIES AND FREEING SPEECH: THE ARGUMENT AGAINST CODES

It is by the goodness of God that in our country we have three unspeakably precious things: freedom of speech, freedom of conscience, and the prudence never to practice either of them.

MARK TWAIN

For a number of years, conservative student organizations have held "affirmative action bake sales" at colleges across the country. Brownies, donuts, and other baked goods were advertised at lower prices for black and Hispanic students than for Asian and white customers. Supporters described the sales as satire designed to draw attention to the unfairness in universities' affirmative action policies applied to the petty level of a bake sale. It was political theater designed to spark debate.

The reaction has been decidedly mixed. At William & Mary, the president denounced the bake sale as "inexcusably hurtful" and "abusive." The sale was halted, he claimed, because it "did not meet the administrative requirements we routinely impose on such activities." A lawyer for the student group remarked, "One can hard-ly imagine such tactics being used to shut down a protest that administrators found more to their liking politically." After press coverage a second bake sale was allowed. At the University of Washington, the College Republicans holding the sales were assaulted. Students tore down the signs and threw cookies on the ground. At Southern Methodist University, administrators shut down the Young Conservatives of Texas's bake sale after forty-five minutes because "some folks felt harassed by this discriminatory menu."

Other universities proved more tolerant. Student bake sales occurred without official opposition at the University of Texas-Austin and at Texas A&M. An Indiana University administrator resisted pressure to punish bake sale organizers, saying, "[Affirmative action] is one of the more significant social and political issues of our time. . . . It is exactly the kind of dialogue that should be encouraged on college campuses."

However, in the spring of 2009, Bucknell University administrators shut down a bake sale. First it was closed for an alleged paperwork error. Then, when the Bucknell University Conservatives Club tried again, the bake sale was stopped for its "discriminatory pricing policy." The Bucknell administrator explained the closure this way. "It's a political issue, ok; it needs to be debated in its proper forum, ok, and not on the public property on the campus." A leader of a student rights group responded, " . . . for $40,590 a year in tuition, the very least Bucknell students should be able to ask is that the university live up to its promises of free speech and not selectively censor opinions the administration dislikes."[8]

There are two basic arguments against speech codes: One is that this restriction on free speech violates the Constitution at public universities and

These college Republicans at the University of California, Berkeley, cooked up a free speech issue by pricing cookies based on the buyer's ethnicity.

undermines the stated missions of private universities as well. The second is that speech codes prevent open discussion of ideas and are inappropriate for a university. Students cannot be expected to defend principles of free speech after they graduate if they are educated in a place where rights are granted or withheld depending on the whims of those in charge.

Examples of speech restraints/codes currently being enforced on campuses range from the serious to the silly. DePaul University, a private religious college, denied recognition to the student group Students for Cannabis Policy Reform, saying that it might promote poor health decisions by undergraduates. Syracuse University police announced that they would require students to remove "offensive" Halloween costumes and discipline them because other students could become violently offended. And in 2010, a Yale University dean interfered with a Freshman Class Council decision to distribute a shirt for the Harvard–Yale football game that quoted F. Scott Fitzgerald's line, "I think of all Harvard men as sissies." The dean thought that the word "sissy" could be seen as a derogatory slur against homosexuals.[9]

The constitutional argument is bolstered by the fairly consistent refusal of courts to support the restraints on speech in these codes. Judges have seen campus codes as interfering with protected First Amendment speech. Universities' attempts to rewrite codes—often putting them under the category of "student conduct"—and make them less sweeping have proven unsuccessful. Many campuses have given up attempting to comply with the courts' broadly tolerant First Amendment rulings and have allowed their codes to fade into history. Speech codes, however, are still used in hundreds of universities.

The educational argument behind speech codes is that there are some expressions so contrary to the goals of a university that they should be banned. However, at various times in American history, the exclusion of certain ideas from universities—whether Marxism or atheism—has prevailed, much to the later embarrassment of the academic community. The problem of defining exactly what speech should be sanctioned has bedeviled the drafting of all speech codes. That may be because making some messages off limits sets a precedent of prohibiting thought. In a sense it empowers controversial ideas, implying that they cannot be presented because they cannot be countered through the normal methods of reason and debate. By punishing expression, the codes violate Thomas Jefferson's goal for a university as a place where error is allowed "so long as reason is free to pursue it. . . ."[10]

The university's special commitment to freedom of speech does not mean it should protect misconduct. Free speech advocates do not dispute the need to prevent threats or harassment directed at an individual or to keep classes from being disrupted. They argue, however, that sanctions should relate to conduct and not translate to vague restrictions on expression. A few groups should not need special protection from a few words. Courts have upheld the idea that speech is not absolute, but the legal restrictions are very narrowly defined. Many university speech codes regulate expression that is clearly protected under the law. A former president of the University of California said, "The university is not engaged in making ideas safe for students. It is engaged in making students safe for ideas."[11] Exceptions to the general rule of protecting speech at a university ought to be just that—exceptions.

UNIVERSITIES AND THE RIGHT TO SHOUT

Israel's ambassador to the United States was speaking at the University of California at Irvine. Or at least he was trying to. Every few minutes a student would stand up, shout something critical about Israel, get applauded or jeered by the audience, and be escorted out by police. 'War criminal,' 'mass murderer,' and 'an accomplice to genocide' were some of the interruptions directed at the ambassador by 11 students protesting his appearance.

Labelled the "Irvine 11," the students were arrested and charged with criminal conspiracy to disturb a meeting as well as disturbing a meeting, which are misdemeanors. Their attorney claimed that most cases involving disturbing the peace were not prosecuted unless they included property damage, threats, or violence. She said they were being charged because of who they were—Muslim students. Their trial was set to begin just before the start of the 2011–2012 school year.

Both supporters of the hecklers and of the invited speaker raised the right of free speech in defending their side.

The Council on American-Islamic Relations defended the protest. "Delivering this message in a loud and shocking manner expressed the gravity of the charges leveled against Israeli policies, and falls within the purview of protected speech." Another supporter pointed out that while the students interrupted the speaker they did not shut down his presentation. They voluntarily left the room after each interruption and let the talk continue, at least until the next outburst. He added, "The First Amendment was never intended to be exclusively polite and courteous."

This argument didn't get far with free speech groups or the campus administration. The Foundation for Individual Rights in Education (FIRE) saw the other side as condoning a 'heckler's veto' and concluded it "would make a mockery of the First Amendment." The chancellor of Irvine was equally harsh. "This behavior is intolerable. Freedom of speech is among the most fundamental, and among the most cherished, of the bedrock values our nation is built upon . . . Those who attempt to suppress the rights of others violate core principles that are the foundation of any learning community."

The head of the American Association of University Professors looked for a middle way. He noted that most faculty members regard interruption as unacceptable. But that as long as the speaker is allowed to continue, he thought some brief demonstration against a speaker isn't necessarily an assault on free speech. Adding, "Free speech doesn't mean you are able to trample a campus event." He recalled a memorable protest he attended in the 1960s at a talk at Antioch College by the leader of the American Nazi Party. No one shouted at him though the students considered him hateful. "The audience was totally silent and then, during the question period, no

*one would ask him a question and he began cursing at the audience, but no one would
speak. To me it was incredibly moving . . . There is a tremendous sense of dignity in
silent witness."*[12]

Much of what goes on at a university has been described as a conversation. It is a forthright discussion between teachers and teachers, teachers and students, and students and students. It is about debating and confronting controversial ideas, and challenging authority by learning to present evidence and arguments. It is a conversation that arouses emotions, provides a sanctuary for cranks and crackpots, and often seems pointless, futile, and wrong.[13] It is, however, talk, and a clear boundary between protected speech and prohibited conduct must be established on campus. The essence of a campus is a broad, engaging, and thriving conversation. Censor it, and you've removed something basic to education.

Notes

1. Alan Charles Kors and Harvey A. Silverglate, *The Shadow University* (New York: The Free Press, 1998), 84.
2. For an example, see the guidelines from the University of Maryland at www.speechcodes.org/.
3. Chris Perez, "Acton Gorton's Truly Astonishing Experience," http://www.thefire.org/index.php/article/7029.html; Harvey Silverglate, "2010 Muzzle Awards on Campus," *The Phoenix*, June 30, 2010.
4. Rober M. O'Neil, *Free Speech in the College Community* (Bloomington, IN: Indiana University Press, 1997), "Introduction."
5. *The FIRE Quarterly* 1, no. 3–4 (Winter 2003); *The FIRE Quarterly* 2, no. 1 (Spring 2004).
6. Martin P. Golding, *Free Speech on Campus* (Boulder, CO: Rowman & Littlefield, 2000). Quote is from Alexander M. Bickel, 34.
7. O'Neil, 3–7.
8. FIRE News, "FIRE Victory: Free Speech at William & Mary," www.thefireguides.org, February 2, 2004. Mike McPhee, "BUCC Donut Sale Rejected by Administration," *The Bucknellian*, as quoted in The FIRE Update, e-Newsletter, October 2010.
9. Greg Lukianoff, "The 12 Worst Colleges for Free Speech," *The Huffington Post*, January 27, 2011.
10. O'Neil, 22.
11. Ibid., 21–22.
12. Scott Jaschik, "Student Protests at Speech of Israeli Ambassador," First Amendment Coalition, February 17, 2010. http://www.firstamendmentcoalition.org/2010/02student-protests. "Israeli Ambassador Prompts Debate Over Campus Free Speech," The Pew Forum on Religion & Public Life, March 1, 2011. "Muslim Students Plead Not Guilty . . . " *The Washington Post*, April 15, 2011.
13. Golding, 23.

5 | PUBLIC OPINION

ABORTION AND THE PUBLIC
A Surprising Stability

Suspicion of public opinion is an old American tradition. Many parts of the U.S Constitution—the indirect selection of the president through an electoral college, the long six-year terms for senators, and the nonelected federal judiciary appointed by the president—reflect the fears that popular opinion could fall under the sway of "violent passions." While democratic voices would be heard, the framers worried about frequent and extreme changes of mass opinion. The checks and balances of a divided federal government would, it was hoped, restrain the citizenry.

More recently, political scientists have come to more positive conclusions about public opinion. In *The Rational Public*, their study of public policy preferences over fifty years, Benjamin Page and Robert Shapiro concluded that Americans' opinions about policy are generally quite stable. (Their results were reinforced some years later in a book by the head of the Gallup poll Frank Newport, who concluded that public opinion was usually "coherent, steady and clear.") Not only do the policy choices of the public seldom change, but these opinions are also generally consistent and moderate. In sorting through data from hundreds of polls, these authors thought that when public opinion does change, it does so in incremental and predictable ways. Accordingly, government policies can, should, and usually do rest on the preferences of ordinary citizens.[1]

The following case shows that public opinion is not something produced only by political leaders, nor are people's opinions completely detached from the political process. Attitudes toward abortion shifted in the 1960s, paralleling the social revolution toward women and sexual behavior that occurred at the time. In the face of attempts by political leaders to manipulate and change it, public opinion on abortion has remained remarkably stable since then. This acceptance of legal abortion has been restrained at times by changes in government policies and the framing of the issue by groups trying to sway public opinion. But while these policies affect public preferences, it is more to the point that government policies sooner or later have to adapt to the public that they seek to represent. Public opinion set the boundaries, and the politics of abortion has played out within these broadly accepted borders over the last thirty years. And the boundaries established by popular opinion on this difficult, polarizing issue were clear and sensible.

Spring 2010 saw President Obama nearing a big victory of his young administration as health-care reform became law. But before that could happen, the president had to hold a small ceremony in the White House to sign an executive order stating that no federal money would be used to pay for abortions under the new reform. The ceremony was attended by many antiabortion congressional Democrats. It was not open to the press.

The quiet event was the result of a compromise needed to get the support of a number of House Democrats for the new legislation. It required citizens who wanted coverage for abortions to write two checks to the insurance companies: one for the part that covers abortion and a separate one for the rest of their plan that receives federal money. It affirmed a long-standing rule that prohibits federal government funding of abortion. Antiabortion activists were not completely satisfied, preferring to have the principle included in the law itself rather than in an executive order. Abortion rights supporters didn't like the compromise either, because it placed restrictions on access and stigmatized women who wanted to use their insurance plan for the procedure.[2]

Other battles in the decades-old war over abortion were taking place within the states. Ultrasound technology which can show a fetus on a sonogram was being used to persuade women not to terminate their pregnancy. Three states, Alabama, Louisiana, and Mississippi, required abortion providers to conduct an ultrasound and offer women a chance to see it. Abortion rights groups opposed the laws as interfering with the patient–doctor relationship and disrespecting women's ability to make an informed choice. Advocates said that it humanized the process by putting a face on the baby. One of the few studies of the issue, in Canada, found that most women wanted to see the image but that none reversed their decision to have an abortion. The Alabama law had no apparent impact on the 11,000 abortions taking place each year in the state.[3]

An argument was heard that antiabortion views were gaining popular support in the country. The number of abortions had been falling since 1990, although the rates among poor women had gone up. A 2009 Pew Research Center poll showed a 7-point decline in backing for legal abortions from two years before with 47 percent currently positive and 44 percent opposing. Almost two-thirds of respondents (65 percent) agreed that it would be good to reduce abortions, while three-quarters (76 percent) continued to favor requiring minors to obtain parents' permission for an abortion. Just as interesting had been the drop in the numbers of people who feel that abortion was currently an important issue. Only 15 percent thought it was a critical issue facing the country, though this drop in intensity was greater among supporters of legal abortion than among opponents. Antiabortionists seemed more committed to their positions and less willing to compromise.[4]

Yet this apparent decline in support for abortion in polls and the widespread actions in various states to limit abortion may have been deceptive. As the report of the Pew Research Center concluded about their 2009 poll, not much has really changed. "In spite of the small shift toward opposition to legal abortion, the basic contours of the debate are still intact, with most major groups lining up on the same side of the issue as they have in the past." (The 2008 election of a pro-choice Democrat for president may have contributed to hardening conservative opinion that felt threatened by opponents' control of the federal government.) Divisions based on religion, gender, education, and overall liberal/conservative beliefs continued to track peoples' opinions on abortion. The changes in state laws restricting the use of abortion generally echoed moderate public opinion that supports keeping abortion both legal and limited.

Neither side has achieved a clear victory, because both face a similar dilemma: *Public opinion on abortion has remained the same for almost 40 years.* Beneath the sound and fury of political battles, the millions of dollars spent advertising the positions of the intensely warring rivals, and the unpalatable compromises reached by lawmakers caught in the middle, there is an underlying popular reality. Public opinion on the issue has remained both moderate and largely unmoved.

THE STABILITY OF PUBLIC OPINION ON ABORTION

The consistency of public opinion seems clear. A defining study of polls on abortion (from 1999) concluded that "public opinion on abortion has been remarkably stable" since the *Roe v. Wade* decision of 1973.[5] The Gallup poll shows little change since 1975. In that year, roughly the same percentages of people surveyed said abortion should be legal under any circumstances as said it should always be illegal—21 percent versus 22 percent. Fifty-four percent stood firmly in the middle, wanting abortion legal only under certain circumstances. These positions varied only slightly over the next three and a half decades: By 2010, 24 percent of those polled believed abortion should always be legal, 19 percent believed it should always be illegal, and 57 percent thought abortion should be legal in some circumstances.[6] In his recent argument against "the myth of a polarized America," Morris P. Fiorina concluded that nearly two-thirds of Americans supported *Roe v. Wade*. Other pollsters' findings are similar.[7]

Saying that public opinion on abortion is stable doesn't mean it is one-dimensional. As Everett Carll Ladd and Karlyn H. Bowman put it, "Some questions pull people in one direction, others draw them in another. Opinion is not only clear; it is also complex."

The majority of Americans hold opinions somewhere between unlimited access and total prohibition of abortion. American attitudes are stable because they lie between two important, if seemingly contrasting beliefs—one that abortion is murder, the other that only a woman can make the decision

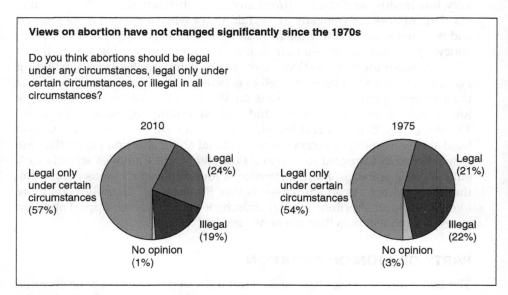

Views on abortion have not changed significantly since the 1970s

Do you think abortions should be legal under any circumstances, legal only under certain circumstances, or illegal in all circumstances?

2010

Legal only under certain circumstances (57%)

Legal (24%)

Illegal (19%)

No opinion (1%)

1975

Legal only under certain circumstances (54%)

Legal (21%)

Illegal (22%)

No opinion (3%)

FIGURE 5.1   Views on Abortion, 1975 and 2010.
Source: Gallup World Poll, July 18, 2010.

to terminate her pregnancy. In a *Los Angeles Times* poll in 2000, 60 percent considered abortion murder. Yet in the same poll, over 70 percent agreed with the statement "No matter how I feel about abortion, I believe it is a decision that has to be made by a woman and her doctor." Americans endorse both the sanctity of life and the importance of individual choice. These positions have been "rock solid" for the last quarter century.[8]

Oddly enough, both pro-life and pro-choice groups can claim majority support for their positions. Activists from the pro-choice camp correctly point out that a majority of Americans disapproves of a ban on abortion. Pro-life groups contend that a majority does not favor abortion on demand—also correct. In fact, most Americans hold an in-between position—legal abortion in the first trimester, but with limits on its use.[9] Nearly two-thirds say abortion should be generally legal in the first three months, but large majorities say it should be illegal in the second and third trimesters. A CNN/USA Today/Gallup poll in October 2003 on whether late pregnancy partial-birth abortions should be allowed found that 68 percent favored making them illegal.[10]

Caught between clashing absolutes, Americans are "situationalists." The situations where the public justifies and opposes abortion are clearly separated. Huge majorities (nine out of ten) support it when the woman's own health is endangered by the pregnancy. Equal support is found where there is a strong chance of a serious defect in the baby or where the pregnancy is the result of rape. In other words, public opinion wants abortion legal in these three *traumatic* circumstances—when the health of the mother is at stake, where there is a defective fetus, or in cases of rape. But in *elective* circumstances, these majorities disappear. The public is conflicted about legal abortion when the family has a very low income and cannot afford any more children; when the woman is married but does not want any more children; or when a woman is not married and does not want to marry the man. In these cases—poverty, unwanted pregnancy, unmarried mother—a narrow majority opposes allowing an abortion.[11]

Attitudes toward abortion are related to demographic factors including age, education, and religion, as well as general political leanings. Education is the strongest predictor of positions on abortion. Opposition to abortion is lowest among college graduates and highest among high school dropouts. Those with the best jobs and the highest incomes are more likely to support legal abortion. Younger voters are more liberal about abortion policy than are older voters. With regard to religion, Protestants and Catholics actually look alike in their attitudes. More difference is found in *how* religious people are: those who rarely attend church—whether Protestant or Catholic—are more likely to support abortion. Regular churchgoers are likely to support abortion in fewer circumstances than are nonattenders.[12]

PARTY OPINION ON ABORTION

The two political parties have staked out polarized positions on the abortion issue. Democratic presidential candidates must pass a litmus test of representing a pro-choice party, just as much as Republican candidates must stand resolutely in favor of a pro-life position. The Democrats 2008 platform reads in part: "The Democratic Party strongly and unequivocally supports *Roe v. Wade* and a woman's right to choose a safe and legal abortion, regardless of ability to pay, and we oppose any and all efforts to weaken or undermine that right." The Republicans spoke unmistakably for the other side in their platform: "We support a human life amendment to the Constitution, and we endorse legislation to make clear that the Fourteenth Amendment's protections apply to unborn children."

But among the *members* of both parties the division is much less stark, and far weaker than among the leaders of the parties. In answer to the question of whether abortion should be legal under any circumstances, legal only under certain circumstances, or illegal in all circumstances there is not much difference between the rank and file of the parties. A little more than 50 percent of Republicans and a little less than 50 percent of Democrats choose "legal only under certain circumstances." Only one-third of Democrats choose "legal under any circumstances" and less than one-fourth of Republicans take the position of "illegal in all circumstances." The majorities of both parties, like the American public itself, are not polarized on abortion. They believe that it should be legal but regulated in various ways.

Pro-life activists who argue that any abortion is unacceptable, even if it involves damage to the health of the mother play a vital role within the Republican party, but compose less than 10 percent of the population. Pro-choice activists, equally important to the Democrats, argue that any limits on a woman's right to choose is unacceptable, also make up less than 10 percent of the public. As mentioned, overwhelming majorities regard rape, birth defects, and threats to the mother's life and health as sufficient reasons for legal abortions. Opinion is less supportive of abortions justified by the mother's age, financial condition, or marital status. The public does not support either extreme on abortion. As political scientist Morris Fiorina put it in his book *Culture War?*, this clear majority are "pro-choice, buts." Or, as that astute politician Bill Clinton described his position, he was pro-choice and against abortion.[13]

THE HISTORIC CHANGE IN PUBLIC OPINION

These views reflect broad historic trends. They developed as part of the country's changing approach to social issues, including sexual morality, the roles of women in society, and the importance of childbearing and families. These trends were all closely linked with a national upheaval popularly known as "The Sixties."

The Gallup poll did not even ask about abortion until 1962, both because it was not an issue and too sensitive to discuss. In that year the media began to cover the plight of an Arizona woman, Sherri Finkbine, who went to Sweden for an abortion. During her pregnancy, she had taken the drug thalidomide, which was later found to cause birth defects, and she feared having a deformed baby. Because her life wasn't endangered by the pregnancy, she couldn't get an abortion legally in her state. At the time, only a bare majority of Americans approved of what she did.

Prior to the 1960s, the idea of abortion, indeed the very word, was considered so unpleasant that the issue was excluded from the nation's political agenda. When public debate over abortion emerged, every state had criminal laws forbidding the intentional termination of pregnancy, with the single exception being to save the life of the mother. These statutes often dated back to the nineteenth century. For example, a Connecticut law written in 1821 made aborting a fetus a criminal offense after its "quickening," or the first evidence of movement inside the womb. By the 1960s, most states had laws on the books making abortion a crime.

With the shift in cultural values in the late 1960s, including the growth of feminism, abortion surfaced as an issue for public discussion. The "boundary-breaking demands for personal freedom" of the decade brought the issue of abortion forcibly to the American public's attention. As part of this "culture of freedom," emphasis was put on individuals' rights to make choices that affected their lives, and this meant questioning the limits of public regulation on private conduct. The feminist movement of the sixties applied that freedom to women's control over their own bodies. Abortion was identified with individual freedom.[14]

This "culture of freedom" energized a social and sexual revolution in thinking. Liberal attitudes toward abortion were spreading on college campuses and among those with few ties to organized religion. Ideas about women's changing role in society were widely discussed, paralleled by growing public support for the women's movement. Federalism played a role when throughout the sixties many states began to pass laws permitting abortion. These early laws usually followed a "model statute" that allowed for abortions in cases of rape, incest, or medical necessity. Other states went further to legalize abortions performed on any medical grounds. As some states passed laws allowing abortions, women traveled to those states to end unwanted pregnancies, which intensified the national debate carried in the media.

College-educated young people were turning away from their parents' beliefs and embracing new ideas about personal freedom. By 1972, most college graduates favored abortion on demand compared to only one-third of people without high school degrees. Among people saying religion should have *less* of a role in national life, three out of five supported abortion. Among those who believed religion should have a *greater* role, only one in five backed abortion on demand. Catholics demonstrated an especially striking change. In 1962, one-third of Catholics supported Sherri Finkbine's right to an abortion. Since 1972, surveys have shown that over three-quarters of Catholics support abortion where there is a strong chance of a serious birth defect.

GOVERNMENT, GROUPS, AND PUBLIC OPINION

To say that the stability of public opinion on abortion reflects long-term cultural shifts is not to say that opinion is unchanging. Both government and activist groups have attempted to influence opinion, and at times have succeeded, at least around the edges. Government—legislatures, courts, and presidents—has announced policies and shown leadership on the issue. Organized interests, both for and against abortion, have pushed specific policies that they felt would gain public support. By presenting their views on this complex issue in a favorable framework, such groups have moved the debate for limited periods. Yet all these political groups' shaping of public opinion had neither the impact nor the durability of the broad social changes brought by the sixties. For policies on abortion to work, they had to operate within the existing boundaries.

In 1973, the Supreme Court, in *Roe v. Wade*, legalized abortion in the first three months of a pregnancy. Not only did this decision reflect the change in public opinion since the mid-1960s, but it helped move that opinion further. One pollster concluded, "That jump in support after the court decision was sharper than in any other two-year period of polling; it signified a switch in position for some ten million adult Americans."[15] The increased support remained high into the 1980s and may have reflected the Supreme Court's prestige as an authority interpreting the Constitution. It may also speak to the polarized nature of the case: forcing people to choose whether abortion should or should not be allowed.

Proabortion groups had helped change public opinion leading up to the *Roe* decision. Activists had pushed for reforming state laws based on an argument of personal liberty. Civil liberties and women's groups identified abortion as a constitutionally protected right of privacy. They were aided by organized medicine, notably the American Medical Association. In 1967, the AMA had passed a resolution supporting liberalized abortion laws, although theirs was an argument for professional control, rather than personal freedom. The physicians framed the issue as a medical one, to be decided by a woman and her doctor, in which political and legal factors had no place.

The themes of professional autonomy and personal privacy were joined by an argument of social policy. Groups concerned with overpopulation, such as Planned Parenthood, had been focused on birth control policies and had historically opposed abortion. Pressured by more radical groups, like Zero Population Growth, Planned Parenthood signed on to the proabortion coalition. Bolstered by civil liberties allies and supporters in organized medicine, Planned Parenthood became an advocate for removing legal barriers to abortion as one method for dealing with the "population bomb."[16]

ABORTION OPPONENTS

The modifying of abortion laws produced stern opposition. "Right to Life" committees were formed in many states to prevent further changes in the laws and to encourage stricter bans. The Catholic Church was the most persistent opponent, although it was joined by fundamentalist Christians and Orthodox Jews. The rise of conservatism in the 1980s, including President Reagan's frequent speeches against abortion, may have led to a slight decline in public support.

Instead of trying to directly overturn the reformed abortion laws—and put themselves outside the widely accepted boundaries of public opinion—opponents framed their antiabortion position around more popular issues. During the 1980s, the most common debate about abortion centered on parental notification and consent for minors seeking abortions. By focusing the discussion around parental notification, public support for this limit on abortion was assured. The need for parents' consent for minors' abortions received over 80 percent support in opinion polls. Since this concern was uppermost in the public's mind, it too may have reduced overall support for abortion.[17]

Abortion is the most common surgical procedure performed on American women—one-third will have one by age forty-five. Yet some extreme opponents have threatened providers and encouraged a climate of fear and shame surrounding its use. Angry picketing and bombings of clinics, verbal threats, and publicized killings of abortion doctors have kept the medical profession from treating abortion as just another part of health care. Only half the number of doctors offer abortion in their offices as did so thirty years ago. Over 90 percent of abortions are provided in specialized clinics rather than in hospitals. In 87 percent of the counties of America, there is no publically known abortion provider. While the medical profession has recently recognized the issue and increased training in medical school in large parts of the country, it is still considered an act of bravery for doctors to offer this legal service.[18]

The Supreme Court's July 3, 1989, ruling in *Webster v. Reproductive Health Services* allowed states to put some restrictions on abortion, which returned the issue to various state legislatures and focused debate on limiting women's access. The initial reaction to the decision was to increase membership and donations to groups on both sides of the abortion issue. Proabortion groups, feeling more threatened by these government restraints, initially saw a dramatic increase in their support.[19]

In the 1990s, opponents of abortion focused on a late-term procedure they called partial-birth abortion, hoping the debate in Congress would shape public opinion. On the floor of the Senate, opponents argued with graphic charts and drawings that partial-birth abortion was no abstract clash of rights; this was infanticide. With the shift in public attention to a late-term procedure, the overall support for abortion dipped. The framing of the policy debate by conservative political leaders once again caused a minor change in the poll numbers, at least for a while.[20] As a Republican senator said, "With partial-birth abortion, you can't miss the baby."

Bills banning partial-birth abortion were passed twice by Congress after the Republicans gained control in 1994, but were vetoed by President Clinton. Upon his veto of April 1996, President Clinton brought five women who had had the procedure to the White House to speak tearfully of their agonizing decisions in dealing with the disorders threatening them and their fetuses. When President Bush signed similar legislation seven and a half years later, he declared, "Today, at last, the American people and our government have confronted the violence and come to the defense of the innocent child."[21]

Pro-choice and pro-life demonstrators line up on either side of the abortion issue on the anniversary of the *Roe v. Wade* decision.

But the 2003 law was halted by nearly four years of legal appeals. Three federal appeals courts ruled against the government because the law did not provide a "health exception" for pregnant women facing a medical emergency. Then in 2007, in a sharply divided 5-4 decision, the Supreme Court made its first ruling on abortion in six years declaring that the law was constitutional. The decision reflected the new conservative majority under Chief Justice John Roberts. Part of the Court majority's argument was that the procedure was so rare that banning it did not place an "undue burden" on women's reproductive choices. The only woman then on the Supreme Court, Justice Ruth Bader Ginsburg, vigorously dissented declaring that the decision was "an effort to chip away a right declared again and again by the court. . . ." The political struggle for public opinion on abortion continues.[22]

CONCLUSION

Thirty years ago, political scientist Austin Sarat concluded, "In the final analysis, the shifting fortunes of abortion politics cannot be attributed to the actions of any group or institution, but rather to the rhythms of the larger culture."[23] The public's acceptance of legal abortion four decades ago was a result of a vast social change in attitudes labeled "the Sixties." A deep belief in personal freedom, decreasing support for religion, increasingly educated youth, and a growing women's movement all led to this acceptance.

Professional and interest groups, state governments, and then the Supreme Court supported this trend and followed it. Since then, opposition groups and elected officials have tried to restrict abortion by marketing their issues around policies like parental consent and partial birth to take advantage of the boundaries of its public support. Nor can one ignore the impact of intimidation, including the bombing of clinics and murder of doctors, in limiting women exercising their right to an abortion.[24]

But underlying the headlines, the polarized debates, and seeming shifts in political sentiment is a public opinion that has remained quite stable over a long period of time. The conclusions of the American public represent a balanced exercise of national judgment. They show the public reacting to available information and reaching moderate opinions as to how abortion should be permitted and limited. These conclusions, of course, may change. Some scholars think that a recent rise in conservative opinion undermining support for abortion may be the result of new ultrasound technology that produces pictures of early-stage fetuses and encourages a belief, especially among young women, that life begins at conception. Others conclude differently—that a younger generation constantly replaces an older one, bringing higher education rates, a larger urban population, and more exposure to modernizing ideas, leading to a long-term liberalizing of public opinion on issues like abortion.[25]

President Obama, among others, has pointed out that many of the issues and divisions that dominate American politics have their roots in the 1960s. That may cause despair that these conflicts have lasted so long, but it is also a reason for hope. Many of the voices on issues like abortion are now in their seventies or have recently died. Both from feminist groups and the religious right the leaders who have set the agendas for the last several decades are "getting quite long in the tooth." At the same time the Millennial generation, born since 1976, were more than a quarter of the voters in 2008. When added to the 20 percent of voters from Generation X, born between 1965 and 1976, there is a growing majority with no direct experience of the 1960s, or arguably much interest. The signs of diminishing popular intensity on issues like abortion underline the point.[26]

For our conclusion, we are willing to suspend our powers of prediction and agree with Drs. Page and Shapiro: "What the public thinks about a given policy now is a very strong indicator of what it will think later."[27] This stable body of opinion sets boundaries around the political choices available to policy-makers. To outlaw abortions now wouldn't be easy. It would require more than a Supreme Court decision, a bill by Congress, or even a constitutional amendment. It would need a revolution in thinking similar to the one that began in the 1960s.

Notes

1. Benjamin I. Page and Robert Y. Shapiro, *The Rational Public* (Chicago: University of Chicago Press, 1992); Frank Newport, *Polling Matters: Why Leaders Must Listen to the Wisdom of the People* (New York: Warner Books, 2004).
2. Lea Winerman, "President Obama Signs Executive Order on Abortion," *The Rundown*, March 24, 2010.

3. Kevin Sack, "In Ultrasound, Abortion Fight Has New Front," *The New York Times*, May 27, 2010.
4. Pew Research Center, "Support for Abortion Slips," October 1, 2009, http://people-press.org/report/549/support-for-abortion-slips
5. Everett Carll Ladd and Karlyn H. Bowman, *Public Opinion About Abortion*, 2nd ed. (Washington, DC: AEI Press, 1999), 1.
6. Gallup World Poll, July 18, 2010, http://www.gallup.com/poll/1576/abortion.aspx
7. See Morris P. Fiorina et al., *Culture War? The Myth of a Polarized America* (New York: Pearson, 2011), Chapter 5, "A Closer Look at Abortion."
8. Clyde Wilcox and Barbara Norrander, "Of Moods and Morals: The Dynamics of Opinion on Abortion and Gay Rights," in Clyde Wilcox and Barbara Norrander, eds., *Understanding Public Opinion*, 2nd ed. (Washington, DC: Congressional Quarterly Press, 2001).
9. Elizabeth Adell Cook, Ted G. Jelen, and Clyde Wilcox, *Between Two Absolutes: Public Opinion and the Politics of Abortion* (Boulder, CO: Westview Press, 1992), 37.
10. See *PollingReport.com/abortion.htm*, p. 1.
11. Cook, Jelen, and Wilcox, 36.
12. Ladd and Bowman, 15.
13. Fiorina, 2011, 89–94. The data on party members' opinions is from Fiorina.
14. See Austin Sarat, "Abortion and the Courts: Uncertain Boundaries of Law and Politics," in Allan P. Sindler, ed., *American Politics and Public Policy: Seven Case Studies* (Washington, DC: Congressional Quarterly Press, 1982), 124–125.
15. Barry Sussman, *What Americans Really Think* (New York: Pantheon, 1988), 192–199.
16. Sarat, 126–128.
17. Clyde Wilcox and Julia Riches, "Pills in the Public's Mind: RU 48 and the Framing of the Abortion Issue," *Women and Politics* 24, no. 3 (2002): 68–69.
18. See Emily Bazelon, "The New Abortion Providers," *The New York Times Magazine*, July 18, 2010, pp. 44–47.
19. Carol Matlock, "Mobilizing for the Abortion War," *National Journal*, July 15, 1989, 1814–1815.
20. Wilcox and Riches, 68.
21. Robin Toner, "For GOP, It's a Moment," *The New York Times*, November 6, 2003, p. A16.
22. Bill Mears, "Justice uphold ban on abortion procedure," CNN.com, April 18, 2007, www.cnn.com/2007/LA/04/18/scotus.abortion/index.html
23. Sarat, 127.
24. See Patricia Baird-Windle and Eleanor J. Bader, *Targets of Hatred: Anti-Abortion Terrorism* (New York: Palgrave, 2001).
25. The first opinion is from Wilcox and Norrander; the second is from Robert Erikson and Kent Tedin, *American Public Opinion*, 5th ed. (Needham Heights, MA: Allyn and Bacon, 1995), 115–116.
26. Fiorina, 245–246. Fiorina points to the following: Feminist icon Gloria Steinem is over 75, Betty Friedan, the founder of modern feminism died in 2006 at 79, and Eleanor Smeal, publisher of *Ms. Magazine* is over 70. On the other side, Pat Robertson, founder of the Christian Coalition, is over 80, Jerry Falwell, who started the Moral Majority, died in 2007 at 73, and James Dobson of Focus on the Family resigned as chair in 2009 at 73.
27. Page and Shapiro, 385.

6 CAMPAIGNS

Hillary Clinton and Sarah Palin

Sexism in the 2008 Presidential Race

In their search for support, presidential campaigns attempt to shape the messages communicated to the public about their candidates. This involves a struggle not only with rival campaigns but with the press. A woman candidate confronts added layers of complexity and stereotypes in projecting an image to the public. Since serious women candidates for president and vice president are still rare occurrences, the 2008 campaigns offer a novel opportunity to see two women competing for the highest offices in the land. How they dealt with gender-related obstacles and opportunities offers insights about campaigns and how the media covers them.

"Frames" is a term used to describe how issues and people are defined in the media. Framing presents and emphasizes certain aspects of an issue or political figure: what is important, what is the range of acceptable debate about the subject, and what conclusions can we draw about them. The framing of an event or a person emphasizes one of many possible readings of the facts; framing directs attention to parts of a reality, while ignoring others. Is a rise in crime linked to and explained by an economic recession or to illegal immigration or lax gun laws or too few police? Does this picture or news report show how attractive or emotional or intelligent is this candidate? "By choosing a common frame to describe an event, condition, or political personage, journalists shape public opinion."[1] Do certain frames— for example, appearance, strength, consistency—change or take on more significance if the candidate is a woman? Gender was a common frame used with both women candidates in 2008 to introduce, explain, or criticize them to the public.

Senator Clinton and Governor Palin handled the frame of their gender in contrasting ways. Clinton stressed her experience and competence in her public image but risked being characterized as unfeminine, unattractive, and unsympathetic. Palin, as a younger newcomer to national politics, emphasized traditional female roles as a mother and wife, while projecting an image of conservative toughness. But her appearance and frontier style could be used to define her as lacking intelligence and preparation for the office she sought. While neither women won the office they sought in 2008, gender was only one of many factors in their defeats, arguably not the most important. Both navigating and taking advantage of simplifying gender stereotypes were tricky and unresolved tasks of the two women's campaigns. In the future, women running for the White House may build on these experiences with greater success.

CONCEPTS TO CONSIDER _____

1. Are **media frames** inevitable in campaigns, because they can be used to present candidates in a simplified and interesting way? Can they be diversified to allow various views of the candidates to be presented to the public? Do they undermine the ability of voters to democratically decide who is the best qualified to fill the elected office?
2. Was the **gender frame** necessary in the media coverage of two candidates for offices that rarely see serious women candidates? Could it have been handled in a way less destructive to the candidates? Can a comparison be made to race—how the first African American nominee was portrayed in the media, and how he handled the issue of race?
3. How did Hillary **Clinton's greater experience** in politics help her overcome the negatives attached to her gender? Did she also miss opportunities to reach women to support her pioneering campaign as the first serious female candidate for president?
4. Was Governor Palin restrained in complaining about gender stereotyping because the McCain campaign had plucked her out of obscurity in part because she was a woman. Did **Palin's conservatism** make her refusal to downplay her feminine appearance more acceptable and more difficult to criticize? Can a conservative opposing many issues promoted by women's groups still be a feminist?
5. Will the next female candidates for president and vice president face the same issues in coverage by the press? What **lessons from the 2008 campaigns** do you think they will learn and apply to their own campaigns for the White House? How successful will they be?

Would you vote for a woman for president if she were qualified in every other respect?

—Gallup Poll, 1937

At the beginning of August 2008, John McCain knew little about his vice presidential pick, Sarah Palin. She had not been on his short list of candidates. This carefully reviewed, or vetted, list of five men had been painstakingly narrowed down, with extensive research and in-depth interviews. But none of them brought the game-changing impact that McCain needed to come from behind to win the presidential election. With a week to go before the August Republican convention, the governor of Alaska who McCain had only met twice came to the top of the selection process. She was seen as someone who could excite the Republican base, mobilize women voters, and reinforce McCain's claim to being a maverick. As a McCain advisor put it, "I'd rather lose by ten points trying to go for the win than lose by one point and look back and say, 'Goddamn it, I should have gone for the win.' "[2] And no doubt about it, Palin was a high-risk choice.

At forty-four, she had been Alaska's governor for twenty months. She had run as a reformer pledging to clean up corruption and had gained an 80 percent approval rate in the state. She had attended five colleges, been a beauty queen, a sportscaster, and a two-term mayor of the tiny town of Wasilla where she lived with her snowmobiling husband Todd and five children. She was conservative: pro-life, pro-guns, and pro-states rights. The governor offered a fresh face in national politics, a common touch, and, as endless observers commented, she was "hot."

She was also unprepared for the media spotlight that now turned ferociously on her. Part of her problem was that the McCain staff hadn't done its homework. They rushed "a vetting so hasty and haphazard it barely merited the name."[3] They hadn't fully researched her background, nor had she been adequately briefed on the foreign and domestic issues she would face as a candidate for vice president. A campaign staff quickly hired to support her knew next to nothing about their new boss. Within the GOP, President Bush was reported to be baffled and the current occupant of the office she sought, Vice President Cheney, told friends it was a "reckless choice." McCain's people were not equipped to defend their surprising selection.

Into this vacuum came the national press with questions and rumors, many related to gender roles. Was her husband a member of a party favoring Alaskan succession? Was her infant son, who had Down syndrome, really her daughter's baby? And that same unmarried daughter's own pregnancy soon became public. A newspaper tabloid accused the governor of infidelity. Her past participation in beauty pageants led to portrayals that edged into stereotypes. Emphasis focused on her physical appearance, her wardrobe, and what could be considered feminine nonverbal communication such as winking. The issue of whether she was qualified for the vice presidency was a legitimate one. But reporters' questions often focused on aspects of her gender in framing this issue of her qualifications.

Prior to Governor Palin emerging the best example of media using gender to present and explain a candidate in the 2008 presidential campaign was Hillary Clinton. A former corporate lawyer she was the first career woman to serve as First Lady. (The next lawyer who became First Lady, Michelle Obama, was initially noted for an outspoken independence characterized by opponents as "an unpatriotic angry black woman." In the course of the campaign, she tamed her image to more traditional, subordinate roles as wife and mother.)

Clinton built her career on her White House experience. She defied convention by fulfilling her husband's promise that voters supporting him would be getting "two for one." Early in the administration she provided vigorous, if unsuccessful, leadership of major health-care reform. She spoke before the UN, led international delegations pushing for human and women's rights, and became known for her strong advocacy for government programs assisting children and families. She also acquired her husband's political enemies, and was tarred with rumors of her involvement in scandals and controversy. She was a polarizing leader in the Democratic party, loved by supporters and hated by others.

In 2000, she became senator from New York, the first former first lady to ever be elected to public office. She was a popular senator who won a landslide reelection in 2006. With her own national reputation and her husband's network of political allies, Hillary became a front-runner for the party nomination starting soon after George W. Bush's reelection in 2004. She maintained that lead in the polls for the next three years. Her announcement in early 2007 that she was officially running excited many women because as her campaign's tagline said, she was "making history."

As the first serious woman candidate for president, she navigated through gender stereotypes by presenting herself as a strong, decisive leader. During the campaign, she told a group of Ohio supporters, "I'm here today because I want to let you know, I'm a fighter, a doer and a champion, and I will fight for you." The governor of North Carolina described her as someone "who makes Rocky Balboa look like a pansy." Her opponents took this frame and found negatives in it. Her gender was a frequent hook for attacks including bumper stickers that read "Life's a bitch so don't vote for one." She was characterized as an emasculator, as abrasive, and as calculating. When she broke down in tears before the New Hampshire primary, commentators questioned the authenticity of the moment. Others, like Lawrence Kudlow of CNBC commented on her "roller-coaster, mood swings." There were news stories about her forced laugh, called a "cackle." Hillary may have been tough; she didn't seem likeable, or feminine.[4]

The reasons behind her failure to win her party's nomination are numerous enough without raising issues connected to gender. Her long political experience and the national coalition she had behind her campaign had raised expectations to an unrealistic level. By being the "inevitable" candidate any setback became that much more deflating. She led a poorly managed campaign with an uncertain strategy; her husband played a distracting role. She appeared as a novel female candidate as well as a Washington-insider with all the baggage that both roles carried. And of course she ran up against, and underestimated, a political phenom named Barack Obama. She may have been "ready to lead on Day 1" but she lost the Iowa caucuses and never quite recovered. She ended up winning 9 of the last 16 primaries and caucuses, compiling an overall total of 18 million votes nationwide before she graciously endorsed Obama at the Democratic convention.

GENDER AND ELECTIONS

Any candidate for national office, especially in the White House, will be subject to intense public scrutiny by the media. The suddenness of Sarah Palin's emergence on the political scene and her relative lack of experience sharpened that scrutiny. For Hillary Clinton, her identity as a First Lady and the almost casual if harsh judgments of her as a woman, for example, her looks, dress, feminism, were part of how she was presented in the media. For the two politicians gender roles were important in a couple ways in how they, like most women candidates, were presented to the public through the media.

First is how a campaign projects an image of the candidate by her words, appearance, and actions. Within the confines of her gender she can shape, to some degree, how she is seen by the press and public, and what being a woman means to her. How central to her public image is her husband, her children and her role in her family, and how traditionally does she define her involvement in her home life—a difficult balance for most career women. For example, women candidates may use only their first name in campaign literature to communicate informality and intimacy, or circulate their pictures posed with their family to emphasize the importance of their roles as wives and mothers. How these women dress also communicates quite a lot.

Perhaps more important are the general frames that the press and public bring to their evaluation of female candidates. Here, media judges what is of interest (or entertaining) to their audience, what information about the candidate should be covered, and with what emphasis. This may mean looking for novel, quirky features of a person's life, qualifications for office or positions on issues, or negative 'gotcha' mistakes that candidates make when campaigning.

There is evidence that female candidates are reported on differently than males. Women often receive more coverage than men on their appearance, personality, and family. Stories on women candidates are more likely to mention children and marital status and to define the candidates by these roles. When Elizabeth Dole, Republican Senator from North Carolina, ran for president, voters were more likely to learn about her appearance or character than her issue positions. Her role as Senator Bob Dole's wife was featured prominently and references to her family surfaced more frequently than those of her opponents. In 1984, Geraldine Ferraro, the first woman nominated for the vice presidency by a major political party, was described as "feisty" and "pushy but not threatening." When she appeared on stage before the Democratic National Convention, NBC anchor Tom Brokaw announced, "Geraldine Ferraro . . . The first woman to be nominated for vice president . . . Size 6!"[5]

The bottom-line question about media framing is this: Does it influence how voters vote? Here things get cloudy. Polls and experiments have indicated that factors including party loyalty, incumbency, and ideology are much more important in influencing how people vote. For instance, the overwhelming number of men who presently hold congressional seats, and thus bring the advantages of incumbency to their campaigns, is arguably the major reason that the percentage of women in congress remains low.[6] A number of experiments failed to find any direct effects of gender on how people voted. As one study concluded, "Voters are not automatically drawn to candidates simply because they are of the same sex; party and political positions are of greater concern when choosing a candidate to vote for."[7]

However, media coverage that stereotypes female candidates may influence voters in evaluating leadership traits. Studies suggest that people do use sex stereotypes when evaluating equivalent male and female candidates. Female candidates are seen as better able to deal with "women's issues" such as education and health. They are also considered more honest and compassionate than male candidates, as well as less likely to be professional politicians. Where information gaps exist cues from stereotypes become more important. For example, in some polls Republicans were less likely to vote for candidates who were females. But further studies showed that it was because the women candidates were thought to be more liberal, that is, strong on welfare spending and social issues and weak on foreign policy and military security. When female candidates who were conservatives emphasized these issues, the lag in support among Republicans disappeared.[8]

The Feminine Bind

Women candidates are caught in a double bind by gender framing. Appearing feminine is a disadvantage to being seen as a leader, especially a national leadership position (like president or vice president) traditionally occupied by men and requiring so-called masculine traits of aggressiveness, dominance, and toughness. Women who attain political positions will often be judged more harshly than men doing the same jobs. Gender roles conflict with the qualities needed for leadership. This means that women candidates may be tempted to play down their feminine sides, while stressing strength and their ability to get the job done. But there's a problem.

Appearing more masculine may make these women less likeable. The public responds negatively to a woman who appears too masculine. She is seen as less sympathetic to the underprivileged, less understanding of more traditional women, less on the side of change. Women candidates have the tricky task of navigating between these conflicting perceptions. Kathleen Hall Jamieson described the double bind this way: "Women who are considered feminine will be judged incompetent, and women who are competent, unfeminine . . . women who succeed in politics and public life will be scrutinized under a different lens from that applied to successful men."[9]

This feminine bind is more important in executive leadership positions in which masculine qualities are identified with the functions and images of the office. Nowhere in American politics is this more true than in the presidency.

Only men have ever been president. Just as important is that many of the functions and symbols of the presidency are associated with masculinity. The importance of serving as a single leader, commander in chief of "the greatest nation on earth" in a dangerous world of terrorists and other enemies, has underlined virtues that have made presidential elections a "masculine space."

In this "space" lurks the question of executive toughness, a preference for military heroes, sports and war metaphors attaching to debates and campaigns. The test is whether the potential presidential "timber" can take on the rituals and real obligations of a king, a father of his people and a warrior-leader. Inspiring confidence in a candidate means having an image that inspires confidence. In many ways, the presidency has become a male-gendered institution where men have played a dominant role in its creation and evolution. Masculinity becomes "natural" in the presidential ideal.[10]

HILLARY CLINTON AND THE TIES THAT BIND

A generation older than Sarah Palin, Clinton was a 1973 law school graduate who came of age during a time when women were first beginning to benefit from the civil rights laws of the 1960s guaranteeing equal employment and educational opportunities. These path breakers believed they had to work harder and play down their sexual identities in order to be treated as equals in male-dominated workplaces. That meant deemphasizing their roles as mothers, wives, and partners, while projecting an identity of asexual competence in

Hillary Clinton's professional competence was seldom questioned; her appearance highlighted by an iconic orange pants suit raised other questions about her public image.

work style and appearance. This image of female independence and lack of submissiveness to men may have made these 1960s feminists threatening to men and women in traditional marriages embracing more conservative values with more conventional lifestyles.

In her long political career, Hillary's independent ways undoubtedly added to her problems. When she married Bill Clinton, she initially retained her surname, Hillary Rodham, until this common feminist practice got such a chilly reception in Arkansas that she switched to using her husband's name. Her sarcastic remark on her career choice in the 1992 presidential campaign—"I could have stayed home and baked cookies"—was long cited by political opponents as reflecting her lack of sympathy for stay-at-home mothers. Her husband's insistence that she was an equal partner in the White House, her failed leadership in reforming health care, and her preference for that symbol of women's professionalism, the pants suit, led to her being seen as elitist, unattractive, and difficult. Her lack of public popularity followed from this widespread view of her distancing herself from her feminine side and the lives of more traditional women.

Ironically, her husband's public infidelity helped her overcome the cold professionalism of her public image. As the "wronged woman" in the Lewinsky scandal, Hillary became a victim, both more human and more sympathetic. Much as she had downplayed her feminine side to emphasize her toughness and competence, it was her vulnerability as a woman that raised her popularity, and may have helped in successfully becoming a senator from New York in 2000. Even in the 2008 campaign, her support seemed to rise when she showed her emotional side by tearing up just before the New Hampshire primary. Detaching further from her image as a "genderless policy wonk," Hillary was able to show strength and to soften her image by expressing sympathy for families in industrial states facing tough economic times. Her criticisms of Barack Obama as not experienced or tough enough for the presidency helped her avoid a too-soft image.

It did not keep her from being attacked. On TV she was referred to in sexist terms as "castrating" (Tucker Carlson) and a "she-devil" (Chris Mathews).[11] Clinton was the inspiration for nutcrackers made in her likeness. Because her only child, Chelsea, was an adult, she didn't have to deal with concerns that she was neglecting her family responsibilities in running for president. She in fact seldom mentioned her identity as a mother in her campaign. Of course as an older woman she endured comments by reporters describing her appearance as "tired," "wrinkled," and "aged." Rush Limbaugh on his radio show made the point more harshly and explicitly, "Will the country want to actually watch a woman get older before their eyes on a daily basis?" The visuals of watching John McCain (the oldest candidate in the race) age were not discussed.[12]

Clinton and her advisors recognized early on the importance of countering the stereotype that a woman president would be too "soft" in dealing with America's enemies. She joined the Armed Services Committee as soon as she entered the Senate. When she announced for the presidency, she publicized thirty admirals and generals who endorsed her. She not only endorsed the war in Iraq but she repeatedly refused to renounce that when she was a candidate despite heavy criticism from her Democratic opponents. Flip-flopping on the vote would have opened her up to charges of being weak and indecisive on military and foreign affairs, thus playing into the stereotype. A story from her campaign in 2007 illustrates Hillary's mind-set. *Vogue* magazine wanted to do a cover shoot and photo spread on the first woman president-in-waiting. Her aides favored doing it as another opportunity to humanize their boss. She turned it down, saying that she was "still trying to convince white men that I can be the commander in chief, and me looking pretty in a dress isn't gonna do that."[13]

By emphasizing their candidate's experience, the Clinton campaign projected her strength and consistency—a way out of the feminine bind. This "gender-masking strategy" may have cost her women's support. As one feminist writer put it, "Why should they show up to support a woman who would barely reveal herself as one?"[14] Unfortunately, this presentation of herself may have made her less sympathetic and left her de-emphasizing her role as an agent of change in an election year when change was a more attractive message, as Barack Obama's success showed.

In some ways Hillary succeeded. Early in 2008, a national poll indicated that 65 percent of Americans thought she had the necessary experience to become president. (On the other hand, only 38 percent of Americans on Election Day thought Sarah Palin was qualified to be president.) This tricky balance of gaining public sympathy while projecting competence and strength was a reflection of the feminine double bind Hillary's campaign faced and only partially navigated.[15]

The challenges Hillary Clinton faced in the split between feminine warmth and masculine toughness in the electoral arena of presidential politics made her a pioneer to those candidates who followed her. On stage at the Republican convention, Sarah Palin reached out to Hillary's supporters, implicitly accepting her debt to her older Democratic rival. "Hillary left eighteen million cracks in the highest, hardest glass ceiling. But it turns out the women of America aren't finished yet, and we can shatter that glass ceiling once and for all."

SARAH PALIN: GENDER COVERAGE

Gender roles, particularly those of a mother and temptress, were seldom far from the portrait drawn of Sarah Palin by the media in the 2008 campaign. Nor, in fairness, was gender far from Palin's own presentation of herself.

The focus on her physical appearance often started with references to her participation in beauty pageants. *The Washington Post* reported that "Palin entered the Miss Wasilla beauty pageant and won, playing the flute for her talent. She went on to compete for Miss Alaska and was a runner up." A later *Post* article covered Palin's appearance from her hair to her "peep-toe pump" and concluded that "Palin seems to dress for pretty rather than powerful." Maureen Dowd, columnist with *The New York Times*, called Palin "Caribou Barbie" blending her attractiveness with Alaska and the National

While her competence was questioned, former Governor Sarah Palin managed to look both fashionable and feminine with her knee high black boots.

Rifle Association. David Wright of ABC said that "Palin can seem like the young, trophy running mate." CNBC commentator Donny Deutsch observed, "Women want to be her; men want to mate with her." A widely distributed Reuters photo shot from behind showed her legs and black high heels framing a young male supporter.[16] In a publicized line, comic actor Alec Baldwin on *Saturday Night Live* said when meeting her, "You are way hotter in person."

Palin's role as a mother was prominently and repeatedly featured in news stories. John McCain introduced her early in the campaign as "a devoted wife and a mother of five." She frequently described herself as a "hockey mom" notably defining that in her acceptance speech as a pit bull with lipstick. An array of newspapers elevated her role as "a spunky mom" (*Daily News*), "the tableau of everyday mom-ness" (*The Los Angeles Times*), and "suburban supermom" (*The New York Times*).

Palin was never merely the passive victim of this media image-creation that she sometimes claimed to be. Reflecting both her own strong personality and a media strategy, she embraced various gender roles. She presented herself simultaneously in a "family-conscious, sexy fashion." Her style included a traditional women's role implicitly rejecting gender neutrality and independence as necessary for proving competence in the male world of election politics. Instead of muting her sexuality she projected it. She and her supporters used animal metaphors which are a common stereotype for women ("foxy," "catfights," "old bat") to project a fierce maternal protectiveness, including phrases like "mama grizzlies" and "Saracuda." At the same time, she was able to embrace a rugged masculinity by vigorously attacking her Democratic opponents. This "split personality" was used by conservative women candidates in the 2010 midterm elections and may provide a road map for future female candidates.[17]

Palin embraced her gender by dressing feminine, wearing her hair long, and emphasizing her role as a mother. Her tight skirts, long hair, high heels, and significant amount of makeup conveyed her femininity. Unlike Hillary Clinton who downplayed her gender and sexuality, Palin embraced hers. She referred to her husband (as "my guy") and acted as the supportive wife in praising her running mate, John McCain. She reinforced traditional feminine identities in her dress and lifestyle, role as a mother, belief in family and church, and in deferring to her husband and running mate. She blended a populist appeal as a Western woman who knows how to gut a moose with a traditional reinforcement of family in welcoming a new special needs infant and a grandchild born out of wedlock. Conforming to these traditional female norms of sexuality and motherhood also allowed her to perform the male roles of attacking her opponents and projecting a tough, aggressive personality on the campaign trail. This feminine packaging may have allowed her to deliver this "masculine" aggressive message in a way that was seen as less threatening by the public.[18]

The public focus on Palin's traditional gender roles was a two-edged sword. It invited a round of questions of whether she could juggle being a good mother and vice president. CNN and ABC reporters, among others, asked whether she could handle raising an infant with special needs and the demands of political office. The announcement that her seventeen-year-old daughter was pregnant intensified the media discussion. CNN's Campbell Brown asked why she had subjected her daughter to this kind of scrutiny by accepting her high-profile candidacy. *The New York Times* put it this way: "With five children, including an infant with Down syndrome and, as the country learned Monday, a pregnant 17-year-old, Ms. Palin has set off a fierce argument among women about whether there are enough hours in the day for her to take on the vice presidency, and whether she is right to try." Two feminist writers commented, "In other words, wait until your children are grown before pursuing such a high-profile career. Once again, this is something that is never asked of men."[19]

Her good looks reinforced the perception that Palin was a dummy. There's an old tradition in American politics of characterizing an opponent as being someone's puppet. Those like Palin who don't have elite universities' degrees or experience in leadership circles tend to be dismissed as a blank slate that someone else may write on. Even within the McCain campaign this view took hold, with Steve Schmidt, the candidate's senior strategist telling other staff, "She doesn't know anything." The focus on her attractiveness may have lowered peoples' opinion of her competence, as a social psychologist's experiment after the election indicated. The feminine bind was still operating in the presidential campaign.[20]

The fall 2008 wardrobe flap took the issue of clothes and turned it against the governor. Politico's website reported that the Republican National Committee had spent over $150,000 to outfit Palin and her family. Each of her five aides had been given permission to spend $28,000 on her outfits and in the chaotic travels of the campaign the amounts spent on high-end items for TV appearances had mounted quickly. The shopping sprees, not completely under the control of the candidate, now threatened her reputation as a down-to-earth housewife. Her response that the clothes weren't really hers and that they would be given to charity after the campaign only partly ended the story. Nasty leaks from the campaign staff referred to her as "a whack job" and "a diva." The clothing scandal became an example for opponents of the hypocrisy of a high-maintenance prima donna. For her supporters this was, again, a sexist media diverting attention from the issues.

Campaign Media Strategy: Palin's Competency Question

[The goal is not to see a] female Einstein become an assistant professor. We want a woman schlemiel to get promoted as quickly as a male schlemiel.

—Bella Abzug, a 1960s feminist and former congresswoman

For much of the first month after her nomination, Sarah Palin was kept from the press. She would give her highly polished stump speech while preparing for a series of anticipated interviews with the network news anchors. Behind this strategy was her staff's feelings that she was unprepared to answer difficult policy questions, and that the press was the "mortal enemy," and should be treated that way. A lot of her time between public appearances was spent memorizing information on 3 x 5 cards that the press might ask her. The McCain staff because of their unfamiliarity with the candidate ignored her reputation in Alaska for having an adept personal touch in dealing with reporters. Whatever the reasons behind the media strategy, the result was that "the least known vice presidential candidate in modern history did not take a single question from the traveling press for the first three weeks of the campaign." After the election, one staffer admitted that they had made "a huge mistake" by not allowing her to talk with the media. The result was both suspicion of her qualifications and resentment from the working press assigned to cover her.[21]

This detachment from the press elevated the importance of the televised interviews that she gave to the network news anchors, with disastrous results. Drawing the most attention was the two-part interview she had with CBS anchor, Katie Couric. Perhaps she was tired, perhaps distracted by her upcoming debate with Joe Biden, or perhaps she simply lacked experience in national politics—whatever the reasons, Palin went into the interview unprepared and unfocused. She placed great confidence in her ability to improvise and this time it proved to be misplaced. The interview, clips of which were replayed on YouTube and cable news programs, was seen as an iconic moment illustrating that the governor was indeed not ready for prime time.

Couric had been advised by her producer to avoid "gotcha" questions to keep from being seen as unfair to Palin. Her question about what newspapers and magazines the governor regularly read to stay informed of events in the world hardly seemed to fall in that category.

But Palin tensed. "I've read most of them, again with great appreciation for the press, for the media."

"Like what ones specifically?" Couric asked.

"All of them," Palin responded, throwing her hands in the air. "Any of them that have been in front of me over all these years. I have a vast—"

"Can you name a few?"

"I have a vast variety of sources where we get our news, too."[22]

It was a simple question, needing a simple answer. Her staffer who brought press clippings to her room each morning looked on in horror at his boss's refusal to answer. Palin had taken affront at what she heard as the implied criticism that a "grizzly momma" on the far reaches of the American frontier was unlikely to keep up with the news.

And there were other flubs in the Couric interviews. When asked to name some Supreme Court cases besides *Roe v. Wade* that she disagreed with, Palin had been unable to cite any. Her inarticulate hedge went like this: "Of course in the great history of America there have been rulings that there's never going to be absolute consensus by every American"—and left it at that. She was asked to name examples of McCain's efforts to regulate the economy. Her reply: "I'll try to find some and bring them to you." And her inability to answer a question on the economy with anything more than incoherent sentences and indecipherable words only underlined the press view that she was in over her head.

Her media frame may have been summed up by a quote that she never actually said. Asked about the relevance of Russia's proximity to Alaska, Palin had declared in her ABC TV interview with Charlie Gibson, "They're our next door neighbors. And you can actually see Russia from land here in Alaska." This led to *Saturday Night Live*'s Tina Fey's satiric portrayal of a ditzy Palin proudly chirping, "And I can see Russia from my house," which for many in the media and many others came to define the governor. Millions of Americans thought the phrase was consistent with her image and that was enough for it to become one of the most quoted lines in the election.[23]

CONCLUSION

Both women candidates running for national office in 2008, Hillary Clinton and Sarah Palin, had to deal with gender stereotypes in the media. They took varying routes with mixed success.

For Clinton it meant downplaying her femininity. Her emphasis on her toughness, experience, and competence was in part speaking to any implicit public doubts about putting a woman into the male bastion of the presidency. Her consistency and conservatism on issues of defense and foreign policy, including the war in Iraq, followed this strategy. It did not keep her from being presented in a negative gender frame, from pants suits to castrating to unattractive.

Palin, the newcomer to national politics, was also the more innovative. She dressed in a feminine way—including long hair, lipstick and heels—and embraced traditional roles of a mother and wife by frequently appearing with her family. Palin also didn't mind performing certain seductive actions like asking her Democratic vice presidential opponent whether she could call him "Joe" and winking at the audience. By identifying with conservative politics and traditional family norms, she could attack opponents without seeming uncomfortably masculine. None of this could remedy her very real lack of preparation for the office she sought or for her lack of familiarity with the issues she was expected to know.

But the issue here is not the imperfections of these two candidates. It is that these flaws, as well as other aspects of their personalities and campaigns, are seen through a gender lens. Hillary was intimidating; Palin was unprepared— but the issue was that these characterizations took on sexist frames in how these candidates were presented in the media. Was that necessary?

As one scholar of the issue has written, the angle that drives stories about women running for high office is the fact that the candidate is female. "Because these reports are fundamentally about women, they often include descriptions of what the candidate is wearing, descriptions of emotions, and much information about personality and character. In other words, they include the kind of information that society regards as relevant to women." While there was progress in the campaign of this frame being replaced by a more candidate-oriented one concentrating on the same issues, the coverage between male and female candidates was never quite equal.[24]

Neither candidate felt comfortable in dealing directly with the characterizations that implied that women because of their gender were somehow less qualified for high office. When Clinton did talk about the "all-boys club of politics" to students at Wellesley, she was criticized for "playing the gender card." There was to be no parallel in either woman's campaigns to the speech on racism that Barack Obama gave after the incendiary remarks of Reverend Wright about black people in America. Both handled the issue indirectly in speeches, advertisements, and appearances. That may indicate how much further women candidates still have to go to get to the White House.

Gender stereotypes are used in elections because they work. For the press, they are an easily understood, often entertaining way to appear to analyze and personalize candidates. For women candidates, gender may be an unavoidable issue but it may also offer some positives such as representing "women's" issues, as well as offering a caring perspective and a more sympathetic response on issues such as education and health care. For the public, gender stereotypes offer a simplified shortcut in drawing conclusions about women candidates' suitability for high office.

The 2010 midterm elections offered hope that both the issue and the stereotypes of gender may be diminishing. There was buzz in the press that conservative Republican women—often labeled "mama grizzlies" when endorsed by Sarah Palin—would change the political playing field for their gender. A record-breaking 145 Republican women filed to run for Congress, but only 52 survived their state primaries and 26 actually won seats—24 in the House, 2 in the Senate. Democratic women, who traditionally run in much larger numbers than Republican women, won 48 seats in the House and 4 in the Senate. In the end the 112th House had 72 women, compared to 73 in the 111th Congress, while the Senate stayed the same with 17 females. This is the first time since 1979 that the number of women in Congress actually dropped. Women still make up less than a fifth of Congress.

And the press . . . remains the press. In a 2010 interview on Fox News, Greta Van Susteren asked Sarah Palin about an issue—with photographs—circulating on the Internet. "Breast implants: Did you have them or not?" Women candidates still had a ways to go.[25]

Notes

1. Kathleen Hall Jamieson and Paul Waldman, *The Press Effect* (New York: Oxford University Press, 2003), xiii.
2. John Heilemann and Mark Halperin, *Game Change* (New York: HarperCollins Publishers, 2010), 363.
3. Ibid.
4. From Diana B. Carlin and Kelly L. Winfrey, "Have You Come a Long Way, Baby? Hillary Clinton, Sarah Palin, and Sexism in 2008 Campaign Coverage," *Communication Studies* 60, no. 4 (September–October 2009), 328–29.
5. Susan J. Carroll and Kelly Dittmar, "The 2008 Candidacies of Hillary Clinton and Sarah Palin," in Susan J. Carroll and Richard L. Fox, eds. *Gender and Elections* (New York: Cambridge University Press, 2010), 58–61.
6. See Barbara Palmer and Dennis Simon, *Breaking the Political Glass Ceiling* (New York: Routledge, 2006).
7. See Richard Matland and David King, "Women as Candidates in Congressional Elections," in Cindy Simon Rosenthal, ed. *Women Transforming Congress* (Norman, OK: University of Oklahoma Press, 2002).
8. Kim Fridkin Kahn, "Does Being Male Help? An Investigation of the Effects of Candidate Gender and Campaign Coverage on Evaluations of U.S. Senate Candidates," *The Journal of Politics* 54, no. 2 (May 1992), 497–517.
9. Kathleen Hall Jamieson, *Beyond the Double Bind: Women and Leadership* (New York: Oxford University Press, 1995), 16.
10. Georgia Duerst-Lahti, "Presidential Elections: Gendered Space and the Case of 2008," in Susan J. Carroll and Richard L. Fox, eds. *Gender and Elections*, 2nd ed. (New York: Cambridge University Press, 2010), 26–27.

11. Andrew Stephens, "Hating Hillary," *New Statesman*, May 22, 2008.
12. Carroll and Dittmar, 70.
13. Paraphrased from Heilemann and Halperin, 101.
14. Rebecca Traister, *Big Girls Don't Cry* (New York: Free Press, 2010), 75.
15. See references in Ann C. McGinley, "Hillary Clinton, Sarah Palin, and Michelle Obama: Performing Gender, Race, and Class on the Campaign Trail," *Denver University Law Review* 86 (March 6, 2009), 715–19.
16. From Carlin and Winfrey, 330–31.
17. McGinley, 721.
18. Carlin and Winfrey, 324.
19. Ibid.
20. Nathan A. Helflick and Jamie L. Goldenberg, "Objectifying Sarah Palin: Evidence that Objectification Causes Women to be Perceived as Less Competent and Less Fully Human," *Journal of Experimental Social Psychology* 45 (2009), 598–601.
21. Scott Conroy and Shushannah Walshe, *Sarah From Alaska* (New York: Public Affairs, 2009), 124–26.
22. Conroy and Walshe, 140–43.
23. Conroy and Walshe, 132. Also see Carl M. Cannon, "Sarah 'Barracuda' Palin and the Piranhas of the Press," *Politics Daily*, July 8, 2009.
24. Erika Falk, *Women for President*, 2nd ed. (Urbana, IL: University of Illinois Press, 2010), 177.
25. See Anne E. Kornblut, "In Primaries, Female Candidates Didn't Make Gender an Issue," *The Washington Post*, June 10, 2010. Howie Kurtz, "Media Notes," *The Washington Post*, June 14, 2010.

7 ELECTIONS

THE REELECTION GAME
An Insider's Candid View

Elections can be exciting. They can be bruising battles between articulate rivals over issues of policies and values, experience, and character. Even their frequent nastiness shows the vigor and importance of an open political marketplace. Elections are the method by which a democracy chooses its leaders in a public contest for popular support. At least, they're supposed to be.[1]

From the viewpoint of those playing the election game, the goal is to win a powerful office. Generally, the person already in the job has the edge in name recognition, money, experience, and a paid office staff. In races for the House of Representatives, these incumbents have even greater advantages because they are able to change the playing field—quite literally. The redrawing of congressional districts after each decade's census offers the political party controlling state government the chance to maximize their favorable districts, while minimizing those of their opponents. In 2002, this advantage produced a House where only four challengers defeated incumbents, the fewest in history. Even the 2010 House election that was considered a disaster for incumbents and resulted in a change of party control from Democrats to Republicans showed only a few incumbents actually losing in the general election. Incumbents ran in 395 races and 54 were defeated (52 Democrats and 2 Republicans) meaning that 13.6 percent of incumbents who ran lost. Most elections remain "choiceless"—merely rubberstamping the nominee of the party that drew the legislative boundaries.[2] What follows illustrates "a normal" reelection campaign for the House seen from the inside.

The following interview with a young campaign manager reflects this lukewarm reality. David "Duke" Hernandez is a twenty-seven-year-old Californian, a former high school wrestler only a few pounds over his fighting weight. Although he sometimes drops phrases from the barrio, he is the son of two teachers and an honors college graduate. In 2002, he managed the reelection campaign of a California congressman we will call Dick Hayes. The story is Duke's, but all names and identifying facts have been changed to allow us to hear an insider's frank views of what happens in the overwhelming majority of the elections where House incumbents keep their jobs in "The People's House."

CONCEPTS TO CONSIDER _____

1. The **advantages of incumbency** come through clearly in this campaign manager's story. Of those mentioned, which are the most important—redistricting, experience in office, public recognition, fundraising, professional consultants, or congressional staff—in explaining the high rates of incumbent reelections? How can a challenger overcome these incumbent advantages?

2. The campaign spends considerable effort **manipulating the electoral process**. Redistricting is an important part of that process. How does the campaign influence the size and composition of the electorate? Would redistricting tend to produce less moderate, more partisan members of Congress dependent on core supporters, as some have charged? How does the campaign staff encourage supporters to vote, while discouraging its opponents from voting?

3. How important is **fundraising** in the campaign? Do the people contributing money have a major influence over the candidate? Could their impact be out of sight of the young campaign manager? Would any campaign finance reform, such as lower fundraising limits, change how the campaign raises money or the influence of money in elections? Would it make campaigning more difficult for incumbents or for challengers?

4. Only a little more than one-third of eligible voters turn out for congressional elections in years when there is no presidential election. Is **voter participation** encouraged or discouraged by the strategy and tactics of this campaign? Does the campaign manager want a large number of new voters to participate on Election Day? Does his realistic description of the inside workings of a campaign make you more, or less, likely to vote?

5. Despite the flaws in campaigns and elections, are there still **benefits flowing from elections**? How does even a reelection to a "safe seat" pressure a member of Congress to leave the bright lights of Washington to meet constituents, talk with interest groups, and raise money? How do elected officials benefit from a campaign? How do voters? How does democracy?

Note: Although this case is in the campaign manager's own words, author comments have been inserted throughout in italics.

The first thing to understand about being a campaign manager for a congressman's reelection is that it isn't very intellectually demanding. It's pretty mechanical. Most of the creative work was done before I arrived on the scene. The redistricting that was done after the 2000 census made all the difference. You could call it an "incumbent-protection racket."[3]

THE REDISTRICTING RACKET

> After the 2000 census, California legislators deliberately drew
> congressional district boundaries in ways designed to eliminate
> competition. . . . Their redistricting scheme took away the voters'
> power to choose.
>
> *Thomas E. Patterson, The Vanishing Voter*

California's 56th District, which Congressman Dick Hayes represents, has usually been marginally Democratic. Hayes first won it in 1996 when it was an open seat, against a moderate Republican woman. He won by a couple of points, outspending her by a lot; a right-wing Libertarian candidate took 5,000 votes, which was more than our margin of victory. 1998 was pretty much a repeat of the first race, with Dick increasing his margin a bit in a lower-turnout non-presidential election year. Then in 2000 the Republicans targeted the district, figuring that with redistricting coming up, this would be their last chance to win the seat. Despite recruiting a strong candidate and putting money into the race, the GOP lost. With [Al] Gore at the top of the [Democratic] ticket winning 57 percent in California, Hayes won the district with 52 percent of the vote, which was three points over a moderate former congressman. So before the 2000 census, the 56th was Democratic, but only by 2–3 percent.

As you know, after the census every state legislature draws up new maps for its congressional districts, which then go to the governor for his approval. The state got one more congressional seat because of population increase. Since in California at the time Democrats controlled the assembly and the governorship, the party was expected to help itself. The party didn't gain as many seats from redistricting as the Republicans did in Texas, because the Democratic incumbents wanted to make sure their own seats were safe. So rather than help the party by moving Democratic voters from their districts to Republican districts and make them close races, most California incumbents took care of themselves by adding Dems to their own districts. This meant increasing the margins of victory for most Democratic incumbent. That's what my congressman did.[4]

The congressman had discussions with a senior staff guy in the state assembly, which I wasn't part of. I heard they ran through the results of some sophisticated computer map programs to figure out how to make the seat safe. Of course, there were a lot of other pols besides Dick interested in the redistricted map. The result was that we cut out an upper-middle-class Republican area and added two Hispanic communities on either end of the district that were overwhelmingly Democratic. Overnight our district went from a 2–3 percent Democratic margin to a pretty secure 12 percent Democratic advantage in registered voters. *In all honesty this redistricting was more important than any campaigning that I did.* (See Fig 7.1)

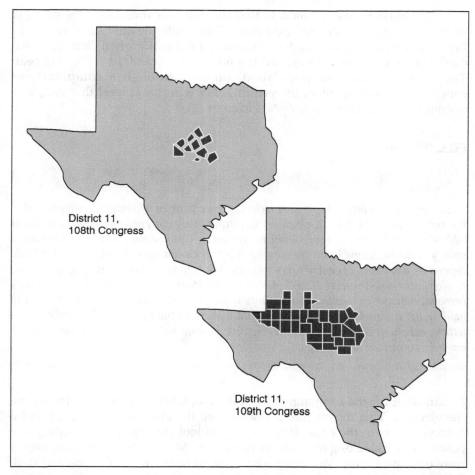

FIGURE 7.1   An example of partisan redistricting: Texas 11th Congressional District, 2002.

The redistricting also managed to pack the Republicans into one neighboring district. So instead of having two marginally Republican districts bordering us, we ended up with one solidly Republican district and one where a Democrat could win—which is what happened when one Republican incumbent was forced to run in this new district and lost to a Democrat in 2002. Meanwhile we doubled our Hispanic population so that it became 30 percent of the district. Hayes actually would have preferred another upscale liberal Democratic area, but lost out to a neighboring Democratic congresswoman who had more seniority and more clout in the [State] Assembly. The congressman now worries about some young Hispanic activist organizing the area and running against him in a future primary. In the future, he is more likely to lose his seat to an insurgent Democrat in the primary than he is to lose to a Republican in the election.

The bottom line for us was that the 56th became a safe Democratic district. Our consultant predicted that 175,000 voters would go to the polls. But whether turnout was high or low would not make any difference in the race. Hayes was likely to exceed the 60 percent standard for a safe seat. The consultant ran the population numbers through a computer and concluded, "I anticipate an uneventful, easy win [for Hayes] this year, and uncomplicated reelections for years to come."

FILL 'ER UP

So this House incumbent begins his reelection race with an advantage of shaping what his voters will look like. Beyond redistricting, this congressman shares a major advantage with other congressional incumbents—fundraising. Having substantial money in the bank long before the campaign begins discourages opponents. Incumbents depend on a network of contributors who want to help for personal and policy reasons. In elections below the level of well-publicized presidential campaigns, a congressman's personal network of wealthy contributors is probably more important than the use of mail or the Internet. Small receptions, fundraisers featuring big-name speakers, and letters and phone calls are ways of mobilizing a connected group of fundraisers that he has been connected to for years.

Fundraising for the campaign had been completed eighteen months before the election. This meant that a year before the election started, we had a million dollars in the bank. It was a way of looking strong and keeping any potential rivals looking for a job out of the race. Most of the fundraising events were done by a hired consultant who brought her own connections and staff. But I saw what she was doing.

Basically, after all his years in office Dick had a network of rich friends. Some of them were connected to the energy and environment sub-committee where he was the second most senior Democrat; but most were just people who liked him. There were not a lot of deals going on when the congressman called. Nobody would ever say, "I like this bill, here's the money." Most had started giving money so long ago they just kept doing it. Many liked to tell their friends that the congressman had called them. And as the fundraising consultant told me repeatedly, "People give money to people not causes."

Most of the money was raised at fundraisers put on by the members of Dick's campaign finance committee, his wealthy buddies. Each would commit to raising, say $50,000, and then would invite fifty friends and business associates to a party at their house for $1,000 each—the legal maximum [per election] at the time. So there's an energy attorney who knows Dick, he teams up with some Hollywood agents who like to keep their hands in politics, they put together the lists, and you've got your event. Rich people don't really care about the events; they'll give the money whether they come or not. They do want to be asked. The only problem this time was convincing them that Dick needed the money for his safe seat. Our consultant liked these parties. As she said, "The $50,000 parties get you what you need pretty quickly. The $10,000 events take forever."

We raised about half the money we needed from these events. A third of the money came from the Dinner Honoring Congressman Hayes, which is held every other year. We raise about $350,000 with about 700 people attending at $500 a ticket. Last time we got Bill Clinton as the guest speaker. The hotel and the meal cost us a pretty steep $60 a person. One of the tricks of fundraising is to keep your costs down. The rest of the money, say $150,000, comes from events in DC—some breakfasts and receptions given by PACs [political action committees]. This gives the interest groups a chance to get some skin in the game. Mostly the unions and energy companies, along with some law firms working for them, show up. Also the other members of Congress, especially the leadership, will help out by giving fundraisers for us.

The congressman was pretty good about making the fundraising calls. A lot of members have to have their arms twisted to get on the phone to ask wealthy people for money. Our fundraising consultant would put together lists of donors, and then Dick would check off the ones he would call. We didn't use either the Internet or mail to raise money. Our consultant thought these only worked in presidential campaigns where you could get ideological giving.

One thing that definitely didn't work was fundraising in the district. Very few of the people we were raising money from lived in the district. We had some "Pancake events" there at $50 a ticket, but that was pretty much for show. Our voters didn't have much money to start with and most of them probably thought that since Dick had plenty of money himself he didn't need theirs to keep his job.

We ended up raising $1.3 million for the campaign and spent about $1.2 million. This was about ten times more than our Republican opponent who I read afterward had raised about $160,000.

GETTING STAFFED

An experienced staff dedicated to its congressman is another ingredient in a successful election. Young people—hard working, loyal, and cheap—comprise most election campaigns. Some of them hope to get jobs afterward, either with the congressman or the party. Some, like a couple that Duke called "tree huggers," were idealists, who were worried about global warming. The congressman's advantage in having already assembled his staff is somewhat limited by the law forbidding the use of office staff (who are government employees) from directly aiding a campaign. While this meant keeping track of which hours a congressional staff spent on government business and which hours they spent on reelection matters, it is a law that seldom keeps these federal employees from being a great advantage to their employer—the incumbent.

So after we have the redistricting down and the money in the bank, me, the campaign manager, walks in. I had started as a volunteer in Hayes's last campaign. I did everything they asked me to do—driver, scheduling, advance [planning] on events, and all-around "gofer." Speaking Spanish helped in the projects, and I worked fourteen-hour days on the phone banks and doing all the junk work anybody asked me for. After the campaign was over, the congressman asked me to join his district office as a field representative. Since I was just out of college, I jumped at the chance. It was a good job, paid about $35,000, and I got to help a lot of compadres with things like Social Security disability checks and veterans benefits. I organized high-visibility events for the congressman and worked for community groups trying to keep the district's naval shipyard open. A lot of my work was keeping in touch with the unions and neighborhood groups to make sure they felt they had the congressman's ear.

I think Dick is an incredibly effective congressman. He focuses on a couple of issues—the environment and alternative energy development—got pilot projects into the district, and increased spending for national programs as well. He also plays by the rules. He'll stand up to local groups when they make demands that he just can't support. Dick is so bright and articulate that he's tough to argue with.

He can be difficult to work for. Staff turnover is high. I remember him hiring a woman who had an MBA and campaign experience to be his AA [Administrative Assistant], which is the top staff job. One evening they worked late, and Dick asked her to drop him off at a dinner reception. When they got there, he told her that he would just be a minute and asked if she could wait for him. He was inside for over an hour while the AA waited in the car. She quit the next day.

We get on pretty well. He reminds me of my dad, strict but pretty fair once you show you'll stand up for yourself. We talk a lot about baseball. We both like the Padres.

In March 2002 he asked me to run the campaign. In the past Dick had hired a professional campaign manager. Now he asked me because he trusted me, and probably because I wouldn't cost much. Because of federal laws, there is supposed to be a firewall between congressional staff and the campaign—federal employees are not allowed to do campaign work. This meant that for the first two months I went half time, working from my home for two days a week and in the district office for three days.

Of course, this was easier said than done. I was supposed to use my own computer and my own phone for campaign matters, but things got sloppy. I'd be talking to the congressman from the district office and he'd ask "what about that fundraising letter?" or about a campaign event. Most of the messages for the campaign came out of speeches written in Washington, and we would design events in the district around themes of the campaign. While he got trips to the district paid for as a congressman, he couldn't go into the new parts of the district unless the event was charged against campaign funds. So we held events in bordering areas. That way we could make it official business.

In June I went full time, and my first job was to set up the campaign office. We could have gotten by without one, but Dick wanted to make sure that the people who had worked in his previous campaigns kept involved in this one. So the campaign office, maybe the campaign itself, was essentially aimed at holding on to supporters. We shared the office—a storefront—with the local assemblyperson. The carpenters' union put up the dividing wall for us—an in-kind contribution. We had twenty phone lines put in, a fax, a copier, and rented computers. Dick hired a field director/volunteer coordinator. She was twenty-four and had been an intern in the office. The office also served as the local headquarters for the Democratic party.[5]

CALLS, CONTACTS, AND THE CANDIDATE

Even a noncompetitive election becomes an opportunity for an incumbent to (re)connect with constituents. Whatever the strength of the congressman's ties with his district, campaign events give him publicity and a chance to address local voters concerns. A campaign energizes supporters and allows important interest groups to gain "face time" with the member. Presidential campaigns have used computers and complicated demographic information to target persuadable voters for mail or phone or personal contact (see Chapter 8). But this congressional effort is much less high-tech in using voter lists to reach likely supporters and urge them to vote for the congressman.

Much of what I did revolved around phoning voters. The phone banks were used most evenings between 5 p.m. and 8 p.m. to call high-propensity voters (people who voted in at least half of the previous six elections) and who leaned Democratic. We excluded diehard Democrats and Republicans, figuring that neither would change their minds. We made about 1,500 calls a night. Our callers, following a phone script, asked if the potential voters were supporting Hayes, and then recorded the yes's and maybe's. If they answered no, we ended the call. The others got a thank you postcard signed by the congressman, adding that if they had any questions to please call headquarters.

My days consisted of making sure the data from the previous night's phoning was entered into the computer and organizing the phone bank for the next night. My biggest problem was to recruit volunteers to make calls for our noncompetitive race. I tried to get groups of supporters to commit to one night. So the local teachers' union might turn out twenty members to come in on a

Election campaigns often depend on the energy and enthusiasm of volunteers to fill in for an expensive full-time professional staff.

Tuesday night. The next night might be an environmental call night for Green groups; another might be held for local elected officials. We got the city's Service Employees Union to make calls in Spanish one evening. We e-mailed or faxed the "Campaign Weekly" newsletter to 1,200 core supporters where we publicized their efforts and gave them credit for their work.

During the day there would be a half-dozen people in the office. They might be interns from the local high school who were getting class credit, or blue hairs [seniors] putting stamps on envelopes, or a guy coming out of a divorce or an unemployed techie with time on his hands. Often the volunteers seemed to be people with something missing in their lives.

Our best help came from organized groups that were clear about what they wanted. We'd have a couple union guys—usually Longshoremen or Teamsters—assigned to take care of us, and they would make sure we got the help we needed. They would drive the congressman around, walk the district with him, make phone calls, and help set up events. They followed legislation affecting the unions and used their access with Dick to talk to him about, say, port security or pension bills in Congress. They were happy about the access they got, even if they were not always happy with the results of the discussions. But they got "face time" with Dick that they would never have gotten in Washington. And when they went to DC, they'd see the congressman, not some junior staff person.[6]

Seeing the candidate in the [home] district wasn't that easy either. Dick only showed up in the district a couple of times a month. While he wanted visibility in the local press to show the folks back home, Dick has a pretty bad case of "Potomac Fever." Most of the time he'd rather be in DC. His kids were in school there, his wife had gotten to like Georgetown tea parties, and he found mixing with the "movers and shakers" a lot more exciting than kissing babies in our farmers' market on a Saturday morning.

Dick had gotten his start in politics as a political appointee in the Carter administration. When he went back into the family business afterward, it just wasn't as exciting. So he took some of his family's money—and there was a lot left over—to use in his run for Congress. He ran one sacrificial race where he lost but learned, and then put it together to win in 1996. Dick was a policy-wonk; he certainly did his homework on the issues I dealt with. He was also a tough-minded liberal who did right by the people in his district. He just didn't want to spend much time with them.[7]

CONSULTANTS AND MAIL

Modern campaigns need professionals. Experts in fundraising, mail, voter contact, and campaign strategy are sought after and highly rewarded. That is not to say that campaigning has become a science. It involves trial and error, judgment calls, and a fair amount of wasted time and money.

The campaign consultants were a group I'll call DNA Associates, who were basically a direct mail firm. They had a national reputation and were already doing a dozen races. When we interviewed them, I wasn't sure who was hiring who. Dick thought we were lucky to get them. They were basically looking either for high-profile races to aid in future marketing or for easy money. At the $35,000 a month they cost, we fell in the latter category. They were pros, and they saw the rest of us as amateurs. We were a business for them—no more, no less.

They did our direct mail and supplied lists of names and numbers for our phone banks. We had a weekly conference call with their top guy and ran everything by him—brochures, messages, and strategy. Although the mailings were taken from stuff written by the congressional staff, DNA went over the message. They targeted the new areas of the district [the ones added on by redistricting], and included a letter by Cruz Bustamante, California's lieutenant governor and the state's highest-ranking Hispanic official. Our messages were traditional Democratic ones: health care, education, and jobs.

Mail ended up being the biggest item in the budget, taking about one-third of a budget that was just over a million dollars. We did eleven mail pieces, four of them going to swing [undecided] voters. We did an environmental piece, a woman piece, and a security/terrorist mailing. We did a mailing to Republicans that had endorsements of Dick by Republican officials. Since education was Dick's big issue, we sent a pamphlet on education that included a note from the president [Republican president Bush] praising Dick's work on the No Child Left Behind education reform. We also sent a mailing to all households with Latino last names that had Hispanic leaders' endorsements.

We sent a lot of mail into the two new areas in the district. To introduce the new voters to the congressman, we mailed Dick's bio to all registered voters in these parts of the district that had been added by redistricting. Dick wanted a strong showing there in order to discourage some Lefty Latino from running against him in a future primary. We tried going door-to-door to register people to vote. (In one of the new areas, Alberta, there were 4,280 registered voters out of 23,180 people.) But it didn't go well. Citizenship was an issue. We found most of the people living there were illegals [illegal immigrants] who couldn't have registered if they wanted to. Families were crowded into a couple of rooms, and most wouldn't talk to a stranger. We put door hangers [brochures] on their doorknobs and left. We pulled the plug on the project after a week.[8]

We spent $50,000 on our field operations. After the fiasco in the new areas, most of the remaining money went into the coordinated campaign of the party. This was the effort by the party to put field [organizers] and mail behind all the Democrats who were running in the area for local, state, and federal offices. Dick ended up giving $150,000 from his campaign funds to other Democrats who were running. He did this through his leadership PAC, and it went to vulnerable candidates as well as to young Latino candidates that Dick wanted to get close to. The amount was considered inadequate by the party, given the amounts Dick had and that his race wasn't close. But it helped Dick's standing with the party and among some of the younger up-and-comers.

THE OPPOSITION AND ELECTION DAY

Often an incumbent's campaign is designed as much for the next election as for the current one; it aims to keep a strong opponent from running in the future. In most instances it works. Opposition party newcomers run in races where they don't have a chance as a beginning step for long-term political ambitions. The race follows a predictable route: the incumbent's party members are turned out on Election Day, and the incumbent wins in a manner designed to discourage future opponents from contesting this "safe" seat. It looks like a democratic contest but it really is closer to a confirmation ritual.

I guess you noticed that I haven't mentioned our opponent. He really wasn't much of a factor. The national Republicans decided that the district wasn't winnable, so they didn't try to recruit a strong candidate to run or direct many bucks into the race. What we ended up with was Frank Grimaldi. He was a young attorney, pleasant enough with a few bucks in his pocket that he could put into his campaign. He had some political ambitions and figured getting his name around town in this election couldn't hurt. The only real danger from Frank was the possibility that he would do better than expected and encourage the Republicans to target the race next time.

Frank put up a few signs, did a couple of radio spots, and got some newspaper ink by accusing Dick of being a carpetbagger who had lost touch with the folks in the district. In the one debate that Dick agreed to do, Frank seemed to wilt when confronting the congressman face to face. Dick knew his stuff and, I think, blew Frank away. We spent about $10,000 on opposition research but most of that was spent investigating Dick's own background. He wanted to see what the Republicans could come up with, especially with the family business—lawsuits, union problems, tax issues, that kind of stuff. Frank never really got much traction in the race.

As we neared Election Day, activities accelerated. We called absentee voters who were registered Dems and who hadn't sent in their ballots. We also visited their homes and left them door hangers to remind them to vote. Our lists weren't perfect. I remember some of our volunteers found Republican signs in the front yards of some of the houses we visited.

Then on the Monday before the election we brought in our volunteers to phone our "yes" universe, from the calls we had made before. We would tell them where their polling station was and what time it opened. And we offered them rides if they needed them. We called all the names in the new areas of the district. On Election Day we got lists of voters who had voted in the morning and called the others to remind them to vote.

I'm not sure how effective the whole campaign was. The congressman was pleased and I ended up keeping my job in the home office. Even a good campaign probably doesn't influence more than a few percent of the vote. It did keep our own key people involved. It also didn't cost much money, and it reinforced the congressman's identity with the district. We won with a little over 60 percent. That means we are now a safe seat and unlikely to be targeted by Republicans in the future. And that was the goal in the first place.

In the next four elections—2004 through 2010—the congressman won reelection with around 65 percent of the vote. His Republican opponents averaged less than 33 percent.

In 2010 California voters passed a ballot initiative, Proposition 20, that took control of congressional redistricting away from the state legislature and put it in the hands of a nonpartisan, unelected commission. That commission—to the shock of many—drew a map of congressional districts that ignored the protection of incumbents. Whether this would cost many incumbent congressmen their jobs was less certain.

Notes

1. A general treatment of campaigns can be found in James A. Thurber and Candice J. Nelson, eds. *Campaigns and Elections: American Style*, 3rd ed. (Boulder, CO: Westview Press, 2010).

2. See David J. Garrow, "Running the House," *New York Times Magazine*, November 13, 2002. Also see Steven Hill and Rob Richie, "The Dangers of Perpetual Redistricting," The Center for Voting and Democracy, July 1, 2003; and The Campaign Finance Institute, Press Releases, Washington, DC, November 5, 2004, at *www.cfinst.org*.

3. "How to Rig an Election," *The Economist*, Print Edition, April 25, 2002.

4. An excellent analysis of the unprecedented GOP gerrymandering in Texas a couple of years after the 2000 census can be found in Jeffrey Toobin, "The Great Election Grab," *The New Yorker*, December 8, 2003.

5. A more complete account of organizing a campaign is in Dick Simpson, *Winning Elections: A Handbook of Modern Participatory Politics* (New York: HarperCollins, 1996), Chapter 3.

6. What these organized interests look like to the congressional staff is reflected in Barry M. Casper, *Lost in Washington* (Amherst, MA: University of Massachusetts Press, 2000).

7. Still the best account of how House members see their districts is Richard F. Fenno, Jr., *Home Style* (Boston, MA: Little, Brown and Company, 1978).

8. Some other reasons for low voter turnout are discussed in Thomas E. Patterson, *The Vanishing Voter* (New York: Vintage Books, 2003).

8 | POLITICAL PARTIES
VOTER TECHNOLOGY
From Targeting to Microtargeting

Reporters have on occasion speculated about the death of American political parties. Noted *Washington Post* reporter David Broder once wrote a book titled *The Party's Over.*[1] (He has since changed his mind.) Still, political scientists point to the rise of candidate-oriented elections where individuals control their own campaigns, to the increased media influence in deciding the outcome of party primaries, and to the reliance on interest groups to channel corporations' fundraising money, all as signs of party decline. Paralleling these factors are voters' indifference to parties: those who declare themselves "independent" of either party, while many others turn their backs on both parties' candidates by deciding not to vote at all.

So what do modern American parties do?

Plenty.

Political parties have become huge fundraising and voter mobilizing operations. Each party—and the candidates operating under the party label—raises as much money as possible. This leads to large sums spent on "party building" and candidate commercials, on voter targeting and get-out-the-vote (GOTV) campaigns, and, of course, on even more fundraising. The two cases below illustrate these trends. In 1980s Colorado, the Republican party effectively used computer technology to help their national and state candidates by locating potential Republican voters and getting them to register. In the 2008 Barack Obama campaign, a candidate for the Democratic presidential nomination creatively employed the Internet and microtargeting to mobilize supporters and raise funds. As the nominee and later president, Obama made sure his party continued to fully use technology to engage his supporters. Both cases demonstrate how parties and their candidates effectively use technology to organize voters for partisan purposes. They also underline why, as Mark Twain said about the rumor of his own demise, the reports of the death of American political parties are, at the least, greatly exaggerated.[2]

CONCEPTS TO CONSIDER _____

1. Political parties have evolved into **service organizations** that provide new campaign techniques to attract electoral support. These techniques include polling, advertising, and public relations, as well as the computer/phone and Internet technologies shown in these cases. Does this mean that the type of people who manage the parties has changed from the days of political bosses? What is the impact of this professionalization?

2. **Voter mobilization**, identifying supporters and getting them to the polls, is now a major task of party and candidate organizations. Does this mobilization make these organizations more democratic? Does it shift power to the voter who must decide to respond to the mail or phone or visit a website? Does Obama's use of the Internet allow for more participation and reverse declining voter turnout?

3. Some political scientists think that there is a **partisan impact of new political technologies**, giving an advantage to those with wealth and power. While the Republicans have been most successful in using technologies in the past, the Democrats have recently taken the lead. How does the Internet, with its expanding fundraising and networking abilities, change the party rivalries? Does it reinforce the dominance of the two parties?

4. **Candidate-centered campaigns** have been accused of encouraging low turnout and special-interest influence—by targeting supporters and using a small group of fundraisers. Do campaigns' use of the Web challenge this idea? How does the Internet expand voter participation? Could the Internet also result in groups that aren't connected being ignored by campaigns?

5. **Microtargeting** transfers the successful technology of advertising to the arena of elections. The goal, however, is not to get consumers to shop for a certain product, but to get citizens to vote for a certain candidate. Does this make civic groups, or organized interests or even political parties less important as channels of information to voters? Does it make the individual voter at their computer the key unit for organizing rather than groups with broader loyalties of party, ideology, or religion?

Back in the spring of 1984, voters in several western states got a phone call—from a computer. A recorded voice announced the following:

> "Good evening. This is Reagan-Bush '84 calling you on a special computer that is capable of recording your opinion. Your answers to two short questions are very important and will take less than a minute of your time. Please answer after the tone.

Question No. 1: If the election for president were held today, would you vote for President Reagan or the Democratic candidate? (Tone.)

Question No. 2: There are a number of unregistered voters in your neighborhood. Is there anyone in your household who needs to register? (Tone.)

Thank you and good night."

In some areas, the telephoned person replied to the questions by pressing a button on his or her push-button phone—5 to indicate support for the president and 6 to indicate opposition. If 6 was pushed, the computer terminated the interview. Pushing 5, however, opened up the voter to a world of high-tech campaigning, courtesy of the Republican party.[3]

ROCKY MOUNTAIN TARGETING

The phone script above reflected the GOP strategy of voter targeting: identifying unregistered Colorado supporters of the party and its candidates, registering them as Republicans, and encouraging them to vote. Using computers and phone banks, the party targeted these key voters so that later they could be contacted about specific issues or taken to the polls on Election Day. Voter targeting demonstrated the party's effectively maximizing its turnout of supporters.

It was the Republican party's answer to the Democrats' advantages in finding and registering new voters. Nonvoters, concentrated in lower-income and minority groups, overwhelmingly support Democrats, if they vote. For example, in 1988 when Jesse Jackson ran for president, at least nine of every ten new African American voters went Democratic. Volunteers for the Democrats could easily go door to door in a black or poor neighborhood and find a large pool of unregistered voters favoring their party.

This meant that Republican efforts to register new voters couldn't mimic the Democratic approach. Republican supporters were likely to already be voters and tended not to live in self-evident ethnic neighborhoods. One Texas Republican party official put it this way: "The thing about Republican precincts, everybody is registered. I walked my precinct, and 90 percent of the people were registered. We have to be selective." Money and technology shaped the Republican registration strategy.

This "high-tech" campaign to locate and register GOP voters created an updated version of the traditional American political machine. Fueled by some $10 million from the national party, Republicans aimed to add 2 million voters to the party rolls. In the old days, the parties would gather loyalists in the back rooms of precincts and hand them "walking-around money" to pass out to citizens to "assist" them in registering and voting. Now the machine operated electronically for the difficult task of identifying solid Republican prospects among the mass of unregistered voters. To find the affluent people who were likely to support Republican candidates and who were not registered, the party's computers ran through a range of lists: mail-order buyers from upscale stores, licensed drivers, homeowners, new utility hookups, and subscribers to the *Wall Street Journal*, to name just a few.

MERGING AND PURGING

Colorado's "political machine" was located in the basement of a Denver bank. Here part-time employees were paid 15 cents above the minimum wage to operate computers costing some $275,000 to reach potential GOP voters. One difference with traditional party activists came in the instructions given to the phone bank operators. "Don't talk politics or issues," the program's manager told them, "This is a paid phone bank. These people don't know politics. I'd as soon not have them try to speak for the candidates. They are not qualified."

The essence of the Colorado GOP registration strategy was a computerized process known as "merging and purging" of multiple lists. It began with a list of registered Colorado voters (1.2 million of them), purchased from the state for $500. Paid party workers first merged this by computer with a list of all licensed drivers over age eighteen (some 2.2 million). They then "purged" all drivers registered to vote, leaving the names of 800,000 unregistered voters who were licensed drivers.

This list was then cut to 120,000 names by eliminating all unregistered drivers who lived in precincts and zip codes with strong Democratic registration numbers as well as Democratic voting histories. The list of 120,000 was matched with another list containing both names and phone numbers, which had been purchased from a commercial firm. About half of the names produced a match of a phone number and an address—absolutely needed if any calls were to be made.

The resulting 60,000 names were the base from which the phone bank with the computerized message operated. The goal of the phone survey—and the computer-generated questions—was to further reduce the list to 20,000 solid Republican prospects. Following instructions on their computer screens, the phone bank employees called the lists. When they reached the person listed—the prospect—they asked if the person was registered. If the answer was yes, the interview ended since the goal was to register the unregistered.

If the response was no, there was a quick series of questions:

- Do you intend to vote?
- Are you likely to vote for Ronald Reagan?
- Would you welcome a letter describing how to register?

The answers were coded by number: 1 for "Yes," 2 for "No," and 3 for "Maybe." Each time the phone bank operator entered a number, the computer responded with instructions to continue the interview or to say thank you and hang up. For example, if the prospect was opposed to Republican candidates, or even undecided, the interview was ended then and there.

For those 20,000 making the final cut, the computer automatically generated a letter from the Colorado state GOP chairman: "I was so glad when you told one of our Republican workers that you wanted to vote." The letter gave the prospect the address of the nearest county clerk where they could register. The names were then sent to their local county Republican executive committee, where someone was assigned to make sure the person actually registered.

The computer could at any time churn out the names of these unregistered people who wanted to support Republican candidates. The list could be sent to the campaigns of the president and senator who were running that year. The candidates' staffers were told: "These people want to vote for you, but they aren't registered. You go out and register them."

REPUBLICAN OUTREACH

Nor did the effort end with registration.

The computers allowed targeting for purposes other than registering likely Republican voters. Using polling, phone bank, and census information, the party could produce clusters of voters who would likely be interested in specific issues. For example, a candidate for the Senate might find from his polls that he was running poorly among women forty-five and older who were single heads of households. His polling told him that this group was concerned about crime. The party lists enabled the candidate to locate the names and addresses of, say, 25,000 women in this category. A letter from the candidate on what he proposed to do about crime could then be targeted only to this group. The Colorado GOP political director, Kay Riddle, justified the effort. "It sounds impersonal and high tech, but actually what it allows us to do is to be very personal, to touch people about what they care about, to talk to them about their concerns, and then to relay that information back to our candidates and legislators."

A similar computerized targeting effort allowed the Republicans to identify potential supporters among an ethnic group that tended to be strongly Democratic. The Republican National Committee developed a list of about 12,000 Hispanic last names. Those names were run against voter registration lists, then cross-tabbed against real estate tax lists. This allowed the party to identify unregistered Hispanics who were homeowners. That list could then be run against the names of buyers of expensive cars, subscribers to financial newspapers, and Hispanic businessmen. The goal was to search for upper-income Hispanics likely to identify with conservative Republican positions. Political director Riddle put it this way: "Our initial target has to be the upwardly mobile Hispanic who has a vision of the future that is similar to Ronald Reagan's. That takes a very sophisticated effort. . . ."

It also took money. The national GOP paid an estimated $7 for every new registered voter, for an estimated $10 million that year. The Democratic efforts, at the time, depended on nonparty organizations registering the poor and minorities in grassroots drives. These were neither controlled nor usually paid for directly by the Democratic party. As a result, no one could be quite sure that the new Democratic registrants actually voted on Election Day.

The Republicans, for their part, had this problem covered by technology and more traditional techniques as well. The GOP designed follow-through programs that included get-out-the-vote drives, absentee ballots, and partisan direct mail. No one would be accusing the party of sitting on their bottoms on the critical day. A state GOP official commented, "We are not going to pay $5 for every new Republican and then let that person stay at home on Election Day. We are going to check those names against our computers all day on November 6, and if some guy hasn't shown up by 6 p.m., we'll carry him to the polls."

Microtargeting: Obama and the 2008 Election

Fast-forward twenty-four years to the opposing party using newer technologies. In the 2008 presidential election, millions of Americans were contacted by Democrat Barack Obama's campaign and many—13 million—signed up for regular e-mails. They would be asked for financial contributions, informed on issues, urged to volunteer, and directed to local rallies and events. The e-mails informally addressed each recipient by name, but this was only the beginning of what the Obama machine knew.

If you were on Obama's list, his campaign team knew your voting history, including the local precinct where you voted, your age and gender,

The information from voters gathered by volunteers making phone calls is useful data for a presidential campaign's microtargeting strategies.

possibly your race. They had a good idea of your income, your credit history, and whether you rent or own an apartment or home. They likely knew which grocery stores you visit and the magazines and catalogs you read, and whether you get your news from cable TV, the newspaper, or online. The websites you visit and how often? Sure. Even what time of day you go through your inbox and respond to mail—a surprisingly useful bit of information.

In fact, Obama's team knew this information and more *regardless* of whether or not you signed up on his website. Along with many political candidates and interest groups, he had significant data on millions of Americans![4]

FROM TARGETING TO MICROTARGETING

As seen in the Colorado example, this is nothing new. Collecting voter data for the purpose of targeting allows campaigns to direct specific messages to people to gain their support (whether it be volunteering, money, or a vote). Targeting is important because political campaigns have limited resources and voters pay limited attention to politics. Therefore, campaigns want efficient communications with voters, ones that will resonate. Why waste time and money on an unread message?[5]

Traditional targeting is a search for a coalition of groups that will produce enough votes to win. The campaign adapts messages to appeal to these groups. For example, if union members are concerned about jobs, a campaign's communications may focus on this issue (through phone calls, mailers, etc.) in high union-membership areas. Younger voters are likely to be less interested in Social Security and Medicare, while they are more interested in issues of war and education. A campaign will tailor its messages accordingly.

Microtargeting takes this strategy to a new level. It shapes messages for *individuals.* For example, if a campaign wanted to locate voters who were both persuadable to vote for their candidate and interested in a certain issue, say gun control, they could do it using statistical techniques. A campaign consultant could use information from voter files that predict whether an individual is undecided. For instance, one variable that often indicates an undecided voter is when a voter identifies with one party but lives with someone who belongs to the opposing party. Each individual can be scored with a probability that indicates their likelihood of being undecided (scores range from 0 to 1). Then the process is repeated to, say, identify hunters by a list of individuals who subscribe to hunting magazines. A second analysis assigns each person a probability of being a hunter. The two scores (undecided and hunter) are multiplied to obtain the probability that an individual is both a hunter and undecided about the election. The campaign mails its literature to the voters with the highest combined score.

To create these targets of opportunity for individualized messages, campaigns require large amounts of data on potential voters. Some of this information comes from states' voter files, which typically include each voter's address, voting precinct, age, gender, and, in some cases, race. Consumer marketing firms already maintain information on individuals' buying habits. If you have ever registered for a product (such as a personal computer), joined an organization's mailing list, or requested a rebate for an item you purchased, then there is a good chance that someone has this information. Commercial direct marketing firms have been using microtargeting for decades and they've built enormous databases on people, which they sell to political campaigns.[6]

Campaigns can also collect their own information on individuals' online behavior. In 2008, visitors to Obama's website had a *cookie* placed in their Web browser. Cookies identified the sites that each individual visited afterward, helping the campaign gain a greater understanding of the individual's interests. With Obama receiving twice as many hits to his website as John McCain, this tool provided a significant advantage in terms of voter identification and targeting.[7] These cookies even allowed Obama to track what time of day members opened their campaign's e-mails. Finding a consistent pattern, they would send all their messages at times when people generally checked their mail. As one Democratic consultant put it, these strategies are effective, for "The marginal benefit of sending some people an email at 2 o'clock vs. 3 o'clock vs. 4 o'clock . . . increases the returns for a fundraising e-mail by 5 or 10 percent."[8]

Finally, campaigns benefit from information given by individuals through public opinion polling and surveys. In a modern political campaign, millions of Americans receive phone calls and home visits by volunteers who collect information, which is then diligently included in a voter information database. The result for the Obama campaign was a database consisting of twenty to thirty data pieces for most individuals.[9] Once this information is collected, analysts study it and attempt to identify the issues and ideas that matter most to individual voters.

PUTTING THE DATA TO WORK

Campaigns may ask 10,000 voters their opinions on the election's key issues. The many questions they ask can be matched with voter file and commercial data. From this information, voter profiles are created. Campaigns can then predict how other people with similar profiles would have answered these same questions. Latte drinkers may be more likely to vote Democratic. Driving an SUV may match up to being a Republican or to being more sensitive to changes in gas prices. Once these profiles are in place, the campaign can adapt its voter contact plan to reach their targets.

Therefore, a candidate with strong gun rights credentials may target subscribers of *Guns & Ammo* with literature on the candidate's position. The candidate will likely not send the same message about gun rights to an individual who shops at Whole Foods and lives in an urban area, as this citizen is more likely to support gun control. A middle-aged mother of three is more likely to care about elementary education, so candidates may focus their outreach efforts to her on this issue, but not send the same message to a single, childless, twenty-five year old. Yale political scientist Alan Gerber described the change that microtargeting brought.

> The basic idea of microtargeting is that in the past, you might target a fairly aggregated level like a precinct, whereas now people are merging lots of data that's aggregated not at the precinct level, but down at the individual level. So you are able to find pockets of voters within some aggregate that are especially attractive to persuade or mobilize.[10]

The explanation here simplifies microtargeting. It is a complex, multidimensional process. In general, no one specific piece of information gives an overwhelming tilt to being a Republican or Democrat, or will predict views on political issues. As Ken Strasma, who worked for Obama, said, "People get hung up looking for a silver bullet. They want to know, is it cat owners or bourbon drinkers or some nice buzz phrase like that. It's when you see the interactions between hundreds of different data points [that patterns emerge]—it's rare that you see one single indicator pop." The broad categories like "soccer moms" that were discussed in previous elections are replaced on a working level with more complex "iPhone owners with master's degrees in their forties who shop at Costco and get frequent flier miles for their credit card purchases."[11]

ENTER OBAMA

Obama's 2008 campaign was history's most successful in using technology for voter targeting. It was not starting from scratch in applying the Internet for fundraising and microtargeting. As mentioned before, corporate America had long used personal data to market its products, which is why an eighty-year-old woman is unlikely to receive a free trial subscription to *Sports Illustrated*. Not surprisingly, the party closely connected to business, the Republicans, were the first to effectively apply targeting technology to politics. In the 1990s, the Republican National Committee put together a database which eventually included information on 175 million Americans. George W. Bush in his 2000 election victory was the first presidential candidate to use microtargeting. Since then, the Democrats have caught up. In 2007, the Democrats consolidated previous databases with VoteBuilder, which allowed their state parties to exchange data and get up-to-date voter information from the national party. In addition, the Democrats have access to a privately owned database, Catalist, which is sold and shared with progressive groups outside the party.[12]

During the 2004 presidential primary, Howard Dean successfully tapped the Internet to mobilize young votes and raise large amounts of money. His campaign built a large e-mail list, though it was never able to integrate the information into one system. Obama, however, with the help of VoteBuilder and Catalist, as well as a disciplined effort by staffers to enter collected information in the central database, set a new standard. The Obama campaign effectively used Catalist to update data from the DNC's VoteBuilder and from its own extensive canvassing activities. With this streamline flow of information, the campaign targeted messages to individual voters at an unprecedented level. Further, they used new tools, such as text messages and personalized e-mail, to deliver the messages. Zephyr Teachout, who ran Dean's 2004 online organizing campaign, commented that Obama took "all our stupid ideas and made them smart."[13]

An example of Obama's microtargeting came when the campaign identified through polling that a number of evangelical Christians were concerned about global warming. These concerns were potentially great enough to overcome their disagreements with Obama over social issues, such as abortion. The campaign then used its database to identify evangelicals who fit into this category, that is, they were younger; they had joined an environmental group; they had subscribed to magazines about wildlife; and so on. The campaign sent materials to these households (especially in swing states) stressing Obama's program to curb global warming. In the election, Obama performed five percentage points better among born-again Christians than John Kerry did in 2004.[14]

This tactic of finding hidden pockets of support allowed the Obama campaign to expand the number of closely contested states where they forced Republicans to compete. By bringing states into play, like Indiana, that were formerly considered reliably Republican, the Democrats' use of microtargeting made Republicans spend money and refocus their strategy. By making some thirty states into battlegrounds in the presidential contest, Obama changed the big picture of the election. Microtargeting gave them the level of precision to find people within Republican groups that could be swayed by the right message.[15]

Another tactic depending on microtargeting that was used in Indiana, where Obama won, was to advertise to moderate women on the issue of abortion. By using radio—classical and rock oldies stations that these women preferred—the Obama campaign narrowcasted the message that McCain favored overturning *Roe v. Wade*. These ads described McCain as an out-of-touch conservative who would not protect women's rights. By reaching moderate women with the message that McCain did not share their values and opposed legalizing abortion, the ads made it easier for them to vote for Obama.[16]

To activate young voters, the Obama campaign set up a site called MyBarackObama.com, which served as the central hub for its volunteer, social networking, and mobilization efforts. On this site, members could create their own Web page, to blog and interact with one another. Over 2 million people joined the site, offering a wealth of information to the campaign. Through this mechanism, as well as using social networking sites such as Facebook, the campaign was able to identify committed followers and encourage them to mobilize other citizens—creating a domino effect. These members placed millions of phone calls, and created more than 45,000 Obama for America volunteer groups across the country.[17]

AFTER THE ELECTION

The massive organization created to put Obama into the White House did not disappear after Election Day. It morphed into Organizing for America (OFA), which continued to contact and mobilize their 13 million online supporters. Rather than trying to win an election, the organization created and sustained support for the president's agenda.

One first-year focus was the debate on reforming the U.S. health-care system. OFA was extremely active. OFA repeatedly e-mailed its members to organize events and to volunteer for reform. Whether the online effort gathered the same intense support that it had for a presidential election was questioned by the press, doubts reflected in a *New York Times* headline of August 15, 2009, that read "Health Debate Fails to Ignite Obama's Web." Yet by March 2010, the final week of debate, OFA directed 400,000 phone calls from constituents to members of Congress.[18] These included calls to Democrats like Representative Brian Baird of Washington who had originally opposed the House health care bill. After receiving an enormous number of calls from his constituents, he voted for the final reform. Democratic National Committee communications director Brad Woodhouse noted that OFA was responsible for nearly three-quarters of all calls to Baird's office in support of the bill.[19]

Entering the 2010 congressional elections, the Democrats hoped to use their advantages in technology and organization to minimize the damage that a president's party usually suffers in the midterm after his election. Millions of dollars were spent mobilizing the groups and people that Obama successfully engaged in 2008, including young people, African Americans, and Latinos. OFA was very active. They reached out to more than 80 million voters, organized some 37,000 neighborhood events using their campaign infrastructure from the 2008 election. Several weeks before the election, President Obama held an online town hall event at George Washington University where he took questions from the audience as well as through Twitter and Facebook. The town hall was the centerpiece of OFA "house parties" held at the same time across the country and recruited by e-mail through the Democrats' massive e-mail lists.[20]

Despite this activity, the Democrats failed to mobilize the voters it had depended on to win the presidency. According to exit polls, 29 million Obama voters from 2008 didn't show up to vote in 2010; 13 percent of Obama voters defected to Republicans for Congress. One of the president's principal support groups, eighteen-to-twenty-nine-year-olds, comprised only 12 percent of the electorate in 2010, as opposed to 18 percent in 2008. Turnout among younger voters was 3 percent less than the previous midterm in 2006. African American turnout was down by 43 percent compared to 2008; Hispanics showed a 40 percent decline. On the other side, senior citizens turned out in force—16 percent higher than the last midterm election. Almost 60 percent of seniors voted Republican, up 10 percentage points from 2006.[21]

Technology was not missing in the president's mobilization of supporters for the 2010 midterm elections. What was missing was supporters' enthusiasm.

CONCLUSION

Technology works. Its use by political parties to win elections is clearly here to stay. The developments of the last several decades—computers, the Internet, and social networks—have made online tactics even more useful to candidates and their campaigns. The successful use of microtargeting by the Obama campaign builds on and fine-tunes the earlier Republican Colorado voter turnout efforts. Whether this is all good for democracy and the public's participation in their government is another question altogether.

For some the complaints fall along partisan lines. A few years ago, Democrats denounced the Republican use of their fundraising advantages to buy expensive technology. When the Internet shoe was on the other foot, as is currently the case, Republicans complained about the Democrats' electoral behavior. Conservative talk radio host Rush Limbaugh argued that Obama's targeting was a form of racism, "He is asking young people, African-Americans, Latino and women to reconnect, to fight who? Who is this fight against?"[22]

Some have argued that the ease with which campaigns can compile personal information raises privacy concerns. How much should elected officials know about our families, our spending habits, our lifestyle, or our beliefs? Robert Richman, founder of the liberal campaign consulting firm Grassroots Solutions, has acknowledged this, "It's pretty scary, the stuff you can get on people."

Leaving aside which party gains from these techniques, the question remains how they affect democracy. Kim Alexander, executive director of the California Voter Project, a nonpartisan public interest group, believes it may be poisoning the political process, stating, "Elections are supposed to be about the give and take of political ideas, but increasingly elections are about going out and trying to get market share."[23] Looking at citizens the way corporations look at customers marks a profound erosion in the idea of how the American people govern themselves. Traditional democracy is not simply the re-presentation of popular opinion as reflected in a vote on Election Day. As consumers we may be treated as atomized individuals, distinguished by gender, income, neighborhoods, subscriptions, and so on—who can be persuaded to buy products and services we may, or may not need.

But as citizens of a democracy, we are more than preexisting opinions and identities. We are groups of citizens in an ongoing dialogue, among ourselves and with our leaders, of how we want to be governed. Through participation in neighborhoods, religions, schools, occupations, interest groups, and political parties, we engage in the messy politics of democracy. At its core lies a more or less deliberative process of negotiations, compromises, and pressures that produce the nation's leaders and policies. Elections and parties are central pieces of this.

And it is politics, not shopping. Elections are how partisans and publics, regions and religions, ethnics and elites gather together to decide on who should lead them. If technology enhances the participation and deliberation that elections require, all to the good. But if it just intensifies the marketing of yet another product by exploiting the vulnerabilities of individual consumers, we may have lost more than an election. We may have damaged our democratic politics.

Notes

1. David Broder, *The Party's Over: The Failure of American Parties* (New York: Harper and Row, 1971).
2. See Paul S. Herrnson, "Fieldwork in Contemporary Election Campaigns," in James A. Thurber and Candice J. Nelson, eds. *Campaigns and Elections: American Style*, 3rd ed. (Boulder, CO: Westview Press, 2010), Chapter 8.
3. The Colorado case is based on Thomas B. Edsall and Haynes Johnson, "Colorado's High-Tech Republicans," in Roger H. Davidson and Walter J. Oleszek, eds. *Governing* (Washington, DC: Congressional Quarterly Press, 1987), 108–113.
4. Mike Madden, "Barack Obama's Super Marketing Machine," *Salon.com*, July 16, 2008. http://www.salon.com/news/feature/2008/07/16/obama_data/
5. C. Daniel Myers, "Telling Voters What They Want to Hear: Exploring the Impact of Micro-Targeting Through a Field Experiment," Presented at the Midwest Political Science Association Meeting, 2004. http://www.princeton.edu/~cdmyers/microtargeting_field_experiment.PDF
6. Madden.
7. Chris Dannen, "How Obama Won it With the Web," *Fast Company*, November 4, 2008. http://www.fastcompany.com/articles/2008/11/how-obama-won-it-with-the-web.html
8. Madden.
9. Myers.
10. Alan Gerber, as quoted by Chad Vander Veen, "Zeroing In," *Government Technology*, January 2, 2006. http://www.govtech.com/gt/97723?id=97723&topic=117671&full=1&story_pg=2
11. For a fuller explanation of microtargeting in elections, see Stephen Baker, *The Numerati* (Boston, MA: Houghton Mifflin Company, 2008), Chapter 3, Voter.
12. Christopher Stern, "Democrats Take Republican Database Model to Target Swing Voters," *Bloomberg.com*, September 18, 2008.
13. Madden.
14. Ibid.
15. Leslie Wayne, "Democrats Take Page from Their Rival's Playbook," *The New York Times*, November 1, 2008.
16. Kate Kenski, Bruce W. Hardy, and Kathleen Hall Jamieson, *The Obama Victory* (New York: Oxford University Press, 2010), Chapter 12, "Spending Differences and the Role of Microtargeting."
17. Christopher Stern, "Obama's 'Gigantic' Database May Make Him Party's Power Broker," *Bloomberg.com*, April 28, 2008. http://www.bloomberg.com/apps/news?pid=20601103&sid=aW_Qty8aiVTo
18. Ben Smith, "Credit to OFA," *Politico*, March 21, 2010. http://www.politico.com/blogs/bensmith/0310/Credit_to_OfA.html

19. Chris Cillizza, "Assessing Organizing for America through the health care lens," *Washington Post*, March 23, 2010. http://voices.washingtonpost.com/thefix/health-care/assessing-organizing-for-ameri-1.html

20. http://techpresident.com/category/categories/2010-midterm-elections

21. http://www.politico.com/news/stories/1110/45107.html#ixzz16iCYZI6e; http://www.nytimes.com/2010/11/01/us/politics/01generationo.html?R=1&rc=twrhp

22. Lynn Sweet, "DNC's Targeting of Obama First Time Voters Triggers Limbaugh Protest," *Politics Daily*, April 26, 2010. http://www.politicsdaily.com/2010/04/26/dncs-targeting-of-obama-first-time-voters-triggers-limbaugh-pro/

23. "US campaigns use voter data to find supporters," *Reuters*, January 21, 2004. http://undecided.com/election/01211.html

9 | INTEREST GROUPS

CLINTON'S HEALTH-CARE REFORM

Harry and Louise Go Public

The next two chapters discuss the role of interest groups in two different political battles to pass health reform. The attempts were similar efforts by Democratic presidents to expand health care to millions of citizens without insurance while controlling the prices of these services. They differed in outcomes. The first in the 1990s by President Clinton failed without even coming to a vote in Congress. More recently, President Obama succeeded in passing legislation in 2010. A critical difference was the involvement of health industry interest groups who opposed the Clinton plan, while generally supporting Obama. Though their strategies and activities were different, the influence of these interest groups was central to the results in both cases.

This chapter outlines the strategy of "Going public" through which health-interest groups opposed the Clinton reform visibly demonstrating national support for their position by mobilizing popular opinion. This strategy is used by presidents, by political parties, and by various organized interests. One common way of going public is through the media, both by advertising and by influencing news coverage. Another tactic involves grassroots lobbying, which includes contacting supporters in states of key officials and getting them to communicate, by phone, mail, the Internet, or personal visits with their representatives. Both sets of tactics require a forceful message that expresses your side's strength and the other side's weakness.

In this 1993 attempt at health-care reform, both the president and his opponents "go public." President Bill Clinton, propelled by his recent election and bolstered by positive public opinion polls, eagerly embraced a national campaign to endorse his number one legislative priority: health-care reform. Confronting him were health industry groups, fearful of their economic fate under the ambitious proposals. Using their ample resources, they joined with Republican rivals of the president to whip up popular fears that expanding government bureaucracies would threaten individual liberties while ruining the existing health-care system.

The outcome was by no means guaranteed.

CONCEPTS TO CONSIDER _____

1. The **expansion of interest groups** is often related to the expansion of the federal government. This case shows the organized responses of industry groups threatened by a major government reform of health care. Note the groups that took the lead in organizing against the reform. Was this a cross section of the entire health-care industry? Who represents the consumers/public, or is that what the debate is about?

2. **Going public** is a strategy to overcome policy roadblocks in Washington. In this case, neither side was certain of the results of a legislative battle within Congress. Both saw the need to mobilize national forces behind their position. How did interest groups ensure that their _media advertising_ and _grassroots organizing_ would have an impact on their Washington targets? Compare the advantages of both sides as they entered the battle.

3. One major struggle was over **framing the issue:** Who would present the stakes of reform to the public in a convincing way? What were the competing frames used by the reformers and the health-care industry? What sort of media and grassroots communications did the interest groups' opposing reform use in presenting their arguments? How did their conservative allies influence the arguments that were used by the interest groups?

4. **Media coverage** clearly had an impact on how the public viewed and understood reform. How did the media coverage change over time? Did the media fail in its coverage by presenting the issue as a horserace and by being distracted by charges of presidential scandals? How successful were the two sides in influencing the media?

5. What was the **influence of public opinion** on the outcome? Was the goal of going public designed to change public opinion or to mobilize targeted support among those already convinced? Why did a newly elected popular president fail to win over public opinion?

The TV ad opens on a middle-aged couple, Harry and Louise, sitting around a kitchen table. They look puzzled. He is reading a newspaper, and she is examining a copy of President Clinton's health-care plan. Harry pipes up:

"I'm glad the president's doing something about health-care reform." Louise replies, "He's right. We need it."

But as the two learn new details about the president's plan, the conversation turns more critical.

HARRY: "Some of these details."

LOUISE: "Like a national limit on health care?"

HARRY: "Really."

LOUISE: "The government caps how much the country can spend on all health care and says, 'That's it!'"

HARRY: "So, what if our health plan runs out of money?"

LOUISE: "There's got to be a better way."

Paid for by the Health Insurance Association of America (HIAA), this simple ad, filmed in a kitchen and known in political circles as "Harry and Louise," first ran in early September 1993—even before President Clinton announced his plan for health-care reform. At least in political circles it created quite a buzz.

Later that month, President Bill Clinton stood before Congress and a national television audience to launch the most important program of his young presidency. He promised universal health care ". . . giving every American health security—health care that's always there, health care that can never be taken away." In stirring words, the president made the need clear. "Our health care system takes 35 percent more of our income than any other country, insures fewer people, requires more Americans to pay more and more for less and less, and gives them fewer choices. There is no excuse for that kind of system, and it's time to fix it."

The issue was joined, the battle lines set. "Harry and Louise" challenged the American president's views of health-care reform before a national audience. In the president's view, reform was a courageous effort to mend a broken, inadequate health-care system that left millions uncovered. In the eyes of industry groups, a power-hungry, inept federal bureaucracy was threatening to ruin a health-care system that was the envy of the world. Which message the public accepted would go far to determine the outcome of reform in Washington.

These arguments reflected a dilemma that existed in the public mind. By September 1993, a large majority of Americans wanted the federal government to solve the nation's perceived health-care crisis. At the same time, equally large majorities had little faith in the federal government's capacity to act effectively. These contradictory views were behind the central messages delivered by the two sides of the national debate.

Perhaps inevitably, an expansion in government as large as Clinton proposed set off a defensive reaction from within the billion-dollar health-care industry. Numerous interest groups, joined by political partisans, began to lobby, organize, and advertise against the reforms. In this sense, the reformers motivated their opposition—the anti-health reform forces. In the end, the ironic result of the administration's far-reaching proposals was to strengthen their opponents.

Both sides pursued a strategy of going public by mobilizing country-wide opinion to support their positions. The new president, fresh from a successful national election campaign, was comfortable in communicating with a broad public. Clinton expected that being in the White House would only increase his public support. Opponents of reform had less choice. The Democrats' control of both elected branches of government in 1993 made Washington appear to be hostile territory. The health-care interest groups were aided by their money, their experience with the issues, and their alliance with conservatives who saw political advantage in helping them. Underlying these advantages was the intensity of an industry with its back to the wall and its vital interests threatened.[1]

HEALTH REFORM: ALIVE ON ARRIVAL

In his campaign for president, Bill Clinton had pledged to make health-care reform a central goal of his first 100 days in office. It was a popular position. The United States had long trailed other industrialized countries in providing universal medical coverage. Because most health coverage was dependent on having a full-time job with benefits, those who were unemployed, in part-time jobs, or poor often had no insurance. This included 15 percent of all Americans. Clinton believed that Health Security was as important for the poor as Social Security was for senior citizens. Indeed, in a simplifying sound bite, the president held up a Health Security card that would function just like everyone's Social Security card.

In his speech of September 22, Clinton laid out one of the most comprehensive domestic policy proposals ever made by a president. The 1,364-page plan included a guarantee of universal health–care coverage, a requirement that employers pay about 80 percent of the insurance costs, the creation of a national health board that would establish national spending limits, and insurance reforms prohibiting cutting benefits to people with preexisting medical conditions. Clinton considered his plan a middle-of-the-road approach—a compromise between market-oriented and government-centered reforms.

Initial popular and press response was enthusiastic. A *Washington Post*/ABC nationwide poll after the speech found 67 percent approved of the president's program, while only 20 percent disapproved. An opposition Republican senator predicted, "We will pass a law next year." A *New York Times* headline read, "The Clinton Plan Is Alive on Arrival."[2]

But there were clouds on the horizon. The reform had been drawn up in secret by a huge White House task force headed by First Lady Hillary Clinton and Ira Magaziner, a bright, politically inexperienced friend of the president. The working group devising the complicated plan was isolated from many of the policy groups in and around government that would be needed to pass the plan in Congress. These interests and experts, who should have been strong allies, felt alienated from the process. Though the First Lady was an effective advocate for reform, her presence inhibited internal debate: Who wanted to go to the president to complain about his wife?

Meanwhile the opponents of reform, on the sidelines watching the drafting process, were not sitting still. With the trillion-dollar health-care industry representing one-fifth of the nation's economy, there were a number of wealthy interest groups with stakes in the outcome of the struggle. Small businesses, health insurers, drug companies, hospital associations, doctors, and chambers of commerce all prepared to mobilize money, ads, and lobbyists for the fight.

Republicans were strongly opposed for reasons beyond health care. Some from the moderate wing of the party favored passing modest reforms. But they were overwhelmed by the conservatives in their party, who viewed the Clinton program as a perfect target for their case against the threats posed by Big Government—fewer freedoms, continued waste, more taxes. (Congressman Dennis Hastert, who would become Speaker of the House in 1999, described the plan in an oft-repeated sound bite as offering "the efficiency of the post office and the compassion of the IRS.") The campaign that followed energized conservative opinion nationwide. A year later, the political momentum gained from defeating Clinton's proposal would aid the Republicans' triumphant takeover of Congress in the 1994 elections.

OPPONENTS OF REFORM GO PUBLIC

As seen in the Harry and Louise ads, opponents of reform were not about to allow the White House to frame the terms of the debate. In the beginning, many businesses connected with health care wanted to negotiate the best deal they could for their industry. This stance reflected resignation to some reform passing. As the tide shifted against the Clintons, opponents jumped at the chance to defeat reform entirely. The battle polarized positions on both sides. Hillary Clinton attacked the health insurance industry (whose trade association funded Harry and Louise ads) for "price-gouging, cost-shifting and unconscionable profiteering."[3]

The health insurance industry led the private groups organizing against Clinton. The cutting edge of this effort was the Health Insurance Association of America (HIAA), a group of midsized and small insurance companies. These companies feared being forced out of business if the reforms passed. There were splits within the industry—with the more reform-minded large insurers, who thought they could survive Clinton's proposals, leaving HIAA. The insurers who remained in HIAA put their political savvy and money into an aggressive campaign of ads and grassroots organizing. Led by a respected former eight-term Republican congressman from Ohio, Willis D. Gradison, HIAA first tried for concessions and then attacked.

On the ad front, HIAA ran three installments of "Harry and Louise," emphasizing evolving themes and trying to wring changes in the health-care plan from the administration. The association spent almost $15 million on these ads, a large share of the $50 million both sides spent advertising in the health-care debate.[4] As one ad followed another, the white, middle-class couple uncovered the horrors of care-by-bureaucracy: It might run out of money; government would be choosing their health plan for them; and younger people could pay higher premiums. These ads framed the industry's arguments and amplified public uneasiness with a reform not being clearly explained by the White House.

Among followers of the black arts of political commercials, "Harry and Louise" gained status because of their impressive impact. Actually, the ads were shown in only a few markets, mainly in the Washington–New York corridor. Their influence grew after Hillary Clinton attacked them. In a blistering November 1993 speech, she accused the insurance industry of lying to the public in order to protect profits. "They have the gall to run TV ads that there is a better way, the very industry that has brought us to the brink of bankruptcy because of the way they have financed health care," declared an unlady-like First Lady.

Inadvertently, Hillary's unplanned outburst increased the news coverage given the industry, a point underlined by HIAA's leader Gradison: "What they did was to give our advertising a much larger audience than it would have had. . . . " The Clintons tried to make a joke out of "Harry and Louise" in a satiric skit at an annual dinner for Washington reporters at The Gridiron Club. President Clinton, representing the "Coalition to Scare Your Pants Off," played Harry. He asks, "You mean after Bill and Hillary put all those new bureaucrats and taxes on us, we're still all going to die?"[5] The result was still more attention for the ads.

Less visible than TV commercials, but arguably more effective, was the interest groups' grassroots organizing. Although dismissed as "Astro Turf" (or artificial grassroots campaigns), paid organizers mobilized public opinion in states and districts of key members of Congress. They recruited local business leaders, patients in doctors' offices, employees of drug companies, and hospital workers. These industry "stakeholders" were encouraged to write letters or phone or visit their elected representatives. Coalitions sprang up using networks of small businesspeople, insurance agents, and medical suppliers. Over $100 million was spent to hammer reform into the ground. In the words of the nonpartisan Center for Public Integrity, health-care reform became in 1993 and 1994 "the most heavily lobbied legislative initiative in recent U.S. history."[6]

HIAA added commercials to their grassroots tactics. Advertising, both print and TV, focused on key battleground states, mostly those represented by conservative Democrats who would be sympathetic to the message, and might be ambivalent toward their party's reform proposals. Every ad included a toll-free 800 number that people could call. Those calling would be entered into a database and urged to write letters or patched through to their member of Congress. (Patching allowed the interest group's phone bank to directly connect callers to their congressional office.) HIAA corralled 45,000 people, generating over a quarter of a million contacts with the media and Congress.[7]

The groups mobilizing to fight the Clinton plan were those with a direct economic stake and those with a more general conservative agenda. Besides the insurers, the Pharmaceutical Research and Manufacturers of America (PRMA) represented leading drug companies worried about price controls on drugs. They, along with the American Medical Association, sponsored numerous free trips for members of Congress. Business associations got involved, including those for large corporations—the Business Roundtable—and small businesses—the National Federation of Independent Business (NFIB). Lobbyists for grocery stores and chains like Burger King that hired many part-time workers without health insurance met frequently with legislators. Conservative groups such as the Christian Coalition sponsored newspaper ads. One featured a picture of a friendly family doctor giving a child shots for immunization, with the warning "Don't let a government bureaucrat in this picture."

This coalition of the health industry, business groups, deficit hawks, and social conservatives operated with a great deal of unity. They shared polls, exchanged intelligence, and targeted legislators needing special attention. They were supported by lists of Republican party donors. They got their arguments on the *Wall Street Journal* editorial page. They listened to conservative talk radio's Rush Limbaugh for comic reassurance. And they took comfort from the spiritual backing of conservative churches. The ranks of these foes of reform expanded and hardened as the fight progressed.

THE WHITE HOUSE CAMPAIGN STUMBLES

The White House effort to promote health-care reform resembled a presidential campaign. Clinton used the same consultants who had led his drive to the presidency. This excluded the health-care experts within the government who lacked campaign experience. The tactics of an election also personalized the battle—focusing attention on the president and First Lady—making it more partisan and expanding the fight into a nationwide media contest. What might have been a narrower Washington debate over legislation leading to a negotiated compromise instead became a bitter public wrestling match with clear winners and losers.[8]

One of the first problems the Clinton administration encountered was how to explain a very complex plan very simply. It was not the White House's fault that health care was, in fact, complicated—reform was hard enough to explain to legislators with experience in the health-care field. It was even more difficult to explain to a skeptical media and a public that wanted reform but feared government "bungling."

White House hopes to use the president to dominate the national news by advocating health care would soon be derailed. Following his speech, the president planned to devote a month to promoting the program, with rallies across the country, leading up to submitting it to Congress in October. But overseas crises intervened. A failed raid in Somalia resulted in eighteen dead American soldiers and brutal televised pictures of a GI's body dragged through the streets. A noisy demonstration in Haiti embarrassingly stopped an American warship from docking. Overheated news from Russia reported the new post-Communist regime of Boris Yeltsin teetering on the brink. These crises demanded the president's attention. In October, he had to cancel all but one of his health-care events. A month that was to launch the campaign instead weakened the president's connection with health care along with its prospects.

Scandals, mostly manufactured, plagued the Clintons. The death in July 1993 of Vincent Foster, a White House aide and close friend of the First Family, sparked widespread conspiracy theories. Although investigated and ruled a suicide, Vince Foster's "murder" became a staple of right-wing radio talk shows. Even more distractions came from the investigations by congressional committees and special prosecutors into the Clintons' Arkansas land dealings, known as Whitewater. Although the Clintons were never ultimately charged with anything illegal, the turmoil took its toll. It diverted the White House by dominating the headlines ("Whitewater: More Questions Than Answers," "How Bad Is It?" etc.). And it weakened the president's ability to communicate on issues—like health care. The president's opponents took advantage of the charges. Conservative talk-show host Rush Limbaugh told his audience of millions, "I think Whitewater is about health care.. . . If people are going to base their support for the plan on whether they can take his [the president's] word, I think it's fair to examine whether or not he keeps his word."[9]

Supporters of Hillary Clinton's health–care reform campaign.

THE BATTLE JOINED, AND BROADCAST

Because of the political storms swirling around the White House, the pro-reform forces found themselves fragmented and outspent, with difficulty unifying their coalition. Part of the problem was stated afterward by the president: ". . . The supporters were always thinking about how they could get a better deal." For example, the powerful AARP (American Association of Retired Persons) was later criticized for questioning the details of the plan instead of immediately campaigning in support. By spring of 1994, when they finally spent $5 million to back reform, it was too late.

During the crucial months following the president's speech—October to December 1993—the opposition had the advertising field to themselves. Groups like the Democratic National Committee were decisively outspent. In this period, the DNC spent just $150,000 for ads, while HIAA and PRMA anteed up $17.5 million for TV and print ads. With the president being distracted by crises and opponents spending a ton of money, it was the enemies of health care reform that got to define the message early to the public.

The media helped. Intentionally or not, the press coverage emphasized the political fight over health care, rather than the substance of the reform and how it would personally affect American families. The emphasis on conflict was considered more exciting, as well as easier to cover. Already noted was how much the media commented on and repeated opposition messages like Harry and Louise. Much of the coverage emphasized the impact of these ads on public opinion, "creating real doubts" among the general public about the Clinton program. Of course, *reporting* widespread doubts about reform looked to supporters to be the same as *spreading* widespread doubts.

Part of the problem the press faced was the sheer size and complexity of the plan. One correspondent for the *Los Angeles Times* said she felt "swamped by the immensity of the policy stuff and the political dimensions. It was so complicated. . . . " When asked how well the administration had explained the plan, she added, "They were awful. The plan was virtually unexplainable, and at first they were just arrogant. . . . Pretty soon, it was all being lost in confusion and fear."[10]

A study of press coverage appearing in the *Columbia Journalism Review* found that the public had actually become *less* informed on the basics of the proposal as the campaign progressed.[11] This development followed the shift in media focus from the seriousness of the health-care crisis to the conflicts surrounding reform. Exceptional efforts by the press to explain the reforms—such as NBC-TV's June 1994 two-hour, prime-time, commercial-free program on health care, financed by a foundation grant—didn't have much impact. As less attention was paid to the consequences of this reform for families, the public ended up getting most of its information from special interest sources. Much of it was slanted. James Fallows, a respected journalist, called the health-care battle "the press's Vietnam War," arguing that "the media failed in a historic way to help Americans understand and decide on this issue."[12]

POSTOPERATIVE POSTSCRIPTS

By mid-1994 it was over. There were futile attempts among moderate Democrats and Republicans to compromise, by passing parts of the president's reform. But despite Democratic control of Congress, despite the commitment from the Oval Office, and despite months of effort by supporters in unions, health-care institutions, and nonprofits, Washington couldn't move on universal health coverage.

On September 26, 1994, almost exactly a year after Clinton had addressed Congress, Senate Democratic Leader George Mitchell made the announcement: A compromise on health-care reform would not be brought up. The Senate majority leader said, "The combination of the insurance industry on the outside and a majority of Republicans on the inside proved to be too much to overcome." The reform never even reached the floor of Congress for a vote. It was a stunning defeat.

One skeptic defined historians as prophets looking backward. It is a warning of how easy it is to look at past political fights including that over health-care reform and make the losers look incompetent, the winners invulnerable, and the outcome inevitable. But to the participants, very little is preordained. President Clinton's assessment of his defeat is one place to start. "Any time you try to change something that's big and complicated, the people who are against it have a better argument because they can be simple and straight. That's number one. Number two, any time you've got something that touches people where they live—and health care is profoundly important to everybody—it's easier for people to be frightened than it is for people to live on their hopes."

The president was insightful without being complete. The opposition's bleak message of fearing Big Government did contribute to the outcome. But the political activities of the messengers were also central. Richard Gephardt, Democratic House majority leader and a commander of the Clinton forces, gave the opponents a backhanded compliment when he downplayed the impact of money on his side's defeat. "It's not money. It's votes. . . I think money had little to do with the outcome. It's the political work they do at home."[13]

Note that Gephardt was referring to the votes of politicians and the grassroots work done in their districts and states. The campaigning funded by committed interest groups convinced elected officials that health reform was not politically viable. They used the modern techniques of public politics to change the views of elected officials in Washington. In his book *Going Public*, Samuel Kernell wrote, "Intense minorities scare politicians more than inattentive majorities for the good reason that the former will act on their beliefs and the latter will not."[14] In this sense, President Clinton was wrong. It was not the public that was scared by the campaign against health-care reform. It was the politicians.

That conclusion is reinforced by the fact that the ads and grassroots efforts may not have changed public opinion on the core issues. From beginning to end, over 70 percent of those polled agreed with the two fundamental goals behind the Clinton reform. One was that all American families should have health insurance. The other was that employers should contribute to paying for their workers' premiums. Thus, even with their uncertainty about the government's ability to deliver on reform, a majority of Americans favored the changes in health care that Clinton was proposing. This striking majority remained unaltered by the campaigns. But majority opinion would not be sufficient by itself to pass health reform. It was a lesson that would be taken to heart by another Democratic president fifteen years later.[15]

What did change toward Clinton's plan was *political* opinion. Control over the national agenda on health care was wrestled away from the new president by a coalition of conservatives and health industry groups. They spread the dubious messages that reform would mean more bureaucracy, less freedom to choose a doctor, and lower-quality care at higher cost. The coalition's commercials, grassroots activities, and lobbying played a critical part. The White House and its supporters failed to respond with a clear, compelling story in favor of reform. President Clinton was hampered by foreign crises, over-hyped scandals, and a process too tightly controlled by his wife and close allies. The media failed to explain the substance of the program and focused on political infighting.

Harry and Louise played their role as well. By the summer of 1994, the reformers' loss of control over public opinion was underlined, ironically, by a Democratic commercial. In July, toward the end of the policy debate, the Democratic National Committee began airing a new TV ad called "Harry Takes a Fall." In the spot, Harry and Louise are in bed. Harry is in a full body cast while Louise's arm is in a sling. Harry has lost his job, his health insurance, and most of his wealth. Louise is blaming Harry for opposing reform. While they helped the Democrats make their argument, Harry and Louise were sending another message: They were now defining the issue for their opponents. Even in politics, imitation is the sincerest form of flattery.[16]

Notes

1. For the perspective of the president in going public, see Samuel Kernell, *Going Public: New Strategies of Presidential Leadership*, 4th ed. (Washington, DC: Congressional Quarterly Press, 2007). For the view of the interest groups, see Allan J. Cigler and Burdett A. Loomis, eds., *Interest Group Politics*, 8th ed. (Washington, DC: Congressional Quarterly Press, 2011).
2. Darrell M. West and Burdett Loomis, *The Sound of Money: How Political Interests Get What They Want* (New York: W. W. Norton, 1999).
3. Haynes Johnson and David S. Broder, *The System* (Boston, MA: Little, Brown and Company, 1997), 202. Much of this discussion relies on this comprehensive history by two reporters of the health–care reform campaigns.
4. West and Loomis.
5. Johnson and Broder, 211.
6. As quoted by Theda Skocpol, *Boomerang: Health Care Reform and the Turn Against Government* (New York: W. W. Norton, 1997), 141.

7. West and Loomis, 85.
8. See Johnson and Broder, Chapter 24, "Lessons: Lost Opportunities."
9. Johnson and Broder, 276.
10. Ibid., 230.
11. Ibid.
12. See James Fallows, *Breaking the News* (New York: Vintage Books, 1997), "The Press's Vietnam War," 205–234.
13. Johnson and Broder, 198.
14. Kernell, 213.
15. Johnson and Broder, 631. More detailed and more negative conclusions about public opinion on health-care reform can be found in Lawrence R. Jacobs and Robert Y. Shapiro, *Politicians Don't Pander* (Chicago: University of Chicago Press, 2000), Chapter 7.
16. West and Loomis, 105–106.

10

INTEREST GROUPS
OBAMA'S HEALTH-CARE REFORM
The White House Networks the Industry

The health–care reform law that President Obama signed on March 23, 2010, was hailed as a major legislative victory. The president had made it his administration's top priority and put behind it the resources of his office and party. But as we saw in the last chapter, the power of the presidency was necessary but alone would not have been sufficient to pass the reform. Early in the process, the Obama White House concluded that they needed support from interest groups in the health industry. The involvement of these groups and the compromises reached with them shaped the bill that emerged.

Political scientists use the term "issue networks" to describe a coalition of policy interests—lobbyists, government officials, and experts—working together to reach a shared objective. The members of these networks are both in and out of government, represent commercial and public interests, and may be lobbyists, congressional and executive branch staff, or think-tank specialists. In the past, these lobbies were called "iron triangles" and described as rigid, autonomous groups that promote narrow policies unconnected to democratic inputs. Contemporary issue networks are seen as more pluralistic. They are ad hoc groupings—flexible and informal, less permanent, larger in size, and more open to new participants than the old iron triangles. These networks are temporary, pragmatic alliances needed to accomplish the overlapping objectives of their members.[1]

The results produced by issue networks are messy. The question of "who won" in a reform as large and complex as health care is unsurprisingly subject to considerable debate. President Obama's supporters see him as having "co-opted" previous opponents into backing reform; others criticize him for having "sold-out" to these interests. Students of interest group coalitions view this lack of clarity as part of bringing together divergent views. ". . . issue networks are not dominated by one powerful set of interests, and hence bargaining, negotiation, and compromise are much more important to the resolution of conflict."[2] Who gained the most may not be as important as the question of whether the results were worth the concessions made on costs and coverage. And, as seen in later efforts to repeal health care, whether the nation believed that the process and results of reform merited the public's support.

CONCEPTS TO CONSIDER _____

1. The **power of interest groups and their lobbyists** is an important question in American politics. What are some examples of lobbyists from the health-care industry dominating the shape of reform? When do government officials—in Congress or the White House—seem to have the upper hand? Do industry lobbyists appear to have greater influence over Congress than over the White House?
2. The health-care **issue network** crossed public and private divisions with members from both government and the health-care sector. Does this make the previous distinction between private lobbyists and government officials an artificial one? Or does it just produce a temporary alliance where the "public interest" is lost in the negotiations with powerful business groups?
3. **Public opinion** often appears confused and indifferent to health-care reform, both while it was being debated and after it was passed. Was that because of the complexity of the issue, its lack of popularity, or the way compromises were reached without much public input?
4. How much of a role does **lobbying money** play in enacting health reform? Could the administration have passed reform without the industry's money? Could it have passed reform with the industry's money opposing it?
5. The argument is made that **the main difference with the Clinton health-care proposal** was the support of interest groups for ObamaCare. What else did the Obama administration do differently from Clinton in its approach to reform, its dealings with Congress, and its substantive positions toward reform? Did Obama act similarly in placing reform on the public's agenda and then aggressively pursuing it?

Harry and Louise were back. Same actors, different message.

"It looks like we may finally get health-care reform," says Harry.

"It's about time," Louise answers.

"A little more cooperation, a little less politics and we can get the job done this time," she concludes.

Looking a bit older in 2009, Harry and Louise were repeating the roles that had helped sink the Clinton plan. But this time they weren't working for the insurance industry and they weren't opposing reform. In a TV ad jointly sponsored by the drug lobby (PhRMA-Pharmaceutical Research and Manufacturers Association) and the liberal advocacy group, Families USA, Harry and Louise had switched sides.[3]

This had come at a cost. In private conversations with White House officials, PhRMA was lured by the prospect of millions of newly insured customers. Both sides exchanged financial concessions including an administration promise not to seek lower drug prices in the Medicare program. To seal the deal, PhRMA pledged to pay for a multimillion dollar media campaign in support of health-care reform. These "secret" concessions did not go unnoticed by liberal supporters of health-care reform. Robert Reich, former secretary of labor under President Clinton, denounced the agreements. "Citizens end up paying for advertisements designed to persuade them that the legislation is in their interest. In this case, those payments come in the form of drug prices that will be higher than otherwise, stretching years into the future."

Given the Clinton failures on health care (discussed in Chapter 9), Obama could be excused for not taking advice from that administration's officials. The Obama White House had learned a vital lesson from their Democratic predecessor: Don't let health-care interest groups unite against reform. Like health reformers before him, Clinton had been outlobbied and outspent by interest groups opposing changes to their industry. This time these interests would be approached differently. As one health professor concluded afterward, "Arguably the most consequential decision that reformers made in 2009 was to work with, rather than against, health system stakeholders."[4]

There was of course a price to be paid for Obama's strategy.

EMBRACING HEALTH REFORM VAGUELY

When Barack Obama entered the White House there were plenty of reasons to believe that health reform would fail again. The Democratic majorities in both houses—59 in the Senate, 257 in the House—were not much greater than the Congress that had not even voted on Bill Clinton's plan in 1994. And in 2009, the economy was in the midst of the worse economic recession since the Great Depression of the 1930s. The federal government already had its hands full: an expensive and unpopular bailout of the banking industry, a $700 billion stimulus program, and soaring budget deficits. American politics remained stuck in a polarized culture war. Republicans had decided that their best chance of regaining power lay in uniting in opposition to all the major initiatives of the young president who had recently trounced them in the polls. With a housing sector remaining in free fall, unemployment hovering near 10 percent, and two expensive unresolved wars, the GOP strategy seemed shrewd.

With these crises filling the new administration's first-year agenda, it was not clear that health-care reform would or should be a priority. During the presidential campaign, Obama had promised to sign health care that provided universal coverage, but had added an important reservation—*by the end of his first four years*. His advisors opposed pushing something as large as health reform in the first year. Chief of Staff Rahm Emanuel, Advisor David Axelrod, and Vice President Joe Biden all thought that it would overload the circuits, distracting from the need to repair the economy. (Emanuel candidly put it, "I begged the president not to do this.") His economic advisors wanted to wait until the economy was in better shape. Democratic leaders in the Senate urged the president to hold off. Public opinion polls showed that for the 95 percent of Americans who had health coverage, insuring those who didn't wasn't a high priority.[5]

Obama stood virtually alone in his White House in pushing for health-care reform. He believed that the escalating costs of health care would eventually bring fiscal disaster, that unless these costs were controlled the federal deficit could not be brought down. Insurance premiums had more than doubled in the last decade and the numbers of uninsured Americans would soon pass 50 million. On the campaign trail, he had heard the painful stories of people thrown into bankruptcy by medical costs, and indifferent treatment by insurance companies. And he remembered his own family history with his mother struggling with insurers as she lay dying of cancer. He knew that as difficult and complex as reform was, it would not get any easier if he waited; like most presidents his power would be more likely to ebb than increase. And the president's ego also played a role. Health care was one of the *Big Things* that he wanted to accomplish as president. Looking back at history, he took a shot at President Clinton when, in arguing with his staff over health care, he said, "he wasn't sent here to do school uniforms."

Obama's strategy could be summed up as doing the opposite of what the Clinton administration had tried. The way to win this time was to stay vague, defer to Congress, and buy off the interest groups that had blocked past reforms. Being nonspecific meant avoiding overly ambitious "dug-in" positions that would win the hearts of liberals but alienate powerful interests in the industry. Out, was the grand Clinton vision of transforming the health delivery system through managed competition and centralized cost controls. In, was incremental, business-friendly reform; small businesses could opt out of the changes and Americans happy with their insurance were reassured they could keep their plans. Even Obama's declaration that the final package would not add to the deficit underlined the limits of the effort. Obama repeatedly warned his staff that the perfect should not be the enemy of the good.

NEUTRALIZING INTEREST GROUPS

In hindsight it's not easy to conclude who seduced who in the White House negotiations with health-care interest groups. From the beginning the industry stakeholders were more willing to accept reform in 2009 than they were in the 1990s. Their motives were clear. Financially they stood to expand their markets with newly insured patients. Politically they made the calculation that reform was likely to pass and so they had better influence its shape from within. The future for the industry didn't necessarily look bright. Employer-sponsored insurance was getting more expensive and less popular, which threatened their profits. And without reform the industry expected the years ahead to bring increased government regulation.[6]

For the White House its strategy of compromise had meant giving up Democratic hopes of a national health insurance program for the entire country. A single-payer, government-sponsored insurance, a la Canada, had long been considered politically unrealistic by Democratic leaders. Now a Medicare-like government insurance program that would compete with private insurers became the centerpiece of reform for liberals. This public option offered the prospect of lower costs and an alternative for those who wished to avoid private insurers. But the price of the administration's negotiations with the industry would eventually mean dropping the public option. The results would be a patchwork of changes that provided federal subsidies allowing patients to choose from private insurance plans. It pragmatically filled in the gaps in the existing system rather than creating a new health system.

Throughout the spring and summer of 2009, meetings were held between industry representatives, Democratic congressional leaders, and White House officials. At these meetings the White House elected not to draft a detailed reform proposal and instead pushed for innovative ways to contain health costs by the industry. Corporate lobbyists agreed to spend millions of dollars on TV advertising supporting health reform efforts and called for fewer restraints by the government on their ability to do business.

A May 11, 2009, meeting at the White House was called a "game changer" by administration officials. At the meeting, drugmakers, the insurance and hospital lobbies, and the American Medical Association representing doctors committed to some $2 trillion in savings in the health-care system over the next ten years. Drug manufacturers agreed to $80 billion in product discounts. Hospitals agreed to accept $155 billion less in Medicare reimbursements in order to avoid cost cutting imposed by the government. Doctors were willing to endorse the health bill in return for abolishing an existing formula in Medicare payments that required cuts in payments to physicians. Other industry groups, like the medical equipment providers, were at the table but didn't reach an agreement with the White House. They faced penalties instead. In this case, the Senate Finance Committee a few months later voted to impose a $40 billion tax on the device manufacturers.[7]

DOING A DRUG DEAL

The drug industry provides a window into the deals that were being discussed over health reform. The pharmaceutical industry lobbyists and executives met with top White House aides dozens of times to hammer out the details. Their top lobbyist was PhRMA president Billy Tauzin, a longtime Democratic congressman who switched parties after Republicans gained control of Congress in 1994. This enabled him to become Chairman of the House Committee on Energy & Commerce where he crafted a bill to provide prescription drug access to Medicare recipients. The legislation benefited the industry by preventing Medicare from negotiating for lower prescription drug costs and threatening to buy imported drugs from abroad. A few months after the bill passed, Tauzin retired from Congress to take the job leading PhRMA for a salary of $2 million. This job change tarnished Tauzin's reputation making him a poster boy for Washington's lobbyist culture. He was taunted in a 2008

Obama campaign ad. At the ad's conclusion candidate Obama points to Tauzin as ". . . an example of the same old game playing in Washington. You know, I don't want to learn how to play the game better, I want to put an end to the game playing."[8]

Backing up Tauzin was an army of lobbyists, a media campaign, and deep pockets of dollars. PhRMA had a total of 165 lobbyists working for it in 2009. Some 137 were former employees of the Congress or the Executive, including two former chiefs of staff to Senator Max Baucus chairman of the Senate Finance Committee that was writing the health-care legislation. Most of the industry's millions of dollars in campaign contributions tilted heavily to Democrats for the first time in decades. On April 15, PhRMA held a meeting with leaders of organized labor, health-care groups, and Democratic senate staff to form two nonprofit groups that would launch advertising to promote reform efforts. The two groups—Healthy Economy Now and Americans for Stable Quality Care—spent $24 million on their advertising campaigns, almost entirely paid for by PhRMA. The contract to produce and place ads went to White House Senior Advisor David Axelrod's former firm.[9]

Led by Tauzin, CEO's from drug companies met with Senator Baucus and administration officials throughout the spring. Although Baucus had initially sought $100 billion in cost cutting by the industry, the negotiators settled on a figure of $80 billion. The industry also agreed to increase their funding to $150 million for a pro-reform advertising campaign. In return the industry was able to restrain several Democratic attempts to lower the costs of drugs. These included restrictions on Medicare negotiations over drug prices, re-importation of drugs from other developed countries, and quicker release of cheaper generic drugs onto the market. In a July meeting in the Roosevelt Room of the White House, Chief of Staff Rahm Emanuel and Tauzin shook hands on the deal. By August, the *Huffington Post* could report that an internal White House memo made clear that in return for industry's drug-price discounts these government measures of cost controls would not be allowed into any final version of reform. Despite various attacks on this agreement from outraged Democrats on the Hill, the PhRMA deal was included fully intact in the health-care reform bill eventually passed in the Senate.

Tauzin proclaimed health-care reform "a once-in-a-lifetime opportunity." The Louisiana congressman had joined PhRMA after he learned he had cancer. He described himself as committing ". . . to the lifesaving work of the people whose miracle medicines had just saved my own." Although liberals attacked the administration for giving away too much, industry officials thought they were the ones who had made too many concessions. After spending $100 million in advertising and agreeing to $80 billion of cost-cutting measures, the drug executives did not agree with Tauzin's bet on reform. A divided board pushed him to resign his post. On February 12, 2010, even before the final legislation passed Congress, Tauzin announced his resignation as president of PhRMA. The White House declined to comment.[10]

AND THEN THERE WAS CONGRESS

Reaching agreements between the White House and major health interest groups was not the same as gaining congressional approval of legislation. Other interest groups, including major business associations like the Chamber of Commerce, remained opposed. Republicans were united in opposition. Liberals were appalled at some of the concessions to business and prepared to challenge them.

And the congress itself, with its two houses, layers of committees, staff and party leaders, presented abundant obstacles to any reform emerging. Already voices could be heard from within the majority Democrats that trouble lay ahead. Senator Tom Harkin, Democrat of Iowa, and chair of the Health, Education, Labor and Pensions Committee (HELP) commented on the White House negotiations: "I can't be bound by someone else's agreement. President Obama never sat down with us."[11]

This is not to say that the White House and its tentative allies were going naked into battle. There were plenty of troops—not always shooting in the same direction. The Center for Public Integrity reported that congressional disclosure forms for 2009 showed that 1,750 companies and organizations had hired about 4,525 lobbyists to influence health reform—8 for each member of Congress. This included 207 hospitals, 105 insurance companies, and 85 manufacturing companies. Trade, advocacy, and professional groups dwarfed them all with 745 registered groups. The center estimates that business spent $1.2 billion lobbying on health in 2009.

With health care consuming 16 percent of the national economy, there was a wide variety of interests represented. The Cigar Association wanted to make sure that a tobacco tax wasn't included; Art Museum Directors pushed for including "creative arts therapists" as mental health professionals; and Dunkin' Donuts lobbied against a proposed soda tax. A vice president for a manufacturer of medical equipment bluntly revealed their motives in opposing the bill, "We don't believe we are going to sell more products as a result of health reform."[12]

Most of the health industry supported reform in principle but withheld final support from the emerging legislation. This meant they could lobby quietly on specific provisions to protect their own business. For example, the American Medical Association spent $20 million lobbying in 2009. While saying good things about reform the AMA leaders wanted to make sure that expanded health insurance coverage wouldn't come out of doctors' pockets. The AMA helped kill a $300 yearly fee for doctors in Medicare, a tax on cosmetic surgery, and Medicare payment cuts for primary care physicians. Each of these had been in the initial Senate bill, but disappeared in the final version. A Princeton University professor summed up the lobbyists impact on reform. "They cut it. They chopped it. They reconstructed it. They didn't bury it. I don't think they wanted to." The lack of serious cost controls, he concluded, were the direct result of industry lobbying.[13]

Unlike the lobbyists, President Obama presented himself as offering broad principles for reform and then keeping aloof from the legislative fights. At best this was a partial truth. Behind the scenes the White House worked not only to preserve the agreements they had reached but also to influence the legislative process. For starters this meant letting the president's congressional allies know that health care was his priority, bills such as climate change were not to get in the way. It also meant elevating the work of the Senate Finance Committee, and its chairman Max Baucus. The finance panel's conclusions provided the lead to the half dozen committees in both houses drafting legislation. The president avoided commenting on the other committees' deliberations but he spoke with Mr. Baucus several times a week. The Montana Democrat was included in many of the meetings with lobbies at the White House. As one congressman admitted, "The House has largely been a sideshow. The Senate Finance Committee is where it really matters."[14]

Unfortunately for the White House, Baucus' committee was unable to meet the president's deadline of passing legislation by August 2009. The delay of the complex legislation came largely from the chairman's hope that he could get bipartisan support within his committee. This centered on his ally and friend, Republican Senator Chuck Grassley of Iowa. But Grassley, up for reelection in 2010, and expecting a right-wing challenge in the GOP primary, dragged his feet. Only when he warned an Iowa town meeting of the bill's "death panels" that meant "pulling the plug on Grandma," and denounced "ObamaCare" despite having agreed in committee on many of its provisions, did Baucus and the White House give up on bipartisanship. The Democratic majority on the Senate committee passed the bill on October 13.[15]

THE PUBLIC'S INPUT

The problem of getting Republican votes in congress paralleled the lack of public support outside of Washington. Throughout 2009, the public focused on a sagging economy, high unemployment, and the bailouts of the banks and auto industry. Why did the government need to spend more on health care? It was a time of public confusion and anger, reflected in noisy town hall meetings during Congress's August recess, the founding of the "tea party" protest movement, and the media amplifying lies about where Obama had actually been born and whether he was a Muslim. Republicans stoked the fires by personalizing policy differences and viewing health care as their opportunity to bring about Obama's "Waterloo." The president had difficulty focusing his message on health care—whether it would reduce costs, or improve quality or introduce security. Even the fraudulent charges that reform meant federal "death panels" that would decide on end of life care served to worry senior citizens that Washington cutting costs might lead to reducing benefits. Simple messages were effective, even if they weren't true.

Part of the president's problem with the public came from his "inside" Washington strategy working against an "outside" Washington grassroots mobilization. Having made a grand bargain with insurance and drug industries, Obama had difficulty branding them obstacles to reform. Trying to win over moderate Republicans and holding on to the interest groups, he had reached compromises, which meant discouraging liberal activists from engaging in protests against their traditional adversaries in the health industry. Unlike historic progressive legislation such as the New Deal, civil rights, and protection of the environment, there were few dramatic expressions of popular opinion supporting health reform. The emphasis on backstage compromises weakened the Democrats' ability to mobilize public outrage against these powerful interests. As two liberal activists charged, "Without a grassroots uprising that challenges business as usual in Washington, we aren't likely to get the change we were promised, much less the change we need."[16]

The administration's dilemma was illustrated in their dealings with insurers. The summer negotiations may have been too little, too late. Liberal supporters of reform denounced "Chief of Staff Rahm Emanuel's disastrous strategy of treating the insurance industry as a partner rather than a nemesis."[17] But the White House had never reached a concrete agreement with the insurers regarding cost cuts. The industry had wanted an individual mandate forcing individuals to buy their products, and a heavy penalty (well over $1,000 per year) for people who failed to buy insurance. They also opposed the public option, popular new taxes of some $70 billion on the industry, and major cuts to programs that encouraged seniors to buy private insurance. As the summer of 2009 faded into fall, congressional committees began reporting out reform proposals that opposed these positions of the insurance companies. It became clear that the Democrats and insurers had irreconcilable differences.

This may have been a mixed blessing for administration officials. They had begun to frame the debate as "health insurance reform." The term polled better than a general reform message because it targeted the unpopular insurance companies. Democrats on the Hill drew up a new public-relations plan that targeted insurers as the enemy. A mid-summer memo from the House leadership told members, "Hold the insurance companies account- able." House Speaker Nancy Pelosi called private insurers "villains."[18] By the fall of 2009, pro-reform groups like Health Care for America Now (HCAN), a broad coalition of labor, consumer, and community groups, sponsored 150 demonstrations at insurance companies across the country. In September, Obama distanced himself further from the industry in a speech to a joint session of Congress. He sounded like a fiery populist:

> More and more Americans pay their premiums, only to discover that their insurance company has dropped their coverage when they get sick, or won't pay the full cost of care. . . . It happens every day. One man from Illinois lost his coverage in the middle of chemotherapy because his insurer found that he hadn't reported gallstones that he didn't even know about. They delayed his treatment, and he died because of it.[19]

Insurers were outraged. The industry responded with grassroots lobbying that echoed their earlier successful efforts against Clinton's health plan. UnitedHealth Group, the country's second-largest health insurance company, asked its employees to call a hotline for anti-reform talking points to use at local events. It urged them to write their senators and local newspapers to oppose "government-run health care." The industry's trade association began a six-state advertising campaign focusing on cuts to Medicare affecting seniors. Six of the largest health insurers contributed some $20 million to other business groups, including the Chamber of Commerce, to create Employers for a Healthy Economy, which funded a national campaign opposing reform.[20]

The White House's uneasy alliance with all the industry groups was fraying badly by the fall of 2009. The administration had built on earlier cooperation in 2006 through 2008 between labor unions and industry stakeholders that had been supportive of reforming health care. In addition, they benefited from the historic fluke that a number of the key players in the traditionally Republican industry were Democrats. But the administration's buying off special interests may have been only a temporary *realpolitik* tactic; a shrewd political calculation that they didn't have enough support to pass health reform without the momentum given them by these groups. Jonathan Alter thinks so. The respected reporter wrote *The Promise*, a supportive chronicle of the Obama administration's first year, based on extensive interviews in the White House. He states, "The idea was to keep interest groups on board long enough so that when the president blasted them and they went into active opposition (as the insurers and hospitals inevitably did), it would be too late to derail the bill."[21]

This may have been true, or it may have been post-game rationalizing for adapting a complex legislative strategy that regularly verged on falling apart. As former heavyweight boxing champion Joe Lewis remarked, "Everybody's got a plan till he gets hit in the face."

STUMBLING TO THE FINISH LINE

The last months of the health fight continued the confusion. Having mostly given up on gaining Republican support, the White House still had the serious challenge of keeping their own party members on board. While congressional Democrats accepted the logic that having gone this far they needed to get something passed, they were still unhappy, especially about the public option. In private the White House had accepted that the public option could not win in the Senate. But it had to go through the motions of voicing support because liberals had focused on this provision to make their stand. House Democrats pointed out that the public option would keep costs down and demanded the president's clout behind his general support for the public option. Obama maintained his strategic vagueness. In response, liberals threatened to run ads against foot-dragging by moderates in the party. Showing his famed temper, Emanuel called them "fucking retarded" and reminded them they were not trying to pass this "through the executive board of the Brookings Institution." Eventually the House would approve a bill, with the public option, on November 9 in a 225-220 vote. But the public option would fail in the Senate and not surface again.[22]

Throughout the fall the Senate stalled out. Progressive senators pushed for a public option and worried about the cost estimates of reform. Trying to keep costs down did not keep individual senators from trying to get last-minute concessions to benefit their own states. Senator Ben Nelson from Nebraska got a $100 million exemption from Medicaid costs for his state that surfaced to public notoriety as "the Cornhusker Kickback." Other compromises were worked out with labor unions and with abortion opponents. The need to keep all 60 Democratic votes to prevent the Republicans from filibustering strengthened these narrow objections and resulted in endless meetings to resolve them. Still at 7a.m. on Christmas Eve morning the Senate approved the bill, 60-39.

One of the things making passage, as Alter put it "more ugly than uplifting," was the tidal wave of lobbyist money flooding Capitol Hill.[23] In the fourth quarter of 2009, spending for lobbying was $955 million topping $900 million in a quarter for the first time in history. This amounted to $20 million a day, a considerable chunk of which was spent on the most important legislation facing congress at the time, health care. The Chamber of Commerce spent $71 million just in the fourth quarter, mostly opposing reform. PhRMA chipped in $26 million and the AMA spent $20 million. The huge American Association for Retired Persons (AARP) spent $21 million in favor of reform. All but a small portion of lobbying money was spent opposing reform or shaping it to reflect corporate needs. This spending came on top of campaign contributions from the health industry of almost $28 million in 2009–2010, most of it going to Democrats. (In 2008, Obama received $19.5 million from health-related donors, much more than John McCain's $7.4 million. Obama raised $750 million overall.)[24]

Passage by both houses didn't put an end to reform's near-death experiences. One grenade was unexpectedly launched from Massachusetts where a special election was held on January 19 to fill the seat of the late Senator Ted Kennedy. The Senator had devoted his long career to the pursuit of universal health coverage and the seat in a reliably Democratic state was expected to stay with the party. It didn't. The Republican victory was framed by the media as a rejection by independent voters of health care and the smelly deals that were being cut behind closed doors. That the Bay State already had a health insurance program similar to what the administration proposed mattered less than the loud message that voters were angry at Washington.

Besides the public disgust reflected in the election, there was the practical result that a new Republican senator made the margins too narrow (59 rather than 60 senators) to stop a filibuster. This meant that the House had to swallow whole the existing Senate bill to keep it from going back to the floor of the upper house. The House now became the obstacle, with abortion opponents, doctors groups, and some Midwestern states taking advantage of Democratic desperation to salvage a few changes. The bill received a final breath of life when an insurer, Anthem Blue Cross of California, announced an astounding 39 percent increase in rates. Coming in the middle of the debate, it reminded the quarreling supporters of the original problems the bill was designed to solve.

Shortly afterward, the House approved the previously passed Senate bill. All 178 Republicans voted no, and the next day the GOP introduced legislation for repeal. President Obama signed the law on March 23, 2010. Ironically, an industry interest group had helped one last time to pass health-care reform.

CONCLUSION

Easily forgotten is what a historic accomplishment passage of the Patient Protection and Affordable Care Act of 2010 represented. As a major progressive domestic reform, it stood as the equal of the Civil Rights and Medicare/Medicaid Acts of the 1960s and the Clean Air and Clean Water Acts of the 1970s. It represented almost a century of efforts to ensure a public responsibility for the health of Americans, a right that is considered basic to citizens in most countries of the world. The law ended discrimination based on preexisting conditions, eliminated price differences based on health status, set up state insurance exchanges, and offered subsidies for up to 30 million uninsured people. It set up important restraints on costs and precedents for increasing services in the future. Yet the legislation was a patchwork mix filling in gaps in the existing arrangements rather than building a new health system. As one scholar concluded, the reform was a product of fragmented American political institutions and was "probably as good as it gets."[25]

Interest groups played a part. Without the cooperation of the industry, however incomplete, health-care reform would not have passed. The price of passage was numerous concessions to industry interests, added costs to consumers and taxpayers, and a less comprehensive bill than was originally conceived. Adding 32 million customers to the health-care system and avoiding price controls gave players like doctors, hospitals, and drug companies reason to celebrate. While they had reservations about the final bill, all three as well as the AARP, supported reform in the end. Insurers, though they had avoided competing with a government-run public option, faced greater regulation in state-supervised exchanges where they would be required to sell their policies. The legislation required them to insure people regardless of their health. The insurers and much of the business community opposed the final bill. Most of the health-care provisions would not kick in until 2014, which left ample time for anxiety and misinformation to spread.[26]

By 2011, only 30 percent of the public said they favored the health reform bill. Forty percent were opposed, and 30 percent were unsure. Confusion about the law was widespread. A quarter of the population thought it contained "death panels" of bureaucrats deciding on end-of-life care; 65 percent believed the congressional budget office said it would increase the deficit, even though these analysts said it would reduce it. President Obama blamed himself for not making the case for the law more clearly to the country. Democrats suffered stunning reversals in the mid-term elections and lost control of the House. The only Democrats running campaign ads about health care were those who voted "no."[27]

And yet despite opponents' slogan of "Repeal and Replace!" health care seemed here to stay. Republican leaders might reassure their voters by attacking the reform, but when it came to actually enacting legislation they would have to satisfy the industry—the drug companies, doctors, and hospitals. As long as these interest groups wanted to keep the overall structure of health care, bills to overturn the reform had little realistic chance of passing Congress. Repeal of health care was a campaign sound bite, not an issue of governing.

Notes

1. For a concise description of issue networks, see Jeffrey M. Berry and Clyde Wilcox, *The Interest Group Society*, 5th ed. (New York: Longman, 2009), Chapter 9, "The Rise of Issue Networks and Coalitions."
2. John R. Wright, *Interest Groups and Congress* (New York: Longman, 2003), 171.
3. As quoted by Jack Kenny, "Healthcare Hirelings," *The New American* 25, no. 20 (September 28, 2009), 20, 21.
4. Jonathan Oberlander, "Long Time Coming: Why Health Reform Finally Passed," *Health Affairs* 29, no. 6 (June 2010): 1114.
5. See Jonathan Alter, *The Promise* (New York: Simon & Schuster, 2010). Much of this section relies on the fine discussion in Chapter 15, Tyrannosaurus Rx.
6. Oberlander, 1115.
7. Gail Russell Chaddock, "Healthcare Reform: Obama Cut Private Deals with Likely Foes," *The Christian Science Monitor–CSMonitor.com*, November 6, 2009.
8. Paul Blumenthal, "The Legacy of Billy Tauzin: The White House-PhRMA Deal," http://blog.sunlightfoundation.com/2010/02/12/, Sunlight Foundation Blog, February 12, 2010.
9. Ibid.
10. David Kirkpatrick and Duff Wilson, "Health Reform in Limbo, Top Drug Lobbyist Quits," *The New York Times*, February 12, 2010.
11. Chaddock.
12. Joe Eaton and M.B. Pell, "Lobbyists Swarm Capitol to Influence Health Reform," *The Center for Public Integrity*. http:/bit.ly/9141XDvia@Publicintegrity.org, February 23, 2010.
13. Ibid.
14. David D. Kirkpatrick, "Obama Is Taking an Active Role in Talks on Health Care Plan," *The New York Times*, August 13, 2009.
15. Alter, 256–57.
16. Robert L. Borosage and Katrina van den Heuvel, "Exacting Change," *The Nation*, June 15, 2009.

17. Peter Dreier, "Lessons From the Health-Care Wars," *The American Prospect*, April 5, 2010.
18. http://www.politico.com/news/stories/0709/25312.html
19. http://www.politifact.com/truth-o-meter/statements/2009/sep/17/barack-obama/obama-says-decision-revoke-insurance-led-illinois-/
20. http://undertheinfluence.nationaljournal.com/2010/01/health-insurers-funded-chamber.php?print=true
21. Alter, 254.
22. Ibid., 407.
23. Ibid., 420.
24. Michael Tomasky, "The Money Fighting Health Care Reform," *The New York Review of Books*, April 8, 2010.
25. Oberlander, 1116.
26. Reed Abelson, "In Health Care Overhaul, Boons for Hospitals and Drug Makers," *The New York Times*, March 21, 2010.
27. Erica Werner, "Obama: My Fault for Not Selling Health Law," Associated Press, September 22, 2010.

11 | MEDIA

AGENDA-SETTING

The News of the Scandal,
The Scandal of the News

Agenda-setting is a major way that the media influence politics. Of the many challenges facing the country, those in the headlines or on TV are usually seen by the public and officials as deserving to be a priority of the nation and its political leaders. If the press discusses crime often and hunger only slightly, for example, crime will likely be seen as a higher priority. This is known as agenda-setting. Of course the media may not be the main political player competing for the public's attention. In the following case, other political actors besides journalists try to influence press coverage to serve their interests.

The media placed President Bill Clinton's affair with White House intern Monica Lewinsky on the nation's agenda and escalated it into a mega-scandal that led to Clinton's impeachment by the House. The scandal dominated the nation's airways for a year. During that time, supporters of the president attacked the partisan motives of his accusers and claimed the scandal had no impact on his official duties. Opponents linked the affair to lying under oath and the president's immorality. And much of the media framed the scandal as a continuing pattern of adultery and dishonesty, deserving of sanction. The public rejected the media's interpretation, separating Clinton's private indiscretions from their robust approval of his job as president.

The Lewinsky scandal shows both the power and limits of media. The press could headline the events and keep them in front of the public and its leaders. Aligned with partisan forces, they could drive the political process to the point of impeachment. Aggressive new media outlets on cable and the Internet expanded their audiences through 24/7 coverage of the scandal. Yet in their "feeding frenzy" the media increasingly looked like racy tabloids—unreliable as news sources. The public, turned off by both the coverage and the use of it for political advantage, reached its own collective judgment that a sex scandal should not undermine a popular president; that setting the agenda at the start did not determine how the issue would be resolved at the end.

CONCEPTS TO CONSIDER _____

1. In placing the scandal before the nation as an important issue, the media engaged in **agenda-setting.** To what degree was this a conscious decision of people in the media, or to what extent did the scandal "take on a life of its own" in a "feeding frenzy" of competitive journalism?

2. As seen in the chapters on abortion (Chapter 5) and gender stereotyping in campaigns (Chapter 6), media shapes how the public sees an issue by defining the problem in certain ways. In **framing** this scandal, the media presented it as part of Clinton's pattern of dishonest behavior that undermined his office. The first press coverage made this link by connecting the affair to testifying under oath. Why didn't this frame convince the public?

3. How was the coverage of the scandal affected by the **economics of the media**? Look for issues of competition between new and old media; promotion of inexpensive talk shows; and broadcast media depending on stories revealed first by print journalists.

4. **White House news management** attempted to protect the president. How did the White House "spin" the coverage in a more favorable light, use leaks to attack opponents, and present the president going about his official duties unaffected by the controversy? How important was the president's celebrity personality? How successful were political opponents of the president in using the media?

5. This case illustrates **adversarial journalism**—the often conflicted relationship between politicians and reporters. Does news that can attract a wide audience give the media an interest in emphasizing political scandals? Is there any liberal or conservative bias in this case of the press's adversarial coverage?

The Lewinsky scandal engulfing the Clinton administration in 1998 was the "perfect" political storm: an unusual buildup of forces that came together to create a public tornado. It began with the most common of elements—a talkative, love-struck young woman, an ambitious secretary, a relentless reporter, a flawed powerful man—swept up into a charged partisan atmosphere. Aggressive prosecutors saw the scandal as an opportunity to energize their stalled investigation of the president's Arkansas real-estate dealings. The press, fueled by leaks and competition from cable TV and the Internet, heated the atmosphere with twenty-four-hour coverage. The destructive, lurid disclosures and the fury from colliding forces held the public's attention for over a year. The storm died out in a Senate vote staged under the protective traditions of impeachment. Its lasting impact is debated to this day.

A CHARGED ATMOSPHERE

Mike Isikoff's compact energy unbalanced a charged atmosphere. The *Newsweek* reporter could be fairly described as a bit obsessed with Bill Clinton's sex life. He had pursued this angle since he worked for the *Washington Post*. It had cost him his job. In 1994, he had battled for months to get his editors to publish Arkansas state employee Paula Jones's charges that Clinton had propositioned her in a Little Rock hotel room. Eventually the *Post* became the first major newspaper to print Jones's account of her encounter with the then-governor of Arkansas. But the shouting matches that the awkward, combative reporter had with his bosses led to his suspension, and eventually Isikoff left the paper. Now, in early 1998, he was having a similar battle with his editors at *Newsweek*.

For a year, Isikoff had been investigating a story of the president's affair with a young White House intern named Monica Lewinsky. Through Isikoff's contacts from his reporting on Paula Jones, he had gotten to know Linda Tripp, a former White House secretary with ambitions to publish a gossipy book on the Clinton administration. Tripp had become friends with Monica Lewinsky when both were moved from the White House to jobs in the Pentagon. Lewinsky, as the public would soon learn, was the plump, pretty intern visiting the president at night in the Oval Office. Not surprisingly, the twenty-four-year-old talked about it with friends. More surprisingly, one of these "friends" secretly taped their conversations. Convinced by her literary agent that she needed the "goods" to market her book (titled *The President's Women*) to a publisher, Linda Tripp had bought a $100 tape recorder, taped her friend, and gone to Isikoff with the results.[1]

The story up till now might well have taken its place with numerous other swirling scandals that Clinton had been sailing through for much of his political career. The first nationally publicized charges had come from Gennifer Flowers, an Arkansas lounge singer. She had held a press conference, complete with recorded phone calls between the two, to announce that, yes, she had been Clinton's lover for more than a decade. For maximum impact, the press conference was staged during the 1992 primary race for the Democratic nomination. Surviving this required Clinton to appear on CBS News's *60 Minutes* holding hands with his wife, Hillary, to deny any intimate relationship—a half-truth at best, since Clinton admitted "having caused pain in his marriage"—but insisted he wanted to move on (what is known by reporters as a "non-denial denial"). Following that, other women surfaced with tears, tales, and tabloid contracts. There were enough of them for the public to believe Clinton practiced adultery, and for the press to disbelieve anything he said on the subject.

If the press was primed to distrust the president, others were out to prove him legally unfit for office. The office of the independent counsel with a mandate to investigate the president made this scandal different from the preceding ones. In mid-1994, Kenneth Starr had taken over as independent counsel investigating a shady land deal in Arkansas labeled Whitewater, in which the Clintons had invested. A previous special prosecutor had cleared the president, but the House and Senate banking committees insisted on reopening the investigation. Starr, who had held high-level positions in two Republican administrations, was backed by conservatives in hopes of a more aggressive inquiry into the Clinton administration. Friends of the president were indicted and later convicted. Although Clinton was never charged in Whitewater, his reputation was tarnished. Lurking in the background was a harassment suit brought against him in 1994 by Paula Jones, with the financial and legal support of Clinton's political enemies. A federal judge ruled that because a president was immune from distracting civil cases, the lawsuit would have to wait until Clinton left office. But in January 1997, a unanimous Supreme Court held that a president wasn't immune; the suit against Clinton could go forward.

On January 17, Clinton testified before Paula Jones's lawyers, who had been briefed about his relationship with Lewinsky. Taken by surprise by their questions about Lewinsky, the president said he did not remember ever having been alone with her and denied having sexual relations with the intern. The day before the president's testimony, Starr had gotten permission from the attorney general to expand his investigation into charges that Clinton asked Lewinsky to lie under oath. Starr took the position that even if he was investigating one crime (Whitewater), if he discovered evidence of another (Lewinsky's perjury) he should investigate it. The president's testimony under oath would eventually lead to the charges of perjury and obstruction of justice that brought the scandal to impeachment. Shaped by Starr's aggressive legal team, the media's coverage of Clinton's lies and sexual indiscretions would grow into a fury.[2]

MEDIA FEEDING FRENZY

> The *New York Times* isn't leaving anything for us.
>
> *An editor of the tabloid National Enquirer*[3]

It was no coincidence that Paula Jones's lawyers had uncovered the Lewinsky affair. They had been getting anonymous calls suggesting that they subpoena Monica Lewinsky and Linda Tripp. The calls came from Tripp as a way to surface Lewinsky and put herself in the middle of the action.[4] When Lewinsky was subpoenaed to testify before Jones's lawyers in late 1997, she panicked. On the Tripp tapes, Lewinsky's hysteria reflected a fear that she would have to either betray the president or commit perjury. She chose the latter route and signed an affidavit on January 7 declaring that she never had an affair with the president. And Linda Tripp, her celebrity-driven motives consistent throughout this tale, went to Ken Starr on January 12. It was the Tripp tapes that allowed Starr to expand his investigation from Whitewater to Lewinsky, after first knowing that Paula Jones's lawyers had the information and would use it to trap the president.

Starr and his team of prosecutors treated Tripp as if they had *almost* won the lottery. They spent the night and the next day debriefing her. Starr needed to prove that the president had tried to get Lewinsky to lie about their affair, which was obstruction of justice—a felony. If Lewinsky was trapped into admitting her affair on tape, they would then pressure her to wear a wire, call the president, and get him on tape obstructing justice. In other words, Starr planned to put a "sting" on the president of the United States.

Having gotten the story from Tripp, Isikoff went to his editors at *Newsweek,* who were reluctant to publish it. Their problem was that on the Tripp tapes Monica never says, "Clinton told me to lie." In fact, at one point Tripp tries to get Monica to say that Clinton knows she's going to lie, and Monica says no. This divided the editors over whether to go ahead with publication. Starr offered *Newsweek* his cooperation—hence, a better story—if they waited.[5] By the next morning, the power of the online media to change press behavior was demonstrated. Matt Drudge, the gossipy writer of the "Drudge Report," had sent out a bulletin on his website that *Newsweek* had killed Isikoff's story about the president's affair with an intern. A media tempest was growing out of anyone's control.

For the next few weeks, the stories poured out in a torrent from television, cable, radio, print, and the Internet. Much of this was built upon the Washington media's adversarial view of the Clinton administration as undisciplined and dishonest. At the very beginning of the young administration, one respected correspondent declared that covering the new White House was like "coming home and finding your kids got into the liquor cabinet."[6] But this attitude now became *a feeding frenzy* of attack journalism where the press goes after a wounded politician like sharks, "creating the news as much as reporting it. . . . "[7] In the words of journalist Bob Woodward, who exposed President Richard Nixon's sins in the 1970s, it was "a frenzy unlike anything you ever saw in Watergate. . . . "

By the Wednesday after the release of the "Drudge Report," the *Washington Post,* quoting "sources," led the mainstream press with an article revealing that Clinton directed Lewinsky to testify falsely. ABC's *Good Morning America* reported that the president had instructed her to deny an affair. This coverage was an early example of questionable interpretations—citing proof of presidential wrongdoing from the same tapes that *Newsweek's* editors listened to and didn't publish because they heard no such evidence. The "sources" were probably the president's opponents in the independent counsel's office. Starr's staff was publicly refusing to comment, claiming that they were not allowed to talk about a witness who might testify before a grand jury. Leaks were another matter.

The media deluge intensified. On ABC, George Stephanopoulos, the former Clinton aide, commented that if the allegations were true "it could lead to impeachment proceedings." CNN found a ten-second video clip showing the president hugging Lewinsky in a rope line of people at a White House lawn reception. It was aired hundreds of times, often in slow motion. MSNBC converted its coverage into what one critic called "all Monica, all the time."[8]

Bill Clinton and Monica Lewinsky.

Media economics played a role: Powered by the scandal, MSNBC used their talk-news programs to launch the new network into a profitable orbit. Their ratings increased 131 percent.

The "new media" (Internet, cable, and satellite) drove the frenzy, and without the restraint displayed by the mainstream media of TV networks, newspapers, and magazines. The opportunities to break a story on the Internet were unlimited, as demonstrated when the "Drudge Report" picked up Isikoff's rejected *Newsweek* story. The traditional media before this scandal would not break news on their websites, preferring to run stories that had first been reported in their major outlet. Now the mainstream press, starting with the *Washington Post*'s initial story, scooped the competition by putting the story online first. This development resulted in errors as well as an "echo effect." Repetition made outrageous claims credible.

Talk shows from *Larry King Live* to *Geraldo Rivera Live* mixed facts, fiction, speculation, and ax-grinding—with no one able to tell the difference. Political scientist John Anthony Maltese said, "Talk is easy and talk is cheap, and the proliferation of these shows led to saturation coverage of the Lewinsky story."[9] Rumors were everywhere. Conservative commentator Ann Coulter mentioned incidents with "four other interns." CNN's Wolf Blitzer reported from the White House lawn that Clinton's close aides were discussing his resignation. *NBC News* anchor Tom Brokaw broke into a pre-Super Bowl program with an "unconfirmed" report that Starr's office was investigating that someone saw the president and Lewinsky in an intimate moment. The *New York Post* declared that the Secret Service found the lovers, with a headline screaming, "Caught in the Act." The *Wall Street Journal* ran a story that a White House steward told a grand jury that he saw the two alone in a study and recovered tissues with physical evidence on them.

These reports were recycled in multiple public outlets in the first weeks as the media raced to keep the news flowing. And, though it didn't reduce their impact, all these stories were false.[10]

WHITE HOUSE NEWS MANAGEMENT: SHELTER FROM THE STORM

Whatever the flaws in the coverage, the fury of the media seemed unstoppable. At first, the White House seemed shell-shocked by the onslaught. As it collectively recovered its balance, aides tried to redirect the charges and protect the president.

On the Wednesday morning that the first article in the *Washington Post* appeared, press secretary Mike McCurry, reading from notes, said Clinton was "outraged" by the reports and denied any improper relationship. When asked what he meant by an "improper relationship," McCurry refused to elaborate. As this was just the latest in Clinton's history of alleged marital affairs, most of the press assumed Clinton was lying. This became clear when he sat down for a scheduled interview with PBS's Jim Lehrer that afternoon and declared that "there is no sexual relationship." Reporters leaped: Why did the president use the present tense? Was he implying a past affair?[11]

Leaks poured out that undercut the White House denials. Clinton had sent Monica gifts, including a book of Walt Whitman poems; his voice was on her answering machine; and she mentioned visiting the White House on many evenings. The White House put its spin on the reports cascading down on them. When the subject couldn't be changed, the next best strategy was to attack: Blame the accusers, point to the right wing, refuse to release records, denounce the press. There were whispers that Lewinsky was emotionally unstable, that the tapes were doctored, and that Starr was out to "get" the president. Cabinet members defended the president's honesty, while aides denounced the "campaign of leaks and lies." Hillary Clinton attacked political opponents, which was an improvement over discussing her husband's extra-marital activities. Whipping up a public backlash against the press could only help the president. Attacking the special prosecutor for unauthorized leaks had the added benefit of truth to it.

One successful example of White House spin occurred when the *New York Times* reported that the president's secretary had told investigators for the independent counsel that Monica and the president had sometimes been alone and that the president had coached the secretary before she testified. The White House fired back. Avoiding the subject of the article, aides appeared on three network morning shows to denounce "these criminal leaks" from the prosecutor's office. (The *Times* reporters had discussed their report with Starr and his staff.) A Democratic congressman requested an investigation into illegally leaked grand jury evidence. That afternoon the president's lawyer gave a rare news conference. As the TV cameras rolled, he asked the federal courts to investigate leaks by Starr's office. The result was to shift the news of the scandal to the issue of leaks. That week, *Time* and *Newsweek* put the leaks controversy on their covers.[12]

Within the administration there was a conflict between the political staff and the lawyers over how much the president should say in public. Ultimately they compromised. Clinton would make a forceful public denial but would not say anything new—which the lawyers preferred. On Monday morning, January 26, after an event publicizing childcare needs, Clinton answered reporters' shouted questions. He jabbed his finger and emotionally declared, "I did not have sexual relations with *that woman*, Miss Lewinsky. I never told anybody to lie, not a single time." The following morning on the *Today* show, Hillary denounced Starr as a "politically motivated prosecutor" and part of a "vast right-wing conspiracy," which the press in their "feeding frenzy" had joined. She refused to answer any questions about her husband's relationship with his intern.[13]

That night, January 27, President Clinton delivered the annual State of the Union address to Congress. With cheering Democrats in the audience and 53 million viewers at home, Clinton reminded Americans of their economic prosperity, of his proposals for the future, and of his stature as president. He never mentioned the scandal, implicitly making the point that such "private" behavior didn't belong in this national ritual of a chief of state. (As one White House aide later wrote, "Separating what Clinton was doing as president from the scandal became a basic strategy.")[14] A *Los Angeles Times* poll found that 75 percent of those asked rated the speech "good" or "excellent." Equally important, 67 percent said that it "kept my attention and I didn't think about the allegations against him." Sunlight seemed to have broken through the clouds over the White House.[15]

THE PUBLIC HOLDS ITS NOSE AND APPLAUDS ITS PRESIDENT—NO MEAN TRICK

Public opinion was to prove the president's most powerful ally. With some wavering at the beginning of the scandal, the public stuck with Bill Clinton, concluding that no, he had not told the truth, and yes, he should stay in office. Clinton's impressive public approval—among the highest of any modern president—steadily held in the mid-60 percent range and, at times, over 70 percent.[16]

Few would have predicted this support when the scandal first broke. Clinton rested at a respectable 60 percent in several polls at the time. By the end of the first week, his approval numbers had dropped to 51 percent. Sixty-two percent believed he had an affair with Lewinsky, and over half thought he had asked her to lie. Even worse for the president, 63 percent in a *Washington Post* poll thought he should resign if he had lied or had asked her to lie. If he had lied under oath and wouldn't resign, 55 percent supported impeachment.[17]

The media's framing the scandal as relevant to the president's official duties mattered less than people's assessment of the peace, prosperity, and moderation that Clinton's presidency represented. Media scholar Kathleen Hall Jamieson wrote that the public drew "a clear distinction between private and public character, between the personal and the presidential."[18] Most people viewed the scandal as the president's private behavior, not connected to his public life or their own lives. The line between public and private was bent (for instance, when the Starr Report released details of the Oval Office incidents), but held firm.

"They love him most for the enemies he has made" is a phrase taken from a nominating speech for another Democratic president, Grover Cleveland, in 1884. Clinton, too, benefited from his choice of enemies. It wasn't hard for the White House to spin the scandal as a political vendetta. The president's allies could point to Republicans' angry rhetoric and the GOP's inability to make congressional impeachment hearings bipartisan. By the fall, Republican leaders, including Speaker of the House, Newt Gingrich, were finding their own personal failings (adultery in Newt's case) being aired on Internet publications like *Salon*. Also helping Clinton was that the women in the scandal were hardly saints. Sympathy for Monica Lewinsky cooled as stories of a previous affair with a married man surfaced. Few believed Linda Tripp was motivated by patriotism and trying to help her "friend." Paula Jones seemed moved by monetary gain from right-wing benefactors. In spring 1998, while Clinton's favorable ratings were over 60 percent, House leader Gingrich stood at 36 percent, Starr at 22 percent, Monica 17 percent, and Tripp 10 percent. Ken Starr's approval ratings would drop later in the year to 11 percent, about the same as Iraqi leader Saddam Hussein.[19]

By the time the surging scandal was channeled into the impeachment process, the Republicans were the big losers in public opinion. In October after the nearly party-line vote in the House to impeach, 62 percent of Americans polled disapproved of the Republican handling of the issue. During the Senate trial, disapproval of the process rose from 41 percent to 56 percent. Perhaps this was a result of an overly partisan media strategy by the GOP, or the popularity of the president, or the prosperity of the country. Or perhaps it was the result of simple disgust with the saturation coverage of a seedy affair. The Washington bureau of the Associated Press moved 4,109 stories on the scandal in 1998 and had twenty-five reporters working regularly on it. In just that one year, there were 25,975 stories on the scandal in the nation's top sixty-five newspapers, and a Web browser search in November 1998 found 622,079 web-pages mentioning Monica Lewinsky or Paula Jones.[20]

TOWARD IMPEACHMENT

> When in doubt, tell the truth. It will confound your enemies and astound your friends.
>
> *Mark Twain*

Between his testimony in the Paula Jones case on January 17, 1998, and his appearance before a grand jury on August 17, the president repeatedly denied, both publicly and privately, any contact with Lewinsky. The essentials of the scandal were in print within days of the first revelation. The president's efforts to delay or derail the independent counsel's investigation failed in July when Lewinsky agreed to testify in exchange for immunity. Facing overwhelming evidence against him, including physical evidence of an encounter, Clinton decided to testify before the grand jury on August 17 and spoke to the nation a few hours later. He admitted an "inappropriate relationship" and that he had misled people about it. However, throughout the looming impeachment process he would continue to give answers that were "evasive or nonresponsive rather than outright falsehoods."[21]

On September 9, 1998, the Starr Report was submitted to the House and immediately released to the public. Whatever facts it contained were quickly overlooked in favor of its graphic sexual descriptions. Each of the ten sexual encounters in the Oval Office was described in shocking detail, the 435-page report was put on the Internet, and juicy tidbits were soon broadcast. One observer called it "the most detailed pornographic government report in history." Press Secretary Mike McCurry was appalled that "all of the filters . . . in the world of journalism evaporated. . . . " Though there was a legal argument that the details of these intimacies were needed to refute the president's denial of a sexual relationship, it appeared to many to be an effort to undermine his public support and embarrass him into resigning.

The relationship between the White House and the press became increasingly adversarial, with enough blame to go around. McCurry, who maintained cordial relations with reporters, resigned as press secretary in October, having been drained by the year's onslaught. During this period, Clinton usually appeared before the press only when a prestigious foreign leader was visiting, such as Nelson Mandela or Czech president Vaclav Havel. Their presence contrasted the newsmen's questions about the scandal with weighty issues of geopolitics. Presidential aides went over the heads of the press by appearing on a daily round of talk shows. By the opening of impeachment hearings before the House Judiciary Committee in November, more than 150 newspapers had called on the president to resign. Many in the press were befuddled that their saturation coverage of the sins of the chief executive had done so little to erode his high public approval.[22]

Despite the polls, and the November mid-term elections—where the Democrats did better than expected—the Republican-dominated House voted on December 19, 1998, to impeach the president (which meant bringing charges to the Senate for trial). In coordinated statements, the White House and House Democratic leaders denounced "the politics of personal destruction." The president's public support reached a high point in the scandal right after the vote—73 percent. Another survey taken the next month after his 1999 State of the Union address, and in the midst of the Senate impeachment trial, showed that 77 percent approved of the speech. Mindful of this public support, the senate could not muster the two-thirds needed to convict and so, as expected, voted to acquit on February 12.

At the end stunned observers noted that "the atmosphere in Washington had been poisoned," that Republicans appeared "disoriented," Democrats "utterly reeled," and the nation was left "in a daze."[23] The public had moved on. While 2 million watched the Senate vote on CNN that night, twice as many were watching professional wrestling on a competing cable station. The scandal no longer dominated the national agenda.

THE NEWS OF THE SCANDAL, THE SCANDAL OF THE NEWS

A number of themes emerge from this scandal: some concern the public, some the president, and some the press.

The country's fascination with the Lewinsky scandal reflected the continuing culture war raging in the United States since the 1960s. For many conservatives, the president's adultery and lying symbolized the decline they saw overcoming the country. Now the decay had seeped into the very pinnacle of national authority. On the other side, liberals worried about the Puritanism and intolerance displayed by the right wing. They saw narrow-minded bigotry dressed up as a posturing morality. The media's exhaustive coverage only intensified the polarization between the two camps.

Public opinion showed considerable stability in riding out the storm. The American people's ability to separate the public job of a president from his private life frustrated both sides. The public supported the job the president was doing, while disapproving of his personal failings and disbelieving his denials. Hardly reluctant to look at the lurid details, the public saw no reason why indulging in media entertainment should contaminate the tasks of governing. The dislike for politicians who exploited the scandal for partisan advantage, and the media who pandered to their increasing audience, may have reflected a general wish that elected officials return to the duties they were being paid to do. Clinton's skill showed in convincing his fellow citizens that he at least wanted to get on with the tasks of his office.

The president was hardly an innocent, even beyond lying and adultery. From his arrival on the public stage, Clinton flourished in low-key informal settings. Avoiding the national press he distrusted, Clinton went directly to the public, often through talk shows. But this media strategy combined with his seductive personality had turned the presidential image into something new. Howard Kurtz, media critic for the *Washington Post,* put it this way: "Bill Clinton dwelt in the same murky precincts of celebrity as Dennis Rodman, Courtney Love, and David Letterman. In a hundred-channel world the president had become just another piece of programming to be marketed. . . . "[24] From this view, the exhaustive exposure given the scandal was a product of the president's celebrity status. Here was a "personal presidency" filled by a man with a compulsive desire to please audiences and a willingness to answer questions about what underwear he wore. As he lived by the talk show, so he would (almost) die by the talk shows. The price of personalizing his presidency was to weaken the press filters that made any aspects of his life off-limits.

The scandal revealed the limits of the media's impact. On the one hand, the role of agenda-setting worked for awhile: Sex, lies, and tapes rose to the top of the country's list of compelling issues. The press had the nation thinking about the scandal, even if it was not able to tell the public *how* to think about it, that is, what frame to use to understand its significance. On the other hand, the flood of news had a diminishing effect which muted its impact on public opinion. By emphasizing sex to attract a large audience, the press may have made the story less politically relevant. Linking adultery to job performance seemed a stretch for most people. Defining the story as sex in the beginning may have minimized its relevance to governing in the end.[25] If the president's behavior didn't live up to the public's expectations, neither did it rise to the level of the "high crimes and misdemeanors" required by the Constitution to remove him from office.

But there was a cost. It was paid in the coin of a chief executive distracted from the issues of world peace and domestic security that a few years later on 9/11 would tragically overtake the country. It was paid by his vice president, Al Gore, who failed to succeed to the presidency in part because he felt he needed to distance himself from the blemished administration he had served. It was paid in a public appalled and enthralled by the lurid chaos engulfing their government. And it was a price paid by a press that, while entertaining a larger audience, may have tarnished their own credibility as democracy's watchdog.

Notes

1. Steven Brill, "Pressgate," in *Brill's Content,* August 1998. See also Mike Isikoff, *Uncovering Clinton: A Reporter's Story* (New York: Random House, 2000).
2. Ruth Marcus, "Starr: Relentless or Reluctant?" *Washington Post,* January 30, 1998.
3. As quoted by Ben H. Bagdikian, *The Media Monopoly,* 6th ed. (Boston: Beacon Press, 2000), xxiv.
4. Brill, "Pressgate." Much of this account of the early press coverage is taken from this extensive report used to launch Brill's media journal.
5. Brill, "Pressgate."
6. See John Anthony Maltese, "The Media: The New Media and the Lure of the Clinton Scandal," in Mark J. Rozell and Clyde Wilcox, eds., *The Clinton Scandal and the Future of American Government* (Washington, DC: Georgetown University Press, 2000).
7. See Larry J. Sabato, *Feeding Frenzy: Attack Journalism and American Politics* (Baltimore: Lanahan Publishers, 2000), 1.
8. The quote is from Brill, "Pressgate."
9. Maltese, 200.
10. Maltese, 200. Also see Howard Kurtz, *Spin Cycle* (New York: Touchstone, 1998), 307–308; and Joseph Hayden, *Covering Clinton* (Westport, CT: Praeger, 2002), Chapter 5.
11. Kurtz, Chapter 17.
12. Kurtz, 309–310.
13. Maltese, 205–206.
14. Sidney Blumenthal, *The Clinton Wars* (London: Penguin Books, 2003), 361.
15. W. Lance Bennett, *News: The Politics of Illusion,* 5th ed. (New York: Longman, 2003), 234.
16. Molly W. Andolina and Clyde Wilcox, "Public Opinion: The Paradoxes of Clinton's Popularity," in Rozell and Wilcox, Chapter 9. For a critique of GOP willingness to ignore public opinion, see Lawrence Jacobs and Robert Y. Shapiro, *Politicians Don't Pander* (Chicago: University of Chicago Press, 2000), Chapter 9.
17. Andolina and Wilcox.
18. Jamieson is quoted by Bennett, 231.
19. Andolina and Wilcox, 188.
20. Doris A. Graber, *Mass Media and American Politics,* 6th ed. (Washington, DC: Congressional Quarterly Press, 2002), 316.
21. Richard A. Posner, *An Affair of State* (Cambridge, MA: Harvard University Press, 1999), 30.
22. Hayden, 91.
23. For an account of impeachment, see Peter Baker, *The Breach* (New York: Scribner, 2000).
24. Hayden, 96.
25. See Julie Yiortas and Ivana Segvic, "Revisiting the Clinton/Lewinsky Scandal: The Convergence of Agenda Setting and Framing," *Journalism & Mass Communication Quarterly* 80, no. 3 (Autumn 2003): 567–582.

PART III

THE INSTITUTIONS

12 | CONGRESS

LEGISLATING GLOBAL WARMING
The Tragedy of the Climate Bill

The "tragedy of the commons" refers to the dilemma where people pursuing their short-term needs act in a way that ultimately undermines their long-term interests. The term comes from herdsmen grazing their cattle on a common pasture where each rationally wants to increase the size of their own herds, until they have destroyed the pasture and with it their livelihood. The common good (and it could be the ocean for fishermen or the atmosphere for all of us) is destroyed if its exploitation is not brought under control. This was the dilemma facing Congress in 2009 and 2010 when elected representatives recognized global warming as a long-term problem which they were unable to address because of negative immediate consequences to their home states' economic interests.

Political scientists have long pointed to the difficulty of organizing issues that produced general benefits for society but concentrated the costs on particular organizations that would form an intense opposition. (The opposite is also true with those issues with concentrated benefits paid by diffused costs. For example, sugar and milk subsidies may inflate prices for consumers, but are easy ways to organize farmers.) This was what happened with a climate bill that could only promise vague universal benefits by preventing a distant disaster while clearly raising the immediate costs of energy for powerful groups of businesses and states. These general benefits offered only limited incentives for political action. That meant that the large affected groups—in this case the earth's inhabitants—were less likely to organize and be represented with the same intensity in Congress.[1]

The problem, if scientists are to be believed, is that carbon-polluting behavior needs to be regulated by the government to prevent a disaster for everyone, but the politics of general benefits and concentrated costs make it difficult to organize around. One solution to the tragedy of the commons is to privatize the common good, such as by fencing parts of the pasture for individual use or granting fishermen exclusive access to parts of the ocean, thus motivating them to harvest prudently. "Cap and trade" and subsidies for alternative energy were creative attempts to reward private behavior that would curb the use of fossil fuels. Immediate problems including loss of jobs, higher energy costs, and an economy in recession proved more important.

This was reflected in the lobbying by regional interests, such as utilities, coal producers, and energy industries. The intense pressures on officials came not from the climate above but the political economy below. As analyst Bill Schneider put it,

> We have a political system that doesn't work unless people are facing a particular crisis. . . . There is an economic crisis. Jobs are the crisis. Climate isn't.[2]

Global warming legislation failed because the particular regional and industry costs overwhelmed the distant general benefits for the climate. The interests that feared these increased costs burdened the House legislation with compensations for their businesses, and derailed similar legislation in the more decentralized Senate that gave greater weight to these state-based interests. Preventing global warming was not sufficient to overcome the immediate costs to American businesses and regions dependent on fossil fuels. Whether this was a reflection of democracy or a failure of democracy depends on your opinion of the outcome.

CONCEPTS TO CONSIDER

1. How did the **decentralized Congress** hinder passage of the climate bill? Did having many different decision makers—in committees, the two houses of Congress, the executive—lead to the bill failing? Or lead to it being compromised beyond recognition?
2. Would a more **centralized political system** have been able to act on the problem of climate warming, more quickly and more effectively? Does that mean that public opinion would be more represented or less represented? Would powerful economic interest groups harmed by the legislation be more influential or less influential in this centralized system?
3. President Obama placed climate warming and energy alternatives on the **national agenda**. And yet the lack of intensity in the administration for pushing this legislation in the Senate was blamed for its defeat. Why did the president hesitate in his support? Did he see defeat as inevitable? Did he have other priorities? Or did he think that alternative policies within the administration and on the state level would accomplish the same goals.
4. Is the **"tragedy of the commons"** an elitist notion? Are we sure that ill-understood future environmental disasters are more important than present-day jobs and expenses? If you were a member of Congress, which way would you have voted? And how would you explain that vote to your constituents?

You have to save your seat before you can save the world.

—*a warning often given to freshman congressmen*

After years of denial, Washington seemed ready to tackle global warming. During his campaign, President Obama had declared that America's oil addiction was "one of the greatest challenges of our generation." After his 2009 inauguration, the new president was advised to lead boldly on carbon pollution "before others hijack or derail it."[3]

The scientific evidence was clear. More than 2,000 scientists on the Nobel Prize–winning International Panel on Climate Change declared that carbon from burning fossil fuels was warming the planet, causing drought, melting glaciers, rising sea levels, and disease. The Arctic ice cap was already less than half the

Morgan City, Louisiana in May 2011 suffered from floods in a year of extreme weather that some observers traced to global climate change.

size it was fifty years ago. U.S. government agencies predicted that if nothing was done to cut these greenhouse gases the Southwest would become another Dust Bowl, and Florida would flood. Key West would be under water in the next century. Of course the poorer countries of the world would be even more seriously affected than the developed countries. Even before 2010 was over, it was declared the warmest year since modern records began in 1880.[4]

Despite opponents' attempts to muddle the science, government experts had for years warned about this trend. An administrator of the US National Oceanic and Atmospheric Administration (NOAA) could state in the mid-90s that "there's a better scientific consensus on this than on any issue I know—except maybe Newton's second law of dynamics." As early as 1988, a NASA scientist testified to Congress on the human causes of global warming and the need for immediate action. In that same year, a notably nonradical British prime minister, Margaret Thatcher, warned in a speech that with global warming, "we may have unwittingly begun a massive experiment with the system of the planet itself."[5]

Public opinion polls showed that many Americans were concerned about global warming, though not very concerned. In a 2006 national survey 44 percent of the public rated global warming as "very important," though it was only eighteenth in a list of things they were worried about. By 2009, three-quarters of Americans thought the government should regulate the release of greenhouse gases, and 62 percent declared they would support regulation even if it increased prices. Some 71 percent agreed that steps to reduce emissions would help the US economy become more competitive.[6] Eight in ten of those younger than thirty supported federal regulation of emissions while among seniors about four in ten were supportive. With Democratic majorities in both houses and a new president making the issue a priority, legislation might be expected to politically focus and reflect this national support.[7]

Neither the scientific evidence nor supportive public opinion meant that a politically viable policy solution would match the planet's needs. Scientists thought that carbon emissions had to be reduced by 50–80 percent to prevent an environmental disaster. No country could do this alone, and developing giants like China and India were refusing to accept any limits, positions similar to that of the United States under George W. Bush. With an international conference on climate in Copenhagen at the end of 2009 (which ended inconclusively), it was hoped that the new administration would provide American leadership to break the impasse.

The most straightforward way of limiting carbon would be to tax it, making polluters pay. But for American politicians in an economy floundering from the most severe recession since the Great Depression, passing a new tax on consumers for every activity that burns carbon-based fuels would be a nightmare. The so-called cap-and-trade system seemed more doable.

CAP AND TRADE: LET THE MARKET FIGURE IT OUT

Under cap and trade, the government would set a yearly limit on carbon emissions and gradually tighten it. It would then issue "permission slips to pollute," giving companies permits for each ton of carbon they burned.

These permits could be bought and sold. The intention was to create a market that would put a price on allowable emissions. Supply and demand would determine how much these permits cost. Tougher standards year by year and fewer available permits would lead to higher prices. Companies would buy permits from each other as long as that was cheaper to do than making the technological changes needed to eliminate their use of carbon. They would pass along the increasing cost of the permits in their prices and presumably consumers would respond by cutting back on carbon-using products. Europe has had a similar system in place for years with mixed reviews.

The results of all this were vigorously debated. The Congressional Budget Office estimated that the costs to a typical family of reducing carbon by 15 percent would be $1,600 a year. Conservative groups did their own studies that found the costs many times more, plus a considerable loss of jobs. Because emissions are a global problem, these reductions by the United States would only reduce the world's total emissions by about 3 percent. Advocates pointed out that this was just a start and that the legislation passed by the House would require reductions of 42 percent by 2030 and 83 percent by 2050. It would also encourage new technologies that would make it cheaper to use alternative energy like wind or sun or clean coal.[8]

THE WAXMAN–MARKEY BILL

The legislation in the House attempting to set this up was called Waxman–Markey, after Henry Waxman of California, Democratic chairman of the Energy and Commerce Committee, and Edward J. Markey, a Democrat from Massachusetts. The bill, which would win approval from Waxman's committee, also had to go through Ways and Means and Agriculture committees. After months of negotiations, the bill was passed by the House in June 2009 by 219–212. Only eight Republicans voted for it, and the GOP denounced it as a national energy tax. President Obama, who actively lobbied for the bill, called it a "bold and necessary step." The bill itself had expanded to over 1,300 pages and even supporters called it a "patchwork of compromises."

The bill required a 17 percent cut in greenhouse gases by 2020, mostly through the cap-and-trade system. By then 20 percent of electricity had to come from renewable sources and energy efficiency. In accomplishing these goals, the bill gave utilities, coal plants, manufacturers, farmers, oil refiners, and other industries special protections to help them in the transition to new ways of using energy. Originally in President Obama's proposal all allowances to emit greenhouse gases would have been auctioned off by the government. The money from this would have been used for tax breaks and energy assistance for the poor. Instead, Waxman–Markey gave away free permits to polluting businesses during a transition period of 10–20 years.

The bill depended heavily on carbon offsets. These were official certificates given for greenhouse gases that *might* have been emitted but were not. U.S. polluters could buy them and pay someone else to reduce emissions instead of doing it themselves. For example, foreign companies might be able to reduce their carbon emissions more cheaply than U.S. firms by planting several acres of trees or building solar power generators. This would provide an equal benefit to the climate at a lower cost. But whether such offsets actually happen overseas, whether they can be verified, or whether they would have happened anyway remains debatable.

There were other parts of the complex bill. New coal-fired power plants were required to produce 50 percent less carbon than existing plants. A tariff would be imposed after 2020 for goods from countries that refused to limit their carbon pollution. Concessions were made to farm groups that included involving the Agriculture Department in regulating parts of the program because it would be more favorable to these interests than the Environmental Protection Agency. Still, forty-four Democrats, mostly from conservative and rural districts, voted against the measure.

WHEELING AND DEALING

Getting the votes needed to protect the world's climate required protecting numerous earth-bound interests. The bill did this by changing *who* pays the costs of cutting greenhouse gases. To satisfy Democrats from coal-mining states, allowances were given to coal-based electric utilities, energy-intensive manufacturers, oil refiners, and the auto industry. Instead of auctioning off these permits—with the money going to energy aid for the poor and a tax cut—the government gave them away, costing the Treasury some $713 billion in the program's first ten years. Coal-based electric companies would get 35 percent or more of the allowances. Energy-intensive manufacturers such as aluminum, glass, or steel would get up to 15 percent of allowances.[9]

Members representing interests affected by the bill battled for concessions. Congressman Gene Green, Democrat from Houston, Texas, demanded 5 percent of the permits be given to oil refiners to deal with the costs of carbon controls. He won 2 percent of the allowances. Colin Peterson of Minnesota got the list of farming activities that would qualify as offsets expanded, bringing a potential windfall to farmers. He then supported the bill. Members of Congress from Georgia, North Carolina, and Tennessee tried to protect utilities from their region by weakening the requirements for renewable energy. The original bill had called for 25 percent of electricity to come from renewable sources like wind, solar, or hydro by 2025. This was weakened to 15 percent by 2020 to gain the votes of congressmen speaking for these southern utilities. Even liberal Democrats got a piece of the action. Bobby Rush, an African American representative from Chicago, withheld his support until a last-minute agreement to provide $1 billion for energy-related jobs for low income workers.

In the months of horse-trading, the bill's targets for carbon use were weakened, its requirements for renewable electricity were reduced, and the incentives for industries were sweetened. While some environmentalists backed the final bill, others like Greenpeace and Friends of the Earth opposed it. Industry was split. The Chamber of Commerce opposed it while some of the nation's biggest corporations including Dow Chemical, Starbucks, and Ford backed it. President Obama welcomed House passage, though he admitted, "I think that finding the right balance between providing new incentives to businesses, but not giving away the store, is always an art . . ."[10]

ON TO THE SENATE

The Senate was expected to be even more difficult. Environmentalists were divided about the complex House bill, and its concessions to industrial polluters. The economic downturn was drawing attention away from environmental concerns, and creating a political atmosphere less welcoming to innovation. The severe recession provided ammunition for opponents, including Sarah Palin who called the House measure "an enormous threat to our economy."[11] The White House which may have been surprised by the swift House passage of the bill did not have it at the top of their agenda for Senate action. Health-care reform came first. The Senate even with a Democratic majority did not have the same strong party control that the House leadership exercised. With independent-minded members, many from energy-producing states, the decentralized Senate presented a number of obstacles. For starters, any climate bill would need sixty votes on the floor to overcome an almost-certain Republican filibuster.

Nonetheless, after months of meetings, Senator Barbara Boxer (D-California), chair of the Environmental and Public Works Committee, along with Senator John Kerry (D-Massachusetts), introduced a climate bill in September 2009. It was similar to the House bill.

The proposal contained a cap-and-trade system that would issue permits for greenhouse gas, gradually lower the amount of emissions allowed, and let companies buy and sell permits to meet their needs. Once again, the bill would give away most of the allowances for the next twenty years to energy-intensive industries and customers relying on fossil fuels like coal. Bonuses for coal-fired plants that stored carbon emissions underground were tripled compared to the House bill—clearly an attempt to win support from mining states like West Virginia. But its overall goals were even more ambitious than those in the House bill. It called for reducing greenhouse gas emissions by 2020 to 20 percent below 2005 emissions, greater than the 17 percent set by the House bill. Of course this was just an opening bid, a proposal open to negotiations and likely to be whittled back in gaining enough support to pass on the Senate floor, if it got that far.

From the beginning, the Senate measure was in trouble. Ten moderate Democratic senators from Midwestern states sent the president a letter declaring that they could not support any bill that didn't protect American industries from overseas competitors not adopting clean energy goals. Perhaps more to the point was that electricity in these states largely came from burning coal, the main source of greenhouse gas pollution. Indiana, represented by Democratic Senator Evan Bayh, derived 94 percent of its electricity from coal, a fact that Senator Bayh repeated each time he was lobbied by his party leaders to support the legislation.[12]

Environmentalists were disappointed by the large numbers of pollution permits that were being given away. Views from within the energy industry were presented by the president of the American Petroleum Institute who described the bill as even more damaging than the House bill. Warnings were heard in the media and from lobbyists that the bill would harm the economy by raising energy prices. The poor state of the economy gave this argument teeth.[13]

The bill Clean Energy Jobs and American Power (S. 1733) was voted out of Senator Boxer's Committee on November 5. The vote was 11-1, with all the Republican committee members boycotting the vote. Committee rules said that at least two Republicans needed to be present to complete the vote and allow the bill to come to the Senate floor. While Chairman Boxer could circumvent the rules and bring the bill to the floor herself, she hesitated, wanting to keep open the possibility that Republicans would later work with her on the bill. Sensing that the legislation was stalled, Senator Kerry began working with other senators, notably Republican Lindsey Graham of South Carolina on possible compromises that could survive a likely filibuster on the floor. At the time Kerry warned supporters, "We have very little time, a lot of pressures, including election pressures, and we are just going to have to be realistic."[14]

THE CLIMATE OUTSIDE THE SENATE

For the next several months, the issue seemed to disappear. The most immediate reason was that health-care reform absorbed the attention of the Senate, the administration, and the public. The Obama administration's priority was health care,—and later financial reform. This would later be cited as a cause for the Senate's failure to act on the climate bill. (One climate activist complained, "What good is health care on a dead planet?") After a yearlong debate, Democrats in both houses finally passed health care in March 2010 with no Republican support.

Interest groups lobbying for and against the climate legislation kept up grassroots activities throughout the country and in Washington as well. Environmentalists argued for Senate action so that the United States could attend the climate-change conference in Copenhagen in December 2009 and push for an international treaty. But at home, the environmental and energy groups were being outspent by a wide margin by oil and natural gas businesses. In the first six months of 2009, anticlimate–bill groups spent over $82 million lobbying Washington, while groups concerned with climate change spent under $19 million. According to the Center for Public Integrity, there were 2,810 lobbyists devoted to climate change, five lobbyists for every lawmaker. Of these only 138 were pushing for alternative energy—the rest were working for fossil fuel interests. Many worked for utilities and had a reputation for being tough. One congressional staffer said, "They're kneecap breakers."[15]

The tensions between global goals and regional interests affected supporters of the bill as well. Environmentalists were not united on whether their message should aim to scare the public with predictions of global warming or seduce it with promises of green jobs. Their opponents focused a blizzard of TV ads calling the bill "anti-jobs, anti-energy." Debates and conferences were sponsored questioning the scientific evidence behind global warming. One moderate Republican senator's office reported that letters were running 100 for and 7,000 against climate legislation. Despite this, a *Washington Post–ABC News* poll in 2009 found that 52 percent of Americans supported the cap-and-trade approach of the House climate bill.[16]

But the year's most politically significant environmental action may have been what didn't happen.

On April 21, 2010, an oil drilling rig leased by British Petroleum exploded causing the worst oil spill in U.S. history, dumping millions of barrels of oil into the Gulf of Mexico over the next several months. It was an unprecedented disaster. And yet, unlike past disasters—the 1990 sinking of the supertanker *Exxon Valdez*, the 1969 oil spill off the California coast of Santa Barbara, and the fire on Cleveland's Cuyahoga River—that channeled public outrage into creating Earth Days and a clean-air law, this environmental horror seemed to have little political impact. Opinion polls didn't budge, gasoline demand went up, and the Senate remained stalled. The public reaction to the spill was anger at BP and preventing future accidents, not the Big Picture costs from pollution resulting from the nation's dependence on fossil fuels. Arguably, the dismal economy and the public's fears of more expensive gasoline trumped all other concerns.[17]

THE EXECUTIVE BRANCH ACTS

Within the Obama administration, the warming climate had to compete with a full agenda from a deteriorating economy, overseas wars, and numerous domestic political demands. The president's first moves on climate were encouraging to his environmental supporters. He appointed Carol Browner, head of the EPA under Bill Clinton and a close ally of Al Gore to be his "climate czar," overseeing the issue from a special office at the White House. His Secretary of Energy, Steven Chu, was a Nobel-Prize scientist, who understood the need to confront global warming. Shortly after taking office, the administration moved on its own to regulate carbon emissions. It required automobile companies to increase their fuel economy of new cars and trucks by 2016, thereby decreasing carbon pollution. The ailing automakers, dependent on Washington for aid, not surprisingly embraced the effort.

The EPA was acting in response to a 2007 Supreme Court ruling, *Massachusetts v. EPA*, declaring that the agency had a responsibility to regulate carbon dioxide as a pollutant under the Clean Air Act. Obama's EPA, unlike the previous Republican administration, appeared eager to take the lead.

It tightened the screws in December by announcing, on the first day of the international climate conference in Copenhagen, that six gases including carbon dioxide posed a danger to the environment and that the agency would draw up regulations on them. By May 2010, EPA released their final rule on greenhouse gas regulations, initiating a phased-in approach that forced power plants and refineries responsible for 70 percent of all emissions to use the best available technology to minimize these gases. The EPA promised to begin enforcing this in January 2011, a deadline that was later allowed to slip.[18]

These administration actions put Congress on notice that the executive branch would act on global warming with or without legislation. They were clearly tactics to get Congress to move, as well as a threat to the energy companies fighting the climate bill. The administrator of EPA put it this way, "There are no more excuses for delay. . . . This administration will not ignore science and the law any longer." Senator Boxer warned, "If Congress does nothing, we will be watching EPA do our job." Senator Kerry added, "..if Congress won't legislate, the EPA will regulate." And this meant that if the powerful energy interests balked at Congress's efforts to curb carbon pollution, federal regulators would be unleashed to do the job. And they would do it without the numerous concessions to business interests incorporated in the cap-and-trade legislation that any bill passing Congress would contain.

Underlining this commitment to act on global warming was an executive order that President Obama issued in October 2009. The order required all federal agencies to measure their greenhouse gas emissions and set specific targets to reduce them in buildings and vehicles. The president reminded the public that the federal government occupies nearly 500,000 buildings, operates more than 600,000 vehicles, and employs 1.8 million civilian workers. Reducing fuel use, cutting costs, using environmentally responsible products, and improving energy efficiency could be expected to appeal to taxpayers. As the nation's largest consumer of energy, the federal government by example was asserting leadership on the environment.[19]

THE SENATE REVISITS THE CLIMATE

A slimmed down version of the climate bill resurfaced in the Senate in April 2010. This moderation of ambitions was not surprising. Republican support for the climate bill—sparse at best—showed no sign of increasing, indeed the leading Republican backer, Lindsay Graham of South Carolina, pulled out of negotiations in late April, charging Democrats with acting in bad faith. Other moderate Republicans, notably Olympia Snowe of Maine made a number of demands for her state, such as exempting home heating oil and protecting Georgia's Bank from drilling, without ever supporting the bill. One person involved said, "She would always say that she was interested in working on it, but she would never say she was with us."[20] The oil spill in the Gulf of Mexico focused attention on federal regulation of drilling. The partisan conflict between the parties intensified, the economy continued depressed, and Republicans sensed that the midterm elections could make them the majority party in one or both houses of Congress. Even the Democrats victory on health-care reform seemed to leave their other legislative priority—the climate bill—embattled and sinking.

In response to this perceived political weakness, Senators Kerry and Joe Lieberman, Independent from Connecticut, discussed the idea of introducing a "utility-only" bill. Such a measure would seek to lower the carbon output *only* of utility companies rather than the entire economy. Since utilities accounted for 40 percent of the nation's carbon output, this seemed a reasonable place to start. A provision to toughen offshore drilling safeguards following the BP oil spill was added, and several senators voiced support. Moderate Republican Senator George Voinovich of Ohio declared that he might be able to back a "utility-only" bill, but would seek to add amendments to increase nuclear power and clean-coal technologies. Predictably electric companies argued that this approach was unfair in discriminating against one sector of the economy, while other sources of carbon emissions such as manufacturing and transportation went untouched.

Early in July, Senate Majority Leader Harry Reid (D-Nevada) said he would introduce an energy bill that reflected these discussions. It would aim to cut pollution from energy utilities and power plants, leaving aside transportation, agriculture, and other polluting sectors of the economy. This scaled-down version of the House bill sought to cut utilities' emissions by 17 percent from 2005 levels by 2020 and 83 percent by 2050. Utilities were required to provide 15 percent of their power from renewable sources by 2021, considerably weaker than the House requirements. Under the bill, individual states would be prohibited from enforcing their own cap-and-trade programs to curb greenhouse gas emissions. In a move to protect Congress's jealously guarded turf, the Environmental Protection Agency would be barred from regulating greenhouse gases as pollutants.

Other senators focused exclusively on what they saw as this executive challenge to legislative power. They signed on to a resolution to veto the EPA's finding that greenhouse gases were a threat to human health. This would prevent the EPA from regulating carbon dioxide without a mandate from Congress. Interest groups representing industry were working the issue in the halls of the Capitol. The president of the American Petroleum Institute called the EPA regulation "intrusive, inefficient and excessively costly." In June 2010, a bipartisan group of senators led by Lisa Murkowski (R-Alaska) backed a resolution prohibiting EPA from regulating climate pollution from utilities, manufacturers, and other stationary sources. The measure instructed the agency to ignore the Supreme Court decision requiring EPA to regulate carbon as a pollutant under the Clean Air Act. Despite some Democratic backing it failed in a 53-47 vote. In a reflection of White House priorities, Carole Browner declared that this was one legislative battle that Obama didn't duck. "We worked very hard to beat the Murkowski amendment back." While declaring his preference for a broad legislative solution, the president was unwilling to "unilaterally disarm before Congress has passed a bill."[21]

By mid-July 2010, what was now called a "utility first" option was also being described as a "last-ditch" attempt to pass a scaled-back climate bill. Proposals for significant investments in energy efficiency and renewal, as well as additional assistance to people hurt by fuel price increases, were attempts to sweeten the package. The problem was that in reducing the bill's scope it was losing its intensely committed supporters without picking up any neutrals or adversaries.

Two meetings that Senator Kerry held on July 13 illustrated the competing pressures facing the senate. In the first, environmental groups including the Sierra club, the Natural Resources Defense Council, and Environment America declared that they would oppose legislation if it included major concessions to relax standards for pollutants like soot, smog, and mercury. Part of the utility-only proposal had concessions to industry that would prevent the EPA from regulating several of these pollutants.[22] That same evening, Kerry met for ninety minutes with the powerful National Rural Electric Cooperative Association (NRECA), representing hundreds of mostly western utility co-ops. By the next day, Glenn English, who heads NRECA, urged senators to reject the "utility-only" approach, saying it discriminated against the co-ops in the Midwest, South, and the Plains states that burned mostly coal to generate electricity. In a jab at Kerry, a New England senator, he noted that northwestern and northeastern states depending on hydropower would not have to pay the price. For other regions, this meant higher electricity bills, a message that English promised to send to lawmakers.[23]

THE SENATE PULLS THE PLUG ON THE CLIMATE BILL

The end of July saw the effort to pass a climate bill through the Senate collapse. Majority Leader Harry Reid who was trying to draw together the different approaches to reduce carbon emissions announced the bill's failure on July 22. "We know that we don't have the votes," he said simply. There was some hope expressed that in abandoning this comprehensive approach the way could be cleared for a more limited bill that would require BP to pay for the cleanup of the Gulf oil spill, tighten household energy requirements, and increase funds for conservation efforts. Such hopeful pragmatism was to prove futile.[24]

In many ways, the bill was not so much rejected as abandoned. The president had stopped pushing for it; he certainly didn't give it the full-court press that includes both serious face time with the chief executive and realistic threats by his staff toward any obstruction. The president's calculation is not hard to fathom. There were alternative solutions available in executive action by his own EPA to regulate carbon emissions, which looked more comprehensive and quicker as the bill was increasingly burdened by compromises. The equally complicated, politically difficult health-care reform was a higher priority for the executive's time and political resources. As one editorial writer concluded, the president didn't sell out his supporters. He prioritized.

"The president had the political capital and the numbers in Congress to pass something big. He chose health care."[25]

Key supporters in the environmental community were alienated by all the industry giveaways, and may have decided that EPA regulation was the cleaner option. Given the Republican strategy of polarizing issues that the Democrats were introducing through a unified opposition, the votes in the political center were simply not there to be moved toward support through rewards. Too few senators had any incentives to pass a rational climate policy that was in the long-term interests of the country. There was no public outcry against global warming, perhaps because "the climate-energy debate got disconnected from average people." We needed less talk, an environmentalist suggested afterward, about "climate" and more about conservation saving money, creating jobs, and preserving resources that people need and use.[26]

But this argument only illustrates the problem. Both the polls that reflected the public's concern with jobs and energy independence, and elected representatives' immediate concern for the interests of utilities and industries in their own states, steered the administration away from their stated priority: preventing climate change. Instead they focused on the particular interests being challenged by the legislation; they accepted the Beltway wisdom that it was impossible to pass a bill without the approval of the polluters. Special interests involved in carbon production were crucial, they had to be persuaded and seduced. The result was handing out hundreds of billions of dollars worth of allowances to pollute and what Obama's own budget director called "the largest corporate welfare program that has ever been enacted in the history of the United States." By the end of the lobbying free-for-all Campbell Soup was getting concessions for the carbon-intensive job of making chicken noodle soup.[27]

Just as bad, little effort was put into mobilizing the public around the global benefits of the law. And yet overcoming the carbon polluters' resistance to change required public pressure: people outraged by a planet in peril. This wasn't done. One critic compared it to President Lyndon Johnson in the 1960s insisting to Martin Luther King, Jr., that he talk only about the expanded businesses and jobs that Southerners would gain when they passed a civil rights bill. As a result, the loudest voices misrepresented the science of climate change, spread fear about loss of jobs, and focused on the costs of these changes to particular industries and regions. They argued for doing nothing; and that's what happened.[28]

CONCLUSION

There aren't many incentives for lots of senators to vote for a reasonable climate bill. Senators from coal states and the South worried that their regions would be disproportionately hurt. The effects of climate change won't be dire for years; and Congress, with its frequent elections, isn't good at accepting short-term pain for long-term gain.

Stephen Stromberg, The Washington Post

The "tragedy of the commons" played out in the inability of the Congress to pass a climate bill. The tension between short-term, regional and business interests and longer-term, devastating global changes was resolved in favor of local votes. This bill, like many attempts to pass alternative energy measures in Congress since the 1970s, fell victim to the struggle between federal goals and intense regional interests. Curbing the use of carbon resources was politically difficult for Senators and representatives who may have recognized climate warming as a legitimate problem but had constituents to represent. In many states, like Alaska, Texas, Oklahoma, and West Virginia, a fossil fuel energy industry is an important part of the local economy. Even the potential of alternative sources of energy is regionally divided, with biomass potential clustered on the West and East coasts while the Great Plains is largely barren of these resources. Utilities in the Southeast didn't support renewable energy mandates because of their dependence on coal and gas from the region. Voters and interest groups from these regions focused on jobs and the economy over the planet's long-term viability. In the House, the representatives of these industries limited the overall targets, were richly compensated to make necessary changes in their energy use, and got the costs of the permits shifted to consumers. In the Senate, because of the greater power given individual senators and the lack of centralized party control, even these compromises failed.

The same state and regional interests that defeated the climate legislation may yet provide a tapestry of solutions to address the problem. Some twenty-nine states have created their own renewable energy standards. Others are using federal matching funds to deploy smart meters for monitoring power use, to provide incentives for clean energy investments, and to encourage an electric vehicle fleet. A regional cap-and-trade program has been operating in ten Northeastern and mid-Atlantic states and may be expanding elsewhere. The executive branch's EPA indirectly reduced global warming gases in July 2011 by imposing new standards on power plants that cut emissions of some pollutants. Conservative groups have proposed increasing federal spending on clean energy to $25 billion a year. Separating energy issues from climate politics by emphasizing conservation, cost savings, and even a bit of patriotism toward the environment may prove more successful in changing peoples' behavior.[29] America's decentralized politics may have derailed congressional action but may also offer alternative means of accomplishing at least some of the same goals.[30]

Meanwhile, an M.I.T. study suggested that the planet was warming much faster than previously thought; melting Arctic Sea ice was releasing even more greenhouse gases in feedback loops that amplified the effects. But this was, as former vice president Al Gore (who backed the climate bill) put it, "an inconvenient truth" for many political and economic interests. The combination of executive branch actions, conservation programs by many of the states, and innovations like the smart grid and wind energy provided fallback solutions. Whether these efforts, without coherent national and international policies to reduce global warming, would be sufficient was doubtful. As one scientist noted, "the laws of physics don't compromise."

Notes

1. See James Q. Wilson, *Political Organizations* (New York: Basic Books, 1974), 330–337. For an interesting update, see Frances E. Lee, "Interests, Constituencies, and Policy Making," in Paul J. Quirk and Sarah A. Binder, eds., *The Legislative Branch* (New York: Oxford University Press, 2005), Chapter 10. The phrase 'The Tragedy of the Commons' is attributed to Garrett Hardin in a 1968 article of that name in *Science* magazine 162 (1968).
2. As quoted by Peter Behr and Christa Marshall, "Regional and State Interests May Dominate Future Climate and Energy Policy," *ClimateWire*, July 26, 2010.
3. Jeff Goodell, "As the World Burns," *Rolling Stone*, January 21, 2010, p. 32.
4. J. Jowit, "Global Warming Pushes 2010 Temperatures to Record Highs," *The Guardian*, July 28, 2010.
5. Maxwell T. Boykoff and Jules M. Boykoff, "Balance as Bias: Global Warming and the US Prestige Press," *Global Environmental Change* 14 (2004): 125–126. For a general treatment of the science behind climate change, see John Houghton, *Global Warming: the Complete Briefing* (Cambridge: Cambridge University Press, 2009).
6. See Anthony Giddens, *The Politics of Climate Change* (Cambridge, England: Polity Press, 2009), 103.
7. Steven Mufson and Jennifer Agiesta, "Limits on Emissions Have Wide Support," *The Washington Post*, June 25, 2009.
8. Coral Davenport et al., "Carbon, from the Ground Up," *CQ Weekly Online*, August 3, 2009.
9. David A. Fahrenthold and Steven Mufson, "Deconstructing the Climate Bill," *The Washington Post*, July 6, 2009.
10. John Broder, "Adding Something for Everyone . . . " *The New York Times*, July 1, 2009.
11. Sarah Palin, "The 'Cap and Tax' Dead End," *The Washington Post*, July 14, 2009.
12. Ryan Lizza, "As the World Burns," *The New Yorker*, October 11, 2010, p. 72.
13. John M. Broder, "Climate Bill is Threatened by Senators," *The New York Times*, August 7, 2009. Steven Mufson and Juliet Eilperin, "Senate's Climate Bill a Bit More Ambitious," *The Washington Post*, October 25, 2009.
14. http://motherjones.com/mojo/2009/11/there-tr-partisan-path-forward-climate-bill
15. Goodell, 33.
16. David A. Fahrenthold, "Environmentalists Slow to Adjust in Climate Debate," *The Washington Post*, August 31, 2009.
17. "Climate Debate Unmoved by Spill," *The Washington Post*, July 12, 2010.
18. http://news.firedoglake.com/2010/05/13/epa-issues-final-ruling-o
19. Juliet Eilperin, "Agencies Told to Reduce Emissions," *The Washington Post*, October 6, 2009.
20. *The New Yorker*, 76.
21. Editorial, "Ms. Murkowski's Mischief," *The New York Times*, January 19, 2010.
22. Josh Voorhees and Robin Bravender, "Kerry, Lieberman Push Their Own Utility-Only Climate Bill," *The New York Times*, July 14, 2010.
23. "Rural Electric Co-ops Say Utility-only CO2 Limits Discriminatory," *Platts*, http://www.platts.com/RSSFeedDetailedNews/RSSFeed/Headlines
24. Carl Hulse and David Herszenhorn, "Democrats Call Off Climate Bill Effort," *The New York Times*, July 22, 2010.

25. Stephen Stromberg, "How Washington Failed on Climate Change," *The Washington Post*, July 29, 2010.
26. Thomas L. Friedman, "Want the Good News First?" *The New York Times*, July 27, 2010.
27. Lee Wasserman, "Four Ways to Kill a Climate Bill," *The New York Times*, July 25, 2010.
28. Ibid.
29. David Leonhardt, "Next Step on Policy for Climate," *The New York Times*, October 13, 2010. Leslie Kaufman, "In Kansas, Climate Skeptics Embrace Cleaner Energy," *The New York Times*, October 18, 2010.
30. Behr and Marshall.

13 THE PRESIDENCY
9/11
Presidential Crisis Dominance

In his classic essay "The Two Presidencies," noted political scientist Aaron Wildavsky divides the chief executive in half. He contrasts the wide powers a president has in directing national security policies with the severe limits a president faces in trying to shape domestic affairs. Wildavsky argues that the overwhelming power a chief executive has in foreign and military matters compared to his restrained influence domestically, especially in dealing with Congress, creates almost separate presidencies. The checks and balances in our federal system means that only in a time of an extraordinary crisis, such as Franklin D. Roosevelt faced in the 1930s Great Depression, can a president succeed in dominating domestic policy. Yet, Wildavsky says, "Serious setbacks to the president in controlling foreign policy are extraordinary and unusual."[1]

In the following case, President George W. Bush confronted both the challenges and the opportunities set in motion by the terrorist attacks on September 11, 2001. The resulting national security crisis gave the president a rare, if temporary, dominance over the political system as well as unquestioned national leadership. These first attacks on American soil since Pearl Harbor concentrated government policymaking in the hands of a wartime commander in chief. How he used the powers of his office to rally public opinion behind him and to direct the government's response marked the weeks immediately following the attacks.

As the crisis faded, the limits to presidential power surfaced. Supporting these restraints were rival institutions, such as Congress, the opposition political party, the media, and interest groups, all of whom had priorities and perspectives different from the chief executive.

CONCEPTS TO CONSIDER _____

1. The president, as chief of state, is often portrayed as a **symbol of national unity**. Filling the government's top political office and elected by the entire country, he represents the nation in rituals that elsewhere are reserved to royalty. How did the president in this crisis use his symbolic role to rally the country at the disaster sites, in religious ceremonies, and in public speeches? What impact did this symbolic role have on the president's actual political power?

2. The individual **personality of a president** is part of executive power. Note the incidents when President Bush acted in a way that reflected his own energy and inclinations—his first tentative reactions to the attacks, the creation of the so-called Bush Doctrine, the assertion of his authority over crisis decision making, and his emotional reaction to the tragedy.

3. While he was publicly rallying the nation, the president was carrying out his **roles as chief executive and commander in chief**. Look for examples of President Bush managing the bureaucracy by selecting a lead agency for the invasion of Afghanistan or by choosing a military strategy. Did his refusal to blame anyone in government for the 9/11 disasters show a chief executive protecting subordinates he depended on?

4. The **president's influence over media** during the crisis was impressive. How did the president simplify and focus media coverage of 9/11 and the government's response? How did press framing of 9/11 reflect the government's priorities? Did the media surrender its role as an independent watchdog of government in echoing a nation's outrage?

5. **Bipartisan congressional deference to the executive** was apparent in this crisis, but was neither permanent nor complete. How did Congress cooperate with the president, from leadership meetings to congressional resolutions? Later, did Congress assert its independence, from "sunset" provisions in the USA Patriot Act to federalizing airport security?

On Tuesday morning, September 11, 2001, four teams of nineteen Arab terrorists took control of four California-bound jets shortly after they left three East Coast airports. Using the planes as "smart bombs," they crashed into both towers of the World Trade Center and the Pentagon. (The fourth plane, apparently thwarted by passengers, crashed into a field in Pennsylvania.) New York's huge 110-story towers collapsed to the ground, killing some three thousand people, while almost three hundred were killed at the Pentagon. A stunned nation watched the doomsday images on television, over and over.

The national reaction dramatized the sense of panic. Immediately after the planes hit, all commercial aviation was grounded and the nation's airports

Stunned New Yorkers watched as the World Trade Towers burned.

were closed. Employees were ordered out of the U.S. Capitol and White House. As rumors of further attacks spread, landmarks such as Disneyland, Mount Rushmore, and the Seattle Space Needle were evacuated. All three stock exchanges shut down for the week. Major League Baseball called off its games, marking the first time since World War I that a national emergency had canceled three days of games. Americans worried that September 11 might be just the beginning of horrors to come.

THE FIRST HOURS

"On September 10, 2001, George Bush was not on his way to a very successful presidency." These words, written by a former Bush speechwriter, were not far off the mark. The economy was slumping and corporate scandals filled the headlines, as did stories of the president's laid-back work habits. Memories of the embittered 2000 election remained fresh. Bush's approval rating stood at 51 percent in early September, lower than any president after eight months in office, except for Gerald Ford, whose popularity suffered after his pardon of Richard Nixon.

Following 9/11, both public and political opinion instinctively looked to the president. As chief of state he embodied the nation, but his role did not stop at symbols. He was also expected to define the enemy, to set out a course of action for the government, and, understandably, to provide reassurance to the country. Underlying President Bush's initial actions lay a whispered doubt: Was this commander in chief—barely eight months in office, elected by a minority of voters, and with almost no foreign policy experience—up to the job? A *New York Times* editorial bluntly declared that the president "remains an untested figure." (A year earlier, the electorate had been divided over candidate Bush's ability to deal with an international crisis: 45 percent thought he could; 46 percent were uneasy.)[2]

The first hours of the crisis were not reassuring to those with doubts about the personal character of the new chief executive. For starters, it took the president most of the day just to get to his office.

His morning had begun in an elementary school in Sarasota, Florida, where he was plugging his education reform, No Child Left Behind. When he first got news of the attacks, he continued reading to a class of students and then took twelve hours to return to the White House. His appearance afterward was described as "tentative, tense, and shocked."[3] Because of security fears, Air Force One had taken a zigzag course returning to Washington, first to an air base near Shreveport, Louisiana, and then to a command post in Omaha, Nebraska, where Bush conducted a meeting of the National Security Council by videophone to Washington. While the Secret Service worried that the attacks hadn't ended yet, the president's political aides had to face another issue: How could President Bush communicate control and confidence to the nation from a bunker in Nebraska? Or, as a *USA Today* reporter noted, "Not since the British burned the White House in 1814 has a President been persuaded by security concerns to avoid the capital."[4]

Arriving back at the White House that night, President Bush gave a brief talk from the Oval Office. A "somber" chief executive sitting alone at his desk assured the 80 million people watching that "Our country is strong. . . . Terrorist acts can shake the foundation of our biggest buildings, but they cannot touch the foundation of America." He declared that the government would continue "without interruption," that the search was underway to find those behind the evil acts, and that both allies and members of Congress would stand together to win the war against terrorism. He ended by asking for prayers for those who grieved and promised, "America has stood down enemies before, and we will do so this time."

A PRESIDENT'S PUBLIC RESPONSE

> The general public is much more dependent on presidents in foreign affairs than in domestic matters.
>
> *Aaron Wildavsky*

In the coming days, the president expanded on these themes. He was shown offering support to victims and rescuers, demonstrating national unity, defining an unseen enemy, and executing a strong military response. His major audiences at home were Congress and the American public. And he moved skillfully to gain the support of both.

Congress was reminded of its physical dependency on the executive in a graphic way. Unlike the executive branch, Congress had no evacuation plan on September 11. Members of Congress wandered around, prayed with the chaplain, or went home. Rumors circulated of more planes heading to Washington. Vice President Dick Cheney ordered that the leaders of Congress be taken to a secure location in a West Virginia resort. When one Republican senator demanded in a phone call to Cheney that the leadership be returned to Washington so that Congress could convene, the vice president refused. The senator pointed out that Congress was an independent branch of government not under executive control. Cheney's reply: "We control the helicopters."[5]

On his first full day back in the White House after the attacks, the president used the national attention focused on him to define the challenge and position himself leading the nation's response. He escalated his language, calling the attacks "more than acts of terror; they were acts of war," thus laying the foundation for military action. News reports showed him calling leaders of Britain, France, Germany, Russia, and China. His press secretary described the president as "rallying an international coalition to combat terrorism." He was photographed meeting with his security advisors and then with congressional leaders on new defense spending. The House passed a resolution of support, and Secretary of State Colin Powell sent stern public messages to other countries: "You're either with us or against us."

As the week went on, George Bush demonstrated the power of the presidency as both a single human being and a branch of government. In a way that only an individual chief executive could do, he personally connected to the range of feelings washing over Americans, from sadness to anger. He comforted victims, thanked rescue workers at the Pentagon and at the World Trade Center site, and reflected the nation's raw wounds. Two days after the attacks, when he got off the phone after talking with New York mayor

President Bush at ground zero. This picture of the president with a firefighter by his side at the site of the destroyed World Trade Towers on September 14, 2001, became a symbol for a rallying nation.

Rudolph Giuliani, a reporter described him this way: "The president's eyes glistened with emotion as he blinked to hold back tears. 'I'm a loving guy,' he said. 'And I'm also someone, however, who's got a job to do and I intend to do it. And this is a terrible moment.'"[6]

A president has been described as a "democratic priest-king," and this religious image was apparent in much of what Bush did that first week.[7] When he declared a national "day of prayers and remembrance," his proclamation read, ". . . in the face of all this evil, we remain strong and united, one nation under God." During a televised service at Washington Cathedral on September 14, Bush said, "The commitment of our fathers is now the calling of our time. We ask almighty God to watch over our nation and grant us patience and resolve in all that is to come."

The president was also the commander in chief, rallying the country for what lay ahead. In that same cathedral service, Bush talked tough: "This conflict was begun on the timing and terms of others; it will end in a way and at an hour of our choosing." Two days after the attack, the president declared, "The nation must understand this is now the focus of my administration."

In the coming days, the president pointedly did *not* do certain things. As head of the executive branch, he publicly demonstrated loyalty to the bureaucrats under him by not blaming anyone in the government for not anticipating the attack. Although the hijackings represented an enormous intelligence failure, the president showed his confidence in the CIA by being photographed meeting with its director. Bush also tried to separate the terrorists from the religion they claimed to represent. He posed at a meeting with American Islamic leaders, declaring that the hijackers had nothing to do with peaceful Muslims. The president made clear that he didn't want his political agenda completely disrupted by terrorism. He pointed to education reform—No Child Left Behind—as remaining his top domestic priority.

PLANNING THE GOVERNMENT ATTACK

> Domestic policy . . . can only defeat us; foreign policy can kill us.
>
> *President John F. Kennedy*

The president's support for the executive branch agencies in charge of national security was not just patriotic posturing. As the chief executive, he was dependent on the bureaucracy for a response to the terrorist attacks. He didn't need a public debate among the agencies degenerating into a blame-game on who was at fault. Bush first turned to the military when he was on Air Force One flying to Washington on September 11. Phoning Secretary of Defense Donald Rumsfeld, he said, "The ball will be in your court." But even in a national emergency, moving the bureaucracy to action would not prove to be a slam dunk.[8]

On a conference call later that day with the National Security Council, the CIA reported with "near certainty" that Osama bin Laden was behind the attack. At least three known operatives of al-Qaeda were on the passenger lists of the doomed airplanes. While the president wanted a strong response to the terrorists based in Afghanistan ("I don't want to put a million-dollar missile on a five dollar tent."), he would find that the military had no plans for invading that country or for dealing with bin Laden's terrorist network. The CIA, however, was ready. Its plan to overthrow the Taliban rulers of Afghanistan was already making its way to the president for approval on September 11. Now some wondered whether the bureaucracy had moved fast enough to counter this long-identified threat.

Not every policy decision was reached systematically in the initial confusing hours of the crisis. In his speech on that first night, the president made what journalist Bob Woodward called "one of the most significant foreign policy decisions in years"—the so-called Bush Doctrine. His statement— "We will make no distinction between those who planned these acts and those who harbor them"—announced a policy that could lead to conflict with any number of countries. It was a personal decision made in discussions with speechwriters by a president who trusted his own gut instincts. Bush had consulted with his National Security advisor, Condoleezza Rice, who after initial hesitation went along. Secretary of State Colin Powell, hurrying back from Peru at the time, had not been involved in the policy pronouncement.[9]

How would the response by various agencies of the executive branch be managed? Vice President Cheney raised the issue of coordination to the president. A savvy bureaucratic in-fighter, Cheney offered to chair a war cabinet of the principals who would develop options for the president and streamline decision making. Instead, Bush kept the reins of power in his own hands.

He asserted that as commander in chief he would chair the full meetings of the National Security Council. When he was not attending, his National Security advisor, Ms. Rice, would run the meetings of principals. Bush wanted to signal that he was calling the shots. Cheney, knowing that his job was to serve the president, accepted a lesser role.

By September 15, in a weekend conference at the Camp David presidential retreat, the key decisions were made. The president approved an antiterrorist war on many fronts—intelligence, finance, diplomacy, and military. The attorney general and the FBI were directed to preempt future strikes and to request new authority from Congress to track, wiretap, and stop terrorists—a decision reinforcing the USA Patriot Act already before the legislature. Bush signed a presidential intelligence order giving new broad authority for CIA covert operations against al-Qaeda, which included intelligence operatives in some eighty countries and the use of deadly force against the terrorist leadership. The president approved all of the CIA requests, rejecting Defense Department efforts to scale back the role of its rival agency. The military was permitted to use missiles, bombers, and "boots on the ground" in Afghanistan. They were prodded to negotiate base rights and speed their forces into position for an invasion. The issue of expanding the war to other countries was deferred— though not for long. On November 21, just seventy-two days after the terrorist attacks, President Bush asked Secretary of Defense Rumsfeld to secretly begin constructing a war plan for Iraq.[10]

Bush was aware of his crucial role in linking these closed-door executive decisions to his public/ceremonial activities. As quoted by Bob Woodward, the president remarked later,

> "I knew full well that if we could rally the American people behind a long and difficult chore, that our job would be easier. . . . I am a product of the Vietnam era. I remember presidents trying to wage wars that were very unpopular, and the nation split." He pointed to a portrait of Abraham Lincoln that hung in the Oval Office. "He's on the wall because the job of the president is to unite the nation."[11]

CONGRESS SALUTES

Many of the president's apparently symbolic activities following the attack had a policy goal: to maintain the support of the public and the Congress for the military plans he was drawing up with his security advisors.

As the initial confusion following the attacks faded, Congress united behind the president, at least for a while. Congress's deference to the president in the midst of an international crisis followed a long tradition in American history. Wars have centralized power in the executive office and elevated presidents like Abraham Lincoln, Woodrow Wilson, and Franklin Roosevelt. Despite its constitutional powers to restrain a president, including funding for military operations, Congress has rarely refused to support a war. In a fast-moving crisis, Congress lacked the information and expertise to challenge a president, especially a modern chief executive with his access to the resources of the executive branch. Congress was hardwired to believe that a president *should* control foreign policy in a crisis. Public opinion weighed in behind the president, demanding a united front against foreign enemies and shunning partisan "bickering" by Congress.[12]

Not surprisingly, then, the first congressional response reflected near unanimous support for the president. On September 14, after little debate, all but one member of Congress voted for a Use-of-Force Resolution to give the president the authority to retaliate against those responsible for 9/11. The resolution was described by one scholar as "stunning in the breadth of authority it granted." It allowed the president to "use all necessary and appropriate force against those nations, organizations, or persons he determines planned, authorized, committed, or aided the terrorist attacks that occurred on September 11, 2001, or harbored such organizations or persons." It was the legal basis for war against Afghanistan. But it could have been used against Iraq or Iran or Saudi Arabia, if they had aided the terrorists. Essentially, Congress signed a blank check: declaring war and then leaving it to the president to decide who the enemy was.[13]

An unusually close working relationship between the president and congressional leaders continued in the weeks that followed. Every Tuesday or Wednesday at 7:00 a.m., the leaders of both parties in Congress met with the president for breakfast. No aides were permitted at these private meetings of what was called the "Gang of Five." Out of these unprecedented meetings came a supplemental appropriations bill to fund disaster relief and military operations. The head of the Democrats in the House, Minority Leader Richard A. Gephardt, reflected the political atmosphere and the legislature's deference to the executive: "We are working together here in the Congress in a completely nonpartisan way. There is no division between parties, between the Congress and the president."[14]

THE PRESS AND PUBLIC RALLY ROUND THE FLAG

It's hard to do jokes because, as you know, Bush is smart now.

Jay Leno

There also wasn't much division between the media and the executive. In its coverage of the attacks and of the president, the press became, in one scholar's words, "a patriot." In analyzing the attack, reporters soon dropped the historic analogy with Pearl Harbor, perhaps because the administration was concerned that it implied a lack of preparedness by the government. The iconic visual that came to represent the attack switched from the burning towers to the more inspiring photo of firefighters raising the American flag, Iwo Jima–like, at the site. The White House was allowed to frame the reasons for the attacks: The terrorists hated the fundamental principles of the American system. As Bush put it, "They hate our freedoms." And in a later speech he said, "We wage a war to save civilization itself." The advantage of this frame was that it put the nation in a position of having its basic values under attack and thus forced to respond. If the alternative to "Why do they hate us?" was "Why do they hate our policies?" that might change the responses arising from the attack. This latter frame focusing on government actions was dismissed by the administration and ignored by the press.[15]

The president's personal character showed remarkable improvement in the image arena. The media, which had formerly been skeptical, if not cynical, about the president's intelligence, now saw few flaws. Earlier, George W. Bush frequently appeared as someone on the losing end of a war with the English language. The press used these slips of the tongue as a sign of incompetence. Now his verbal fumbling was either ignored or considered unimportant. Perhaps the media's less negative approach reflected the public's wish to see in the president the qualities they needed from their leader. Even comics kept their hands off the chief executive. In the months before 9/11, Bush was the target of 32 percent of the jokes on late-night television. In the two months following the attacks, he was the target of only 4 percent.[16]

Americans' rallying behind their government and president after 9/11 was attributed to instinct. But with leaders of the opposition Democrats and the mainstream press following the patriotic path of loyalty to national symbols—and the presidency was one—it would be surprising to find loud dissent voiced among the general public. Americans faced an international threat they hadn't thought much about before—a 1998 poll showed that only 4 percent of the public identified terrorism as an important issue. Now demonstrations of solidarity, mixed with vengeance toward the enemy, were the immediate, near universal and expected public response.

The president's ratings skyrocketed, from the low 50s to over 90 percent approval, an almost unprecedented rise. Even rarer was how long Bush's support remained high. Some six months later, it had only barely dropped. This support was paralleled by a rise in trust for all government institutions. The thirty-year decline in trust for the federal government, rooted in the lies and tragedies of Vietnam and Watergate, was reversed temporarily by the trauma of the terrorist attacks. Strong backing for an armed response was also evident. An *ABC News/Washington Post* poll taken on the evening of September 11 showed that 90 percent advocated the use of the military against those responsible for the attacks. This aggressive nationalism extended to those suspected of aiding terrorism who were detained in the United States without benefit of normal civil liberties protections. A *Newsweek* poll found that 86 percent of the public supported the government detention of accused terrorists.[17]

What had been a widespread public cynicism toward politics—reinforced by the media frenzy of the Lewinsky scandal and the nasty partisan controversies in Florida over the 2000 election—dissolved in an outpouring of patriotism. American flags were hung from highway overpasses next to signs proclaiming: *These colors don't run.* Even if these nationalist sentiments would fade in time, they would define the public opinion boundaries of Washington politics for months to come.

LIMITS OF BIPARTISANSHIP

> The Constitution is "an invitation to struggle for the privilege of directing American foreign policy."
>
> *Edward S. Corwin, The President: Office and Powers, 1787–1957*

In the weeks following September 11, criticism of the president was limited, feeble, and angrily put down when it surfaced. Only when important, conflicting domestic interests were in play did cracks appear in the chief executive's dominance. Then Wildavsky's division between presidential strength on national security and weakness in facing domestic interests more easily applied.

On issues touching the war, where patriotic appeals didn't ensure loyalty, the president's GOP supporters were prepared to use heavier clubs. In February 2002, Senate Democratic Majority Leader Tom Daschle told reporters that he believed the war on terrorism was successful but he worried that the administration's efforts to expand the war lacked "a clear direction." A Republican House leader struck back calling the remarks "disgusting." Trent Lott, Senate Minority Leader, attacked: "How dare Senator Daschle criticize President Bush while we are fighting our war on terrorism, especially when we have troops in the field?" And Rep. Tom Davis, chairman of the National Republican Congressional Campaign Committee, accused Daschle of "giving aid and comfort to our enemies," which just happens to be the legal definition of treason. Few of his fellow Democrats came to Daschle's defense.[18]

But bipartisanship had its limits. Congress was willing to quickly pass the administration's USA Patriot Act, which loosened the restraints governing surveillance activities. But congressional concern for the consequences on individual privacy led it to "sunset" the most controversial provisions, meaning they would expire in 2005 unless Congress voted to renew them. As the country moved further from 9/11, Congress stiffened resistance to presidential initiatives, including drilling in the Arctic Wildlife Reserve and judicial nominations. The White House argument that dissent on these domestic issues would hurt the war effort was seen as strained at best.

Beneath the surface unity, Washington interest groups didn't change their goals. They reframed their arguments to speak to the new crisis. Now the preferred response to terrorism depended on the lobbyists making the pitch. The airline and insurance industries, which suffered huge losses from the attacks, made their case for assistance. More of a stretch was the travel industry, which wanted a $1,000 tax credit for family vacation expenses, or large corporations' request for a $15 billion retroactive tax break, or the makers of traffic signs wanting federal money so that Americans could more easily escape from terrorist attacks, or the California date growers who lobbied for California dates being included in Afghan food packages. As one lobbyist frankly admitted, "What happened was a tragedy, certainly, but there are opportunities. We're in business. This is not a charity."[19]

Bipartisan congressional cooperation with the president floundered on the issue of airport security. The fact that all the al-Qaeda hijackers had passed through security checks led many Americans to fear flying. Airport traffic declined, and Congress examined what it could do. The problem wasn't hard to locate. Airport security guards, some getting $7 an hour, made less than fast-food restaurant workers. Turnover was high, training was haphazard, and security breaches were frequent. For congressional Democrats, the solution was to create a new agency in the Department of Transportation where professional screeners could be hired and trained. Such legislation easily passed the Senate, 100-0.

But the majority Republicans in the House took a dim view of expanding federal employment. They wanted to continue to have private companies handling airport security, though with better standards, salaries, and training. They also worried about the difficulty in firing incompetent security personnel protected by civil service rules. Not as loudly expressed was the GOP concern that this reform meant 40,000 new federal employees, who could be expected to join a Democratic labor union, look to the Democrats to protect their interests, and donate campaign funds to Democratic candidates. Ideologically, Republicans preferred solutions resting on private corporations, which were also more likely than government workers to contribute to GOP fundraisers.

Public opinion made the difference. Anxiety about security was reinforced by press stories of private firms hiring convicted criminals as screeners and cutting corners on safety to save money. People felt more confident having federal employees responsible for airport security. At the same time, the crash of American Airlines Flight 587 in Queens, New York, just two months after the 9/11 attacks seemed to mobilize public opinion. Although the crash had nothing to do with terrorism, the public pressure about airline safety grew. The White House and congressional Republicans caved. While some concessions were made, such as allowing federal screeners to be dismissed for incompetence, the bill that resulted was a Democratic victory over the president.[20]

A CALL TO ARMS

The climax of the initial response to the attack came in President Bush's speech to a joint session of Congress on September 20. Using the Capitol as his stage and the Congress as his cheering chorus, a president not known for rhetoric gave an inspiring speech. He called on the nation to unite to destroy terrorism. "Tonight we are a country awakened to danger and called to defend freedom. Our grief has turned to anger, and anger to resolution. Whether we bring our enemies to justice, or bring justice to our enemies, justice will be done."

He framed the challenge as one that Americans had faced in the past. "They hate our freedoms—our freedom of religion, our freedom of speech, our freedom to vote and assemble and disagree with each other. . . . We have seen their kind before. They are the heirs of all the murderous ideologies of the twentieth century . . . They follow in the path of fascism, and Nazism and totalitarianism. And they will follow that path all the way, to where it ends: in history's unmarked grave of discarded lies."

Bush saw a long, difficult campaign to which he committed the resources of the nation. He pledged, "The advance of human freedom—the great achievement of our time, and the great hope of every time—now depends on us . . . We will not tire, we will not falter, and we will not fail." And when Bush concluded, "In our grief and anger, we have found our mission and our moment," he wasn't speaking only of the nation. He was speaking of his presidency.

In time, the national unity behind the president would fade. A short, apparently successful conflict in Afghanistan was followed by a far different involvement in Iraq. Misleading presidential justifications that Iraq had weapons of mass destruction and was closely allied to the al-Qaeda terrorists undermined the public support that followed 9/11. As the costs and casualties of the Iraq War mounted, the gaps in military planning became more apparent and an end to the violence grew more distant. Political leaders, the press, and the public refused to rally behind the president as they had after 9/11. The doubts about presidential leadership of foreign policy surfaced in the 2004 election. They fully blossomed in the 2008 presidential election where President Bush's unpopularity contributed to his party's loss of the White House. Critics pointed to the administration's incompetence, lack of candor, and arrogant unwillingness to accept responsibility for mistakes. Some sense of closure to 9/11 may have come with the killing of the leader of al-Qaeda by American forces. But it occurred 10 years later under a different administration with credit going to a Democratic president.

This loss of support reflected a system working the way it was designed. The period following the terrorist attacks was the exception. Even in foreign policy, presidents remain part of a government where, as one of the framers of the Constitution, James Madison reminds us, "Ambition must be made to counteract ambition."[21]

Notes

1. Aaron Wildavsky, "The Two Presidencies," *Trans-Action* 4, no. 2 (December 1966): 7–14. The article has been widely reprinted, and the quote can be found in Peter Woll, ed., *American Government: Readings and Cases* (New York: Longman, 1999), 306.
2. James M. Lindsay, "Deference and Defiance: The Shifting Rhythm of Executive-Legislative Relations in Foreign Policy," *Presidential Studies Quarterly* 33, no. 3 (September 2003): 537. The quote in the first paragraph is Lindsay's, a former Bush speechwriter.
3. Frank Bruni, *Ambling into History*, 255, quoted by Kathleen Hall Jamieson and Paul Waldman, *The Press Effect* (New York: Oxford University Press, 2003), 146.

4. *USA Today*, September 12, 2001, as quoted by *National Journal*, September 15, 2001, 2856.
5. Jeremy D. Mayer, *9–11: The Giant Awakens* (Belmont, CA: Wadsworth/Thomson, 2003), 24.
6. "Emotional Bush Promises Victory," *Boston Globe*, September 14, 2001.
7. See Thomas Langston, *With Reverence and Contempt: How Americans Think About Their President* (Baltimore: Johns Hopkins University Press, 1996).
8. Bob Woodward, *Bush at War* (New York: Simon & Schuster, 2002), 19. The internal national security discussions leading to the invasion of Afghanistan are taken from the Woodward book. Woodward, an editor at the *Washington Post*, was given unique access to the participants in these meetings and granted extensive interviews that included the president. His book can be considered the administration's version of the executive branch planning for the war in Afghanistan.
9. Woodward, *Bush at War*, 30–31.
10. Bob Woodward, *Plan of Attack* (New York: Simon & Schuster, 2004), 1. Bush's Secretary of the Treasury Paul O'Neill says that the president had brought up using force against Iraq as early as January 2001. See Ron Suskind, *The Price of Loyalty* (New York: Simon & Schuster, 2004), Chapter 2.
11. Woodward, *Bush at War*, 95.
12. See Gary C. Jacobson and Samuel Kernel, *The Logic of American Politics in Wartime* (Washington, DC: Congressional Quarterly Press, 2004), 9–16.
13. Lindsay, 538.
14. *CQ Weekly*, September 15, 2001, 2124.
15. Jamieson and Waldman, Chapter 6, "The Press as Patriot."
16. Jamieson and Waldman, 157–161.
17. Mayer.
18. As quoted by Lindsay, 538.
19. David E. Rosenbaum, "Since Sept. 11, Lobbyists Use New Pitches for Old Pleas," New York Times on the Web, www.nytimes.com, December 3, 2001.
20. Lindsay.
21. The phrase is from James Madison, *The Federalist* #51.

14 | THE BUREAUCRACY

THE *COLUMBIA* AND *CHALLENGER* SHUTTLE DISASTERS
Organization Groupthink

Modern government needs bureaucracy. To deliver the mail, to fight the wars, to clean the environment, to manage the schools, and to launch shuttles into space, an organization of experts and staff is required. These administrators are what keep America's government among the most competent, least corrupt in the world. But there's a price to be paid for relying on specialized bureaucracies. The risk is they can develop interests of their own, often seeing the world through the eyes of their agency's mission rather than the citizens they serve. They may also be so tightly directed or politically pressured that they ignore the experts on which their organization depends.

The National Aeronautics and Space Administration (NASA) is a highly regarded federal agency, with accomplishments in space exploration that include putting men on the moon and robots on Mars. Yet our case study, somewhat unfairly, focuses on the agency's two most spectacular disasters—the *Columbia* and *Challenger* shuttle accidents. Both occurred because of flawed technology—foam insulation hitting the *Columbia* at takeoff, and O-rings eroding on the *Challenger* rocket boosters. People in NASA knew about both risks before the tragedies occurred. But bureaucratic pressures led to these flaws being minimized, the people raising them ignored. The immediate causes of the accidents were technical; the underlying reasons were organizational.

The accidents occurred seventeen years apart, the *Columbia* in 2003, the *Challenger* in 1986, yet the bureaucratic behavior was similar. At the risk of simplifying complex technical and bureaucratic issues, the tragedies shared a common problem of "groupthink," the striving for in-group agreement that overrides a realistic appraisal of alternatives by discouraging independent thinking.[1] While groupthink can promote a loyal, smoothly running team, in this case a downsized organization accountable to high external expectations pressured employees not to break ranks.

Engineering experts' advice was undermined by supervisors needing to keep costs down, to meet a demanding schedule, to retain a vital contract, to emphasize a "can-do" attitude, and to hold on to the procedures that had served them in the past. NASA's very virtues were its vices. A hardworking bureaucracy's dedication to its mission encouraged a culture of consensus that reduced internal conflict, but produced the mistakes leading to both tragedies.

CONCEPTS TO CONSIDER _____

1. Bureaucrats are often represented as unmotivated administrators. This case reveals people dedicated to their **bureaucracy's goals** and committed to maximizing limited resources. How did high motivation lead to errors in implementation? How was NASA cutting corners and ignoring safety to achieve its mission?
2. **Downsizing** the federal government by reducing bureaucracy's employees and budgets is politically popular. This case study shows some of its internal consequences. How did it affect NASA? Since the agency didn't want to give up its shuttle missions, how did it try to achieve ambitious goals with fewer resources? Did privatization—contracting out to private contractors like Morton Thiokol—change how NASA bureaucrats did their jobs?
3. All bureaucracies are structured as hierarchies, with bosses and subordinates, usually divided into specialized areas of expertise. How did this **bureaucratic structure** encourage groupthink and discourage open discussions? How did NASA leadership limit information and control the decisions that the agency made?
4. Making bureaucracies **politically accountable** to elected officials is important. But did NASA's leadership's accountability create the pressures that made the groupthink behind the accidents more acceptable? How did congressional oversight, politically influenced contracts, and public relations concerns affect NASA's operations?

THE *COLUMBIA* CRASH, FEBRUARY 1, 2003[2]

Just sixteen minutes before its scheduled landing at the Kennedy Space Center in Florida, the space shuttle *Columbia* disintegrated during reentry. On that morning of February 1, 2003, flashes of the orbiter debris could be seen across the skies from California to Texas. Even as Mission Control at Kennedy was attempting to contact the *Columbia*, people outside called to say they had seen live television coverage of the spacecraft breaking up. It was a catastrophic accident that cost the lives of the seven-person crew, the first shuttle disaster since *Challenger* crashed on January 28, 1986.

Earlier, as those on duty at Mission Control tracked the *Columbia* descending at eight times faster than a bullet, the first sign of trouble was the failure of four sensors on the left wing. The entry flight director's thoughts flashed back to the launch: A briefcase-sized piece of foam insulation had broken off from *Columbia*'s external fuel tank eighty-one seconds after liftoff and slammed into the left wing. A team of experts had studied photos of foam flying off and dismissed its importance. The Mission Management Team had unanimously agreed. This failure in the left wing had to be a coincidence.[3]

But seven months later the head of NASA's Research Center would declare, "In four simple words, the foam did it."[4] The foam, traveling 500 miles per hour, had punched a hole as big as a dinner plate in the ceramic edge of the left wing. It was invisible to the astronauts in orbit. As the shuttle reentered the atmosphere, heat passed through the hole and melted the inside of the wing. Foam had caused the accident, but a cluster of bureaucratic attitudes had led to the disaster.

Two sets of decisions and nondecisions preceded the events in the sky on that morning in February. The first was what happened in the months and years before the launch that led to a NASA mind-set that foam was "no big deal." The second was what occurred once the foam had struck and the shuttle was in orbit. Here a series of decisions about what to do, specifically whether to get military spy satellites to take a picture of any damage, sealed *Columbia*'s fate. In both arenas, an organizational culture—call it groupthink or "group pride"—led to a disaster that eerily paralleled the *Challenger* disaster seventeen years earlier.

COLUMBIA: FOAM OVERSIGHT

> . . . For twenty years NASA management had lived under the belief that foam could cause no damage.
>
> *Dr. Douglas Osheroff, Nobel laureate and member of the Columbia Accident*
> *Investigation Board*

In every one of the 112 shuttle missions before *Columbia*'s January 2003 liftoff, foam had hit the shuttle, including some severe strikes. On *Columbia*'s first shuttle flight in 1981, 300 protective heat tiles had been dinged by a shower of foam. During the twenty-one years since, orbiters had returned with an average of 143 damaged tiles, including thirty-one with scars measuring more than an inch. The foam, used to insulate the external tanks, had been deemed an "accepted risk" despite a clear rule against debris strikes that had existed from the beginning of the shuttle program. No substitute was found for the foam (which looked and felt like its cousin, Styrofoam), and efforts to reduce its thickness had not solved the problem. The more it fell off and struck the craft without causing an accident, the more the bureaucrats agreed among themselves: Foam was a nuisance, not a "safety-of-flight" issue.[5]

This view was put to the test at the launch of the shuttle *Atlantis* in October 2002, when a mailbox-size chunk of foam struck the rocket booster. Both the size of the debris and the fact that it had hit near a critical electronics box had caused jaws to drop when film of it was shown at the Flight Center. Working-level engineers wanted the foam loss to be declared an IFA— In-Flight-Anomaly—a critical failure that had to be fixed before the next flight or proved not to threaten vehicle safety. Engineers saw the largest piece of debris to come off the space vehicle as a dangerous threat. Yet the argument

One of the last photos of the doomed US *Columbia* space shuttle re-entering earth's orbit on February 1, 2003.

they faced from their bosses was that the size of this debris was unique, that it did no damage, and that there was no available alternative. Instead of being classified as an IFA, it was put under a milder "Plans/Studies." Responding to pressures to keep to the schedule, supervisors stifled dissent. One engineer who resisted this group pressure and to signing the flight readiness statement for the next shuttle was privately given a brief history of foam loss, how it had been handled in the past, and how it had never interfered with a launch before. After listening to his superior, he signed.

Senior managers discussed the foam issue, along with other concerns, at the Flight Readiness Review for the shuttle *Endeavor*'s November flight. The fuel tank manager who presented the foam issue to the meeting had not been worried by the strike on the *Atlantis*, equating it to a Styrofoam cooler lid hitting the window of a car—distracting but not dangerous. In his seven-minute presentation, he dismissed safety concerns as no more relevant than they had been for all the previous flights. He promised to report back on possible fixes for the foam problem. The meeting participants took no formal action and set the due date for a report on the issue after the next shuttle launch. Essentially, the problem was buried.

The *Endeavor* was launched on November 23. As the fuel tank manager had predicted, the shuttle suffered no serious foam damage. The issue never came up at the next Flight Readiness Review for the *Columbia*. A senior NASA manager, looking back at the *Endeavor*'s Readiness Review, would later conclude, "That was one of the things we really missed as an agency."[6]

External pressures played a role in the decision to continue with the *Columbia* launch as planned. NASA was in the midst of a large downsizing, with its shuttle workforce having dropped 42 percent in the decade before the *Columbia* launch—from 30,000 to just over 17,000. It had been reducing its budget and employment by eliminating civil service jobs and increasing the use of private contractors operating outside. Despite the downsizing, NASA was still over-budget and behind schedule in assembling the space station, which was the primary task of the shuttles. If it didn't meet its goal of assembling crucial parts of the space station by early 2004, it risked losing support from the White House and Congress. NASA was not just politically accountable; it was "on probation." The Columbia Accident Investigation Board (CAIB) later reported that the managers' need to keep to their schedule "appeared to have influenced their decision" not to treat the foam loss as an IFA. NASA was "slowly accepting additional risk in trying to meet a schedule that probably could not be met."[7]

COLUMBIA: FOLLOWING THE LAUNCH

The story that emerged was a sad and unnecessary one, involving arrogance, insularity, and bad luck allowed to run unchecked.

William Langewiesche, Atlantic Monthly

Shouts of "Oh my God!" filled the auditorium. Launch engineers were watching film of a large chunk of foam smashing into the *Columbia*'s left wing at the shuttle's takeoff a few hours before. It had come from the same area of the fuel tank as the one that had broken off in October's launch of *Atlantis*. But this debris was by far the largest piece to hit the orbiter. It wasn't clear from the pictures exactly where it had struck or whether the debris cloud contained foam, ice, or bits of the shuttle's heat tiles. It *was* clear that this time it wasn't the rocket booster that was hit. It was the orbiter itself.

The film reviewers concluded that the vehicle might have suffered damage from this unprecedented strike, but that they couldn't tell conclusively from these pictures. They suggested getting the military to use their spy satellites to take pictures of the shuttle in orbit. Rumors soon spread at Kennedy that the shuttle might be landing early. Some managers put out reassuring e-mails downplaying the likely damage from the foam and emphasizing the strength of the heat tiles in the wing edge area.

The mission managers responded to the film with minimal concern and a desire to get on with the mission. Worried engineers on the working-level Debris Assessment Team found that they had to clearly prove that a safety issue existed before the shuttle management would request a spy-satellite image of the left wing. (As the CAIB later noted, proving something is *unsafe* reversed the usual requirement to prove that a situation *is safe*.) Senior managers pointed out the extra time that would be spent maneuvering the *Columbia* into position for the pictures, the halting of scientific experiments, and the uncertainty whether the new images would be very clear.

They doubted that the foam had sufficient density to damage the spacecraft. Managers also made the fatalistic argument that even if there was damage, it couldn't be repaired in orbit. The NASA supervisors, under budgetary and political pressures, were interested in how to keep the foam problem from affecting the schedules of future shuttles, not in generating information undermining their decision.

Some frustrated engineers used a computer program called Crater, which could predict damage from debris fragments on a spacecraft. From the foam chunk's size, direction, and impact site, the model calculated that the strike would have disastrously penetrated the heat tiles. But senior managers dismissed the Crater model as not appropriate for large debris. They assumed that the foam had hit heat tiles—not the wing edge—and couldn't have damaged them. Other engineers requested, through informal channels, Air Force photos of the left wing. When the chair of the Mission Management Team found out, she simply terminated the request with the Department of Defense. The photos were never taken.[8]

According to the CAIB report, the organizational culture of NASA deterred working-level engineers from vigorously pushing their safety concerns. Rodney Rocha, described as a smart, stubborn, veteran NASA engineer, was upset by the foam strike. He had pushed for satellite photos and argued with others about the likelihood of shuttle damage. At a pre–Mission Management Team meeting where the foam strike was discussed, Rocha and other engineers felt that the dangers were minimized and the meeting rushed. Yet Rocha sat and said nothing. It was a large meeting with a consensus among the supervisors that there was no safety-of-flight issue. Although they talked about heat tile problems, no mention was made of possible damage to the wing edge panels. Reflecting on his resentment at this groupthink, Rocha recalled his feelings as the meeting ended: "I felt like going in there and interrupting or waiting until they got through and just saying, . . . I just want you to know that we are not finished,' but I didn't. I didn't do any such thing. . . ."[9]

An atmosphere of intimidation prevailed, and with it came an unspoken fear of reprisals for criticism. The Debris Assessment Team's concerns never made it up to the Mission Management Team supervising the shuttle. Senior managers never asked the engineers about their concerns. The safety representatives were too few and too passive. No one challenged the shuttle managers' decisions, including the assumption that rescuing the *Columbia* was impossible. Later, the head of the CAIB concluded that launching a second shuttle in time to attempt a rescue would not have been easy but was conceivable. Indeed, it was the rescue of the *Apollo 13* crew in 1970 from its seemingly certain disaster in space that had given the agency much of its heroic public image. A NASA astronaut said, "You give us a challenge, we know the problem, and it is amazing what you can do."[10]

But in the *Columbia* tragedy, NASA's directors never confronted the problem because they never accepted that they had a problem. Even worse, it had all happened before.

CHALLENGER: JANUARY 28, 1986

I think I'm hearing an echo here.

*Sally Ride, former astronaut and member of the two commissions
that investigated both the Columbia and Challenger disasters*

Seventeen years earlier, the space shuttle *Challenger* had been postponed four times before it took off in 1986 on its tenth mission. A little over a minute into the flight, a massive explosion destroyed the spacecraft, killing the crew of seven. It was the space program's worst disaster yet and a remembered tragedy for the millions who watched on TV. The commission created to investigate the explosion found design flaws in the O-rings of the solid rocket boosters, but also identified NASA's faulty decision-making system as a cause of the accident. A look back at a key meeting the night before the launch illuminates how this accident was "rooted in history." Flaws in how critical group decisions were arrived at would lead to this first shuttle disaster.

On the night of January 27, 1986, thirty-four people sat at tables in three different states and held a tense two-hour teleconference. These were managers and engineers from NASA's Kennedy Space Center in Florida, the Marshall Space Flight Center in Alabama, and, in Utah, representatives from Morton Thiokol, the private contractor who had built the solid rocket boosters. They were discussing the next day's launch of the *Challenger.* Several meetings had already taken place focused on whether it was safe to launch the shuttle. The debate centered around whether the O-rings that sealed the joints of the boosters would hold.

The engineers from Morton Thiokol, led by Roger Boisjoly, presented their doubts about the O-rings. The booster contained two levels of seals, a primary and a secondary seal. Both seals were designed to be resilient enough on take off to expand and close up the joints. If the primary O-ring did not seal, hot gas could be blown through to the secondary O-ring, possibly causing it to fail and resulting in a catastrophe. Boisjoly and the engineers had seen some evidence from previous flights that when the temperature at launch was cold, the O-rings lost their ability to seal. Because the weather at the launch the next morning was predicted to be an unusually chilly 18 degrees, the Thiokol engineers recommended against launching.

Thiokol engineers had never before recommended against a launch. Boisjoly's team of engineers had been studying the O-ring problem for several months, without much support from management. Although the evidence was mixed, their engineering hunches and safety concerns had led to the pre-launch meeting. The teleconference the night before the launch was in itself unusual, since such presentations were usually made face-to-face two weeks before a launch. And the predicted cold temperature for the next day was below that of any previous launch. NASA was venturing into uncharted territory.[11]

As in the *Columbia* disaster almost two decades later, both internal and external pressures were pushing for the launch. Everyone at the meeting was familiar with NASA's mission-oriented, low-cost bureaucratic culture. This meant that whatever priority was given to safety in speeches had to compete with concerns of schedule and expense in practice. Where once the burden of proof was on engineers to show beyond a doubt that it was safe to launch, now Morton Thiokol was expected to prove that launching *Challenger* would *not* be safe. If NASA accepted the engineers' recommendation not to launch below 53 degrees (the previous lowest temperature of a launch), the managers would be agreeing to a new criterion for all launches—a costly complication in meeting tight schedules for future missions.

An underlying conflict existed in the bureaucratic hierarchy between managers and engineers. Earlier in NASA's history, the professional opinions of technical people—scientists and engineers, no matter what their rank—were given great deference. Over the years, a more top–down system of bureaucratic accountability had developed. Managers and engineers fell into a relationship of superior and subordinate. The experts began to act like "cowed bureaucrats," and the free flow of information up and down the agency was restricted.[12] Anything that "slowed" the progress of space flights, which in this case included safety concerns, was discouraged. The managers challenged the engineers' observations from previous

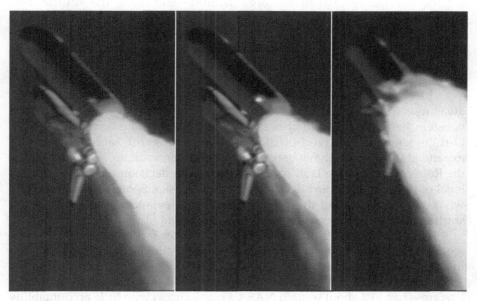

This sequence of photos shows the space shuttle *Challenger* at takeoff on January 28, 1986, as its right solid rocket booster begins to explode.

flights, questioning whether they could be considered "hard data." Near the end of the January 27 meeting, a supervisor asked one of the engineers, "Am I the only one who wants to fly?" and requested one of them to "take off his engineering hat and put on his management hat."[13]

While NASA officials at the teleconference disagreed that low temperature led to O-ring erosion, they were reluctant to overrule the engineers at the meeting. At this point, Thiokol managers asked for a smaller private caucus with their engineers. Here the lead person said that "a management decision was necessary." The four senior executives then held a brief discussion and voted unanimously to reverse the original engineering recommendation. They returned to the teleconference, from which the engineers were now excluded, and announced that Thiokol had reexamined the data and supported the decision to launch. The launch managers at Marshall and Kennedy did not know that the Thiokol engineers still objected. One manager at Marshall asked, "Does anybody have anything more to say?" No one spoke. The dissenters had been silenced. The disastrous launch went ahead the next morning.

CHALLENGING MANAGEMENT

The Thiokol engineers were battling the weight of management in trying to stop the launch because of their concern for the O-rings. They were subordinates in a bureaucratic hierarchy; and their objections were dismissed as observational and intuitive, rather than quantitative and scientific. A cost-conscious culture and an array of political and economic pressures all pushed for the overriding goal of the organization—launching the shuttle. Not surprisingly then, their immediate supervisors never communicated the engineers' objections to superiors at NASA (who weren't at the teleconference) because these supervisors viewed this decision as one appropriately made at their level. Reflecting the flawed communication flows in the agency, they kept the information to themselves.[14]

Rejecting the engineers' concerns came in part from the managers' awareness that concerns with the O-rings, as well as other risk factors in the boosters, had been raised in prior launches. As the missions continued and the O-rings showed damage but didn't fail, the range of "acceptable risks" expanded. NASA may have been "playing Russian roulette," as a member of the Rogers Commission later concluded, but each decision accepting a higher level of risk made the next decision that much easier. Soon it became routine, what one scholar called the "normalization of deviance." Step by step, the shuttle management descended into poor judgment.[15]

Financial and political pressures were another fact of life for those overseeing the shuttles. Budgets were tight. The public climate that NASA operated in was not as supportive of the shuttle program as it had been during the "space race" to the moon in the 1960s. For the *Apollo*'s journey to the moon, Congress had just about written NASA a blank check, with little accountability to the rest of the government. But now the shuttle program had to be sold as a business, with NASA claiming it could pay its own way by ferrying scientific experiments and commercial satellites to space and back. As a result, the shuttle was publicly positioned as a routine "operational program" rather than the more risky "developmental system." The four reusable shuttles were put on an ambitious schedule of seventeen missions a year with twenty-four scheduled for 1988. This meant speeding up the turnaround time of shuttles between launches, and making sure the 60 million components and thousands of countdown activities would not interfere with any of the takeoffs.

As the demands increased and the resources tightened, the need for political support steered NASA away from the technical culture on which the space agency had built its reputation for quality. Contracts were awarded to private contractors for most shuttle activities, which meant that the original "dirty hands" approach of NASA technicians doing the work themselves changed into supervising for-profit companies. Nor were these contracts devoid of political calculations. One agency critic said, "NASA was organized from day one so that all fifty states would have NASA contracts. . . ."[16] Politics might mean placing a U.S. senator in orbit, or choosing a New Hampshire woman to be the "First Teacher in Space" for public relations purposes. (That teacher, Christa McAuliffe, was lost with the other six crew members aboard the *Challenger*.)

The corporation managers were aware of these pressures surrounding the shuttle program. As contractors they could be expected to respond to their bureaucratic employers, not just to the engineers whom they employed. Privatization of the space program had led to Thiokol's $1 billion contract with NASA, which was up for renegotiation with a serious possibility that it would be put up for bidding to competitors. A phone call was scheduled for the day after the *Challenger* liftoff to discuss the contract. All the managers knew this. One can only imagine the impact on Thiokol when one NASA official said during the heated teleconference, "My God, Thiokol, when do you want me to launch, next April?" Immediately following this comment, the Thiokol executives asked for the private meeting with their engineers.[17]

CONCLUSION

Diane Vaughan, a Boston College professor and expert on bureaucracy, wrote an exhaustive and penetrating scholarly study of the 1986 *Challenger* disaster and NASA's organizational culture. Her widely reviewed book was used to improve safety programs, and she consulted on reducing risks for organizations ranging from the U.S. Forest Service to hospitals. Eventually, she was called to testify before the Columbia Accident Investigation Board at a public hearing. She was asked if NASA ever contacted her after the book came out. She replied, "No. . . . Everybody called. My high school boyfriend called. But NASA never called."[18]

Whatever the NASA bureaucracy learned from the first disaster of the *Challenger* resulted in only limited changes, too few to prevent the second accident. Investigators of the *Columbia* noted the similarities with the earlier crash: cost and schedule pressures, the increasing acceptance of risk, the top–down communications, and the ignoring of engineers' concerns. In the words of one CAIB commissioner, ". . . They basically relaxed back to the kind of thinking that they'd had that had produced the loss of the *Challenger*." NASA's dedication to accomplishing its goals led to ignoring safety. Once again groupthink was used to throttle dissent. Rather than break ranks or speak against the consensus, the engineers involved in *Columbia* would give up or convince themselves that everything was OK. When someone differed from the party line "they were intimidated or ridiculed," which were, the investigators noted, "not very positive management techniques."[19]

While organizational dysfunctions became the focus for both investigations into the shuttle disasters, this should not obscure the issue of individual responsibility. "NASA" didn't approve the shuttle launches, the "agency" didn't intimidate engineers, and the "bureaucracy" didn't overlook safety. People did. Individuals in authority responded to pressures, evaluated information, and made decisions. They also made mistakes for which they were accountable. Nor is NASA the only institution in which groupthink exists. A Senate report in the summer of 2004 showed that the CIA's exaggeration of Iraqi weapons of mass destruction served the political purpose of supporting Bush administration officials' policy of going to war. The Senate panel blamed "a broken corporate culture and poor management."[20] But here, too, blaming systems and communications and bureaucracy, rather than individuals, may lead those responsible to evade responsibility.

POSTSCRIPT

After the *Challenger* crash, Roger Boisjoly, a leader of Morton Thiokol's dissenting engineers, was called before the Rogers Commission. He testified that he disagreed with his managers in their interpretation of the events leading to the launch decision. Thiokol management subsequently removed him from their investigation team and criticized him for "airing the company's dirty laundry." He was isolated from NASA and their efforts to redesign the O-rings. Chairman Rogers publicly criticized Thiokol for retaliating against those who opposed the decision to launch. In an effort to clear the air, Boisjoly asked for a private meeting with the company's three top executives. He found them unreceptive. He saw his position as untenable.

An organization was punishing an individual employee for his dissent, for being right. On July 21, 1986, less than six months after the *Challenger* blew up, Boisjoly requested an extended sick leave from Morton Thiokol and eventually resigned. Reflecting on his experience later, he wrote, "I have been asked by some if I would testify again if I knew in advance of the potential consequences to me and my career. My answer is always an immediate 'yes.' I couldn't live with any self-respect if I tailored my actions based upon the personal consequences. . . ."[21]

Notes

1. Paul 't Hart and Marceline Kroon, "Groupthink in Government: Pathologies of Small-Group Decision Making," in J. L. Garnett and A. Kouzmin, eds., *Handbook of Administrative Communication* (New York: Marcel Dekker, 1997), 309–328. Also see "Groupthink of Irving Janis" Chapter 18 in Em Griffin, *A First Look at Communication Theory,* archived under www.afirstlook.com.

2. Following both the *Challenger* and *Columbia* disasters, independent investigating commissions were set up: the Rogers Commission (named for its chairman William Rogers, former secretary of state) following *Challenger* and the Columbia Accident Investigation Board, CAIB (chaired by retired Admiral Harold Gehman), after *Columbia.* The investigators produced volumes of reports that provided the basis for the writings by scholars and reporters, and much of what follows in this chapter. The conclusions of the two commissions were similar in blaming bureaucratic mismanagement and the striving for group consensus under the pressures of costs and schedule.

3. Michael Cabbage and William Harwood, *Comm Check . . . The Final Flight of Shuttle Columbia* (New York: Free Press, 2004), Chapter 5.

4. From "Talk of the Nation," National Public Radio, August 26, 2003.

5. Cabbage and Harwood, 56–59.

6. Ibid., 66–72.

7. Maureen Hogan Casamayou, "The *Columbia* Accident," in Richard J. Stillman II, *Public Administration: Concepts and Cases,* 8th ed. (Boston: Houghton Mifflin, 2005), 117. Also Cabbage and Harwood, 206.

8. From Cabbage and Harwood, Chapters 5 and 6.

9. As quoted by Cabbage and Harwood, 257, 258.

10. See William Langewiesche, "*Columbia's* Last Flight," *Atlantic Monthly,* November 2003, 85.

11. Diane Vaughan, "The Trickle-Down Effect: Policy Decisions, Risky Work, and the *Challenger* Tragedy," *California Management Review* (Winter 1997): 92–95.

12. From B. S. Romzek and M.J. Dubnick, "Accountability in the Public Sector: Lessons from the *Challenger* Tragedy," *Public Administration Review* 47 (1987): 227–238.

13. Russell P. Boisjoly, Ellen Foster Curtis, and Eugene Mellican, "Roger Boisjoly and the *Challenger* Disaster: The Ethical Dimensions," *Journal of Business Ethics* 8 (1989): 217–230.

14. Ibid., 224.

15. Vaughan.

16. Greg Klerkx, *Lost in Space: The Fall of NASA and the Dream of a New Space Age* (New York: Pantheon, 2004), 254.

17. Michael T. Charles, "The Last Flight of Space Shuttle *Challenger,*" in Richard J. Stillman, *Public Administration: Concepts and Cases,* 8th ed. (Boston: Houghton Mifflin, 2005), 118–119.

18. Cabbage and Harwood, 203.

19. Ibid., 201.

20. *Washington Post,* July 10, 2004.

21. Boisjoly et al., 229.

15

THE SUPREME COURT

WATERGATE AND
U.S. v. NIXON
The Supreme Court Referees

The justices of the Supreme Court sit atop one of the three branches of the federal government. They head an important policy-making institution. The Supreme Court acts as an agent of the national government in interpreting, applying, and creating rules that, as seen in other cases, can range from abortion to affirmative action. At times the Court resolves disputes between groups, or even between the other branches of government. In its rulings, the Court may act to guard its own powers and the status of the judicial branch. By interpreting and enforcing the law in this case, these nine policymakers became referees for the political system they help govern.

In *United States v. Nixon*, the Supreme Court confronted the national crisis called "Watergate." The 1972 wiretapping of Democratic party headquarters by agents of President Richard Nixon and the cover-up, scandal, and resignations that followed mark the surfacing of several toxic flowers of modern American politics. Much of what we have focused on in this book blossomed here: The ascendancy and dangers of secret executive power; the bitter partisan conflicts inflamed by a festering war; the rise of a cynical, adversarial media; the far-from successful struggle to limit the excesses of campaigns and political money; the acceptance of scandals and investigations as a legitimate channel of opposition; and the public's declining confidence in their government. All these bloomed in Watergate.

Watergate began in the Republican White House's near obsession over confidential information being leaked to newspapers by dissenters, most spectacularly in the *Pentagon Papers*, a secret government study of the decisions leading to the Vietnam War. After going to court proved unsuccessful in stopping publication, the Nixon administration tried to prosecute those responsible and then to halt other leaks by using undercover espionage agents. These same semi-government operatives would later plant wiretaps on the Democrats for purely partisan motives—the president's reelection. The exposure of their illegal activities poisoned the political atmosphere, isolated the president, disgusted and disillusioned the public, and led to Nixon's unprecedented resignation.

By the time the scandal reached the Supreme Court in the case of *U.S. v. Nixon*, Congress was closing in on the president. No reconciliation was possible between the branches. The constitutional issue centered on whether Nixon could use the doctrine of "executive privilege" to withhold taped conversations that would prove his wrongdoing. The president claimed that the judiciary had no right to judge his actions. Questioning the power of judicial review turned the case into an institutional challenge of the Court itself, one demanding a unified response from the nine "politicians" who saw their branch's authority at stake.

CONCEPTS TO CONSIDER _____

1. The constitutional principle of **separation of powers** was evident throughout Watergate. After the president violated the law to undermine legitimate opposition, other branches of government moved to check this expanding executive power. Note that a district judge first exposed the cover-up, Congress began its investigation (after press stories leaked by the executive bureaucracy), and ultimately the Supreme Court entered the dispute. Was it important that this expansion of presidential power occurred in wartime? How was the Constitution's separation of powers reinforced by partisan politics?

2. The Supreme Court has been called a **political institution**, with its own policy preferences and goals. From the partisan nature of their appointments to their consensus ruling supporting their institution and resolving the dispute, the justices acted in the political arena. What aspects of the Watergate case up to and including the final decision illustrate the Court's political role?

3. The case opens a window to the Court's internal **judicial decision making**. Why did this decision unite the Court? From speeding up the case, to the conferences in the opinion writing, to the unanimous decision, the Court anticipated the reaction of the public and the other branches. Did the crisis atmosphere make the Court more sensitive to public opinion?

4. The Court not only resolved a heated conflict between the two elected branches of government, it also made law. This **judicial lawmaking** allowed for a wider interpretation of the president's claim of **executive privilege**. How did this debatable legal precedent allow for a compromise unanimous opinion?

5. **Judicial review** as applied in this case allowed an appointed branch to check an elected branch in the name of the Constitution. Did the president's questioning of judicial review affect the Court? Were the constitutional claims by the president undermined by so blatantly serving to cover up criminal behavior?

A "THIRD-RATE BURGLARY"

In the early morning hours of June 17, 1972, five men were caught breaking into the luxury Watergate building in Washington, DC. They were repairing the listening devices they had placed the month before in the offices of the Democratic National Committee. President Richard Nixon was running for reelection and the "plumbers," as the burglars were called, were illegally spying on the opposition. Two supervisors, overseeing the operation from across the street, were also arrested: E. Howard Hunt, a White House consultant and former CIA agent, and G. Gordon Liddy, employed by the Committee to Re-Elect the President (CREEP). The burglars had White House telephone numbers in their pockets.

The cover-up of White House and CREEP ties to the crime began within hours of the arrests. The problem facing the Nixon White House was that among those involved in the break-in were the president's closest aides, the directors of his campaign, the attorney general, and several high administration officials. Although the president wasn't involved in planning the break-in, he found out about its ties to his reelection within six days of the arrests. The conspiracy he led sought to prevent the exposure of this and other illegal activities. The Nixon gang was responsible for a lengthy list of questionable actions: wiretaps on reporters; the use of tax information by the IRS to target an "Enemies List"; the development of a "Huston Plan" for domestic political spying; and the break-in at a psychiatrist's office to steal embarrassing files on Daniel Ellsberg, who had leaked the *Pentagon Papers* to the *New York Times*. Revealing these crimes would have jailed the president's men and dealt a major blow to his reelection.[1]

The goal of the cover-up was to make it appear that Watergate was limited to the people originally arrested. Documents linking the Oval Office to the crime were destroyed. A cover story was circulated that painted Liddy as a "wild man" who had pulled off Watergate on his own. A stickier problem was that the money used by the plumbers could be traced to the president's election campaign. Presidential aides brought the CIA in to delay the investigation by telling the FBI that tracking the money would endanger one of their undercover operations. Getting the CIA to interfere with the FBI in the name of national security required Nixon's approval. Discussed within a week of the break-in, the president's involvement in this lie, when revealed on tape, would prove key to his downfall.

The cover-up continued through the November 1972 election and beyond. It succeeded in keeping Watergate from harming the president's landslide victory over Democratic Senator George McGovern. Falsehoods to the public were a constant. The president's press secretary called it a "third-rate burglary." At a press conference in August, the president announced that his White House counsel had completed an investigation and that no one in the administration was involved in this "very bizarre incident." (Meanwhile, he privately congratulated White House counsel John Dean on managing a successful cover-up.) On September 15, the seven men arrested were indicted for the break-in. But the U.S. attorneys, taking their cues from the Justice Department, treated the case as minor. No questions were asked as to why the men had committed the crime, on whose orders, and who paid them. The U.S. attorney general called the investigation the most thorough in years, adding that there was absolutely no evidence that others should be charged.[2]

Avoiding exposure led Nixon's conspirators to commit further crimes. Campaign officials perjured themselves in trying to conceal the money going to the burglars. The head of the FBI destroyed material found in Hunt's White House safe. The president's lawyer sat in on FBI interviews of campaign officials and White House staff, and then reported back to his superiors. The burglars were secretly given hush money after their arrests and promised executive clemency if they remained silent. Their silence kept the lid on the scandal and the cover-up through the election and into 1973.[3]

THE COVER-UP UNRAVELS

PRESIDENT: How much money do you need?

DEAN: I would say these people are going to cost, uh, a million dollars over the next, uh, two years.

PRESIDENT: We could get that.

March 21, 1973, meeting from the tapes[4]

The cover-up came apart in 1973 under persistent battering from the judiciary, the Congress, and the press. The pressure—mainly from the other branches of government guarded by the Constitution's separation of powers—turned the conspirators against each other, increased their demands for money and protection, and led to a breakdown in their silence.

While no higher-ups had been named in the trial of the burglars, presiding Judge John Sirica was not convinced that the guilty verdicts reached by the end of January had revealed the whole truth of the crime. Sirica's skepticism was backed by his power (and his reputation—he was known as "Maximum John") to impose sentences of up to sixty years in prison on the convicted plumbers. Press reports added to the climate of suspicion surrounding Watergate. Two young *Washington Post* reporters, Carl Bernstein and Bob Woodward, had been assigned the story at the time of the break-in. Their investigation of the plumbers' links to the White House convinced a wide audience in Washington that this was no ordinary robbery. Woodward and Bernstein kept Watergate on the front page and expanded the coverage to the numerous "dirty tricks" against Democratic candidates. Their stories soon began to include names from Nixon's inner circle.[5]

On February 7, 1973, the Senate voted 77–0 to establish a Select Committee on Presidential Campaign Activities (under North Carolina Democratic senator Sam Ervin) to investigate Watergate and related campaign activities. Worried about their upcoming sentencing, some of the plumbers were raising their demands for more hush money while threatening to reveal other illegal acts done for the White House—blackmail, in short. The Ervin Committee "invited" the president's lawyer, John Dean, to testify. The president, fearing that the scandal would blow wide open, cited "executive privilege" in refusing to allow his counsel or other aides to testify. Realizing that the cover-up was coming apart, Dean warned Nixon that Watergate had become "a cancer growing on the Presidency."[6]

Dean noticed that each of the conspirators around him was hiring a lawyer to "watch his own back." Soon one of the plumbers, facing the possibility of a lengthy jail sentence, wrote Judge Sirica that he was willing to cooperate. Within the White House, the president's closest aides were tightening the defenses around their chief. They were preparing to blame subordinates for the break-in and for keeping the president in the dark about the cover-up. Dean worried that he was being set up as the fall guy. He contacted a lawyer, and by early April he too was cooperating with prosecutors.

THE OTHER BRANCHES CHECK AND BALANCE

> I don't give a shit what happens. I want you all to stonewall it. Let them plead the Fifth Amendment, cover up, or anything else that will save the plan. That's the whole point.
>
> *Richard M. Nixon, March 22, 1973, from the tapes*

As the Ervin Committee began to take public testimony in televised hearings, the president responded that all members of his staff would appear voluntarily before the committee. He appeared to be cleaning house and putting the scandal behind him, dismissing his chief advisors including Attorney General John Mitchell, John Dean, and his two closest aides, H. R. (Bob) Haldeman and John Ehrlichman. Dean soon became a star witness at the committee hearings, accusing the president of involvement in both the break-in and the cover-up. Responding to a Senate resolution, Nixon's new attorney general, Elliot Richardson, appointed a special prosecutor on May 18, 1973, to investigate Watergate. This special prosecutor, Harvard professor Archibald Cox, while technically in the Justice Department, was given virtual independence from the administration. By the end of the month, Nixon publicly admitted a White House cover-up, blamed his dismissed aides, and claimed he had no prior knowledge of Watergate or the effort at concealment.

On July 16, 1973, the scandal took an unexpected turn. A former White House aide, Alexander Butterfield, when asked if there were listening devices in the Oval Office, testified that the president had taped and saved all conversations in his offices. Both Cox and the Ervin Committee immediately requested the tapes. Nixon refused. Asserting executive privilege, he maintained that the Constitution's separation of powers allowed him to withhold such confidential information from the other branches of government. The special prosecutor went into federal court to force the president to turn over nine of the tapes. Cox argued that even a president couldn't interfere with a criminal justice case in a federal court. Nixon's lawyer claimed that the president was the "sole judge of executive privilege" and that the only remedy for presidential abuse was impeachment. The president lost his argument in the district court (under Judge Sirica) and then in the U.S. Court of Appeals.[7]

After a futile attempt to reach a compromise with Cox to turn over the tapes, Nixon fired the special prosecutor on October 20, 1973. This became known as the "Saturday Night Massacre," when both the attorney general and his deputy resigned rather than carry out the president's order, which they considered illegal. Facing a firestorm of national protest, the president retreated. He turned over the tapes to Judge Sirica and appointed a new special prosecutor, Leon Jaworski, who could only be fired with the agreement of the leaders in Congress. The outrage following the Saturday Night Massacre led to voicing what had been unthinkable till then: Nixon should be impeached. (The resignation of Vice President Spiro Agnew on unrelated tax evasion charges in October increased opponents' willingness to see the president replaced by the less controversial new vice president, Gerald Ford.) By February 1974, the House of Representatives asked the Judiciary Committee to begin impeachment hearings. In March, after reviewing the tapes that the president finally released (two of the nine were missing, and the tape recording of the first conversation after the break-in contained a suspicious gap of eighteen minutes), a federal grand jury indicted seven persons and secretly named Richard M. Nixon an unindicted co-conspirator. The grand jury gave its information to the House Judiciary Committee.

Both the Judiciary Committee and the special prosecutor's office requested an additional sixty-four tapes from the president. In April, Jaworski asked Judge Sirica to order Nixon to turn over the tapes. Once again claiming executive privilege, Nixon refused. In late May, Sirica ordered the president to give him the tapes for his examination. The president appealed. On May 24, 1974, Jaworski dramatized the importance of quickly resolving the case by taking an unusual step. He bypassed the U.S. Court of Appeals and asked the Supreme Court to grant *certiorari*—an order to the lower court to send the case to the higher court for review. And so, two years after the ill-fated bugging of Democratic headquarters, the U.S. Supreme Court took the case of *U.S. v. Nixon*.[8]

THE ISSUES BEFORE THE COURT

The political setting involved a president who had undermined his popularity by condoning illegal acts and who many feared was expanding executive power into an "imperial presidency."[9] There were two overlapping legal issues before the Court: separation of powers and its impact on the president's claim of executive privilege.

The president's lawyer argued that judicial review did not apply, questioning whether the Court had the authority to judge the president's actions in this dispute. He based his case on a strict interpretation of the constitutional doctrine of separation of powers. Separation of powers meant a claim to "absolute executive privilege against inquiry by the coordinate Judicial Branch." This interpretation made the president's conversations with White House aides confidential, and only he could decide whether tapes of them should be released. Nixon's clash with the special prosecutor was a dispute *within* the executive branch between the president and a subordinate, which the chief executive had the sole authority to resolve. The president's lawyer suggested that the Court's decision would be advisory, not binding. In short, the Supreme Court could not use judicial review to reverse the president's actions. This challenge to the Court's institutional power would ultimately motivate a unified response from the justices.[10]

For the special prosecutor, the president's claim to executive privilege had no constitutional basis. Even if there was a privilege for executives to withhold information, the idea that the president had nonreviewable power to determine what information would be released had never been established. The federal courts retained the power to review presidential actions involving the special prosecutor. The separation of powers had never been an absolute bar against judicial review, *unless* the courts themselves decided that an issue was outside their jurisdiction. To remove any president from judicial authority was troubling. In his oral argument, Jaworski got to the heart of the matter:

> Now enmeshed in almost 500 pages of briefs, when boiled down, this case really presents one fundamental issue. Who is to be the arbiter of what the Constitution says? . . . In his public statements, as we all know, the President has embraced the Constitution as offering him support for his refusal to supply the subpoenaed tapes. Now the President may be right in how he reads the Constitution, but he may also be wrong. And if he is wrong, who is there to tell him so? And if there is no one, then the President, of course, is free to pursue his course of erroneous interpretations. What then becomes of our constitutional form of government?[11]

Jaworski shaped his argument as if a person named Richard Nixon had important evidence that was needed for a criminal case. He made the stunning point that the president was only using executive privilege in this case to conceal a criminal conspiracy, not the legitimate business of his office. But the prosecutor still had to contend with the president's absolutist claim that the right of executive privilege, protected by the separation of powers, prevented any interference by the courts in the president's refusal to turn over the tapes. These tapes would, the president argued, eventually be made available for impeachment proceedings, thus drawing the Court into a political dispute between the two branches. The Court had to determine whether they could judge this case, whether the president had a right of executive privilege, and whether that right extended to protecting the confidentiality of his conversations. These legal issues, while important, were secondary to the extraordinary political crisis surrounding the case.

THE BURGER COURT WAITS FOR THE CASE

A hard-to-miss aspect of *U.S. v. Nixon* was that one of the parties had appointed four of the nine justices to the Supreme Court. President Nixon had not only elevated Warren Burger to be chief justice, he also appointed Harry A. Blackmun, who like Burger was from Minneapolis (and remained so close to his friend that they were labeled the "Minnesota Twins"); Lewis F. Powell, a prominent lawyer from Virginia; and William H. Rehnquist, the Burger Court's most conservative jurist and later to be chief justice. These appointments were made with an eye to undermining the liberal decisions of the influential reign of Earl Warren, chief justice from 1953 to 1969. In the end, the Burger Court (1969–1986) disappointed many of its conservative backers, leading one scholar to conclude, "No important Warren Court decision was overturned by the Burger Court."[12]

Part of the reason for the lack of a clear direction from the Court was the holdovers that remained on the bench from the Warren Court. Three of them made up the liberal bloc—Justice William Brennan, who was the chief justice's main adversary; William O. Douglas, a maverick and the Court's senior member; and Justice Thurgood Marshall, the first African American justice. The two remaining justices, Potter Stewart and Byron White, were more conservative, but their independent judicial philosophies made them difficult votes to count on. Also questionable was Burger's leadership. Nixon appointed him for his strong law-and-order positions and, perhaps, because he looked like a Hollywood version of a chief justice with snow-white hair and impressive shoulders. He had been active in the Republican party and served on the court of appeals in Washington, DC. On the bench, he could be aloof and pedantic, focusing on minor details rather than the critical issues at stake. A number of the justices simply didn't respect Burger's intellectual grasp of the law.

This interplay among the justices would be an important ingredient in the case they now faced. *U.S. v. Nixon* was to be, as much as any case in history, a negotiated institutional decision to resolve a major constitutional crisis. It was to be unanimous not because of any shared views of the law among the justices, or even much agreement among themselves on the decision they signed. This exceptional decision was reached as a collective compromise because the justices felt that the stakes of the case, for the government and the Court, were too high to allow dissent. They spoke in one voice because their institution was being challenged. Their decision represented "the rule-of-law defended against attack."[13]

THE LAW AND POLITICS OF A UNANIMOUS DECISION

The first issue for the Court was whether to accept the case. When President Nixon refused to deliver the tapes to Judge Sirica in the district court, Jaworski bypassed the Court of Appeals and went directly to the Supreme Court. While he argued that the case should be expedited because of the important constitutional issues at stake, the understood reason was that Watergate had already paralyzed the government for months. In addition, the impeachment proceedings were starting and to wait for as much as the expected year it would take for the Court to resolve the tapes issue was unthinkable. On May 31, 1974, the Court approved this rare procedure and announced it would hear the case. Justice Rehnquist disqualified himself, because he had served in Nixon's Justice Department with several of the defendants who were now on trial.

In discussing the case in conference, the justices quickly agreed on the major points. They concurred that the Court had jurisdiction and that the case should be decided as soon as possible. They further agreed that Nixon's claim of an absolute executive privilege could not stand, but they disagreed on how much deference they owed to this executive claim. These differences among the justices would be reconciled during the writing of the opinion. Justice Brennan suggested a joint decision, written by all the justices. This unusual option was quickly turned down by the other justices, and Burger asserted the traditional right of the chief justice to write the opinion when he was in the majority. What resulted, however, in the weeks after the conference was an unusually collective drafting process, where the weakness of the Court's leadership and its divisions melded together in a rare show of support for their institution. The importance of a public show of unanimity by the Court spurred cooperation among the justices.[14]

Burger's first draft caused unhappiness on the bench. Potter Stewart told his clerks that the chief's paper would have gotten a grade of D in law school and was raised to a B by the efforts of the other justices.[15] The result was what Justice Blackmun called "a palace revolution," with justices taking over different sections of the opinion.[16] Blackmun worked on the statement of facts; the issue of the Court's jurisdiction reflected Douglas's writing; and Powell, Stewart, and Brennan all had a hand in the final section on the president's claims to executive privilege. The irony of having the chief justice accept their revisions and deliver the Court's ruling against the president who had appointed him did not go unnoticed among the justices. The back and forth of various drafts and Burger's accommodations to the other justices' objections made the final opinion something less than a legal masterpiece.

Executive privilege produced the most vigorous conflict. Although all the justices agreed that Nixon's absolute claim couldn't stand, the questions of whether the Constitution allowed executive privilege at all and how far it went provoked disagreement. In his early draft, Burger had recognized this right when the president was conducting what the chief justice called "core functions," such as war powers. He added that in the *Nixon* case this did not apply because the president's claim did not relate to an essential function. Several justices thought that introducing language about core functions implied that the president did have an absolute constitutional authority (which implied no judicial review) over some of his duties, and invited "future chaos." These justices, led by Stewart, wanted a clear assertion of judicial review, worried that Burger was too deferential to presidential power and that this language could give the president wiggle room for not obeying a decision in the present case. Burger eventually dropped his core functions language.

The final decision delivered by the Court did find a constitutional basis for executive privilege. For the president to effectively exercise his powers, the Court found that his claim of executive privilege was "rooted in the separation of powers under the Constitution." However, in the present case there was little to back up the president's claim, and when weighed against the prosecutor's need for the information in a pending criminal trial, it wouldn't stand. So in the process of rejecting a specific claim to executive privilege and demanding that the president turn over the tapes, the Court did establish a general constitutional right that a president's communications should be treated as confidential. The Court established this right for the first time with little backing from the historical record.[17]

CONCLUSION

The dramatic July 24 announcement forcing the president to deliver the tapes came just hours before the House Judiciary Committee began its televised debate on articles of impeachment. It was a devastating moment for the president. Nixon had counted on there being some allowance in the decision for national security matters. He had also thought that there would be at least one dissenting justice. He had hoped there would be some "air" in the Court's ruling. He was told by his chief of staff that the decision was unanimous, with no air in it at all.

"None at all?" Nixon asked.
"It's tight as a drum."[18]

Nixon decided he had no choice but to comply. The wrenching public confrontation between the president and the other branches of government was near an end. Seventeen days later, clearly implicated in the Watergate cover-up by the tapes and facing almost certain impeachment, Nixon became the first president in history to resign.

Columbia law professor Alan F. Westin wrote that *U.S. v. Nixon* was "one of the most predictable rulings in the history of American constitutional law. The political situation was not only hospitable to a ruling against the president but almost irresistibly pressing for it."[19] The Court resolved the government impasse. It restrained a president who was far out of line

President Nixon, the only president to resign his office, delivers his farewell speech to the White House staff on August 9, 1974, surrounded by equally unhappy members of his family.

with the traditions and practices of his office—and who had acted illegally. The justices supported his removal. They accepted their role of guarding the system of government and fulfilled their duty to end the Watergate crisis.

At the same time, the Court showed its more traditional deference to presidential authority. The price of the Court's unanimous agreement was to confirm a broad constitutional right of executive privilege. Although not approving of the president's assertion that he alone could determine the application of executive privilege, insulated from judicial review, the Court did defer to a vaguely defined privilege, which many considered a strengthening of the presidency. As of now, the judicial precedent has not been widely applied nor has it led to other crises over executive power. But this executive privilege was now on the books.

Whatever legal scholars may say, the process of reaching a unanimous decision that resolved *U.S. v. Nixon* and the constitutional crisis it represented underlined that the Supreme Court contained justices with both judicial expertise and political savvy.

Notes

1. U.S. Congress Senate. *Select Committee on Presidential Campaign Activities,* Vol. I (Washington, DC: A Dell Book, 1974).
2. Frank Mankiewicz, *U.S. v. Richard M. Nixon* (New York: Quadrangle, 1975), 13.

3. See Douglas Muzzio, *Watergate Games* (New York: New York University Press, 1982), 15.
4. C-SPAN has excerpts from the Nixon tapes online at www.c-span.org/executive/presidential/nixon.asp.
5. Bob Woodward and Carl Bernstein, *All the President's Men* (New York: Warner Books, 1975).
6. *Select Committee on Presidential Campaign Activities,* 1974, xiii. This is the Ervin Committee's detailed account of the cover-up and related illegal activities by the Nixon White House.
7. A good account of the legal processes can be found in Howard Ball, *"We Have a Duty": The Supreme Court and the Watergate Tapes Litigation* (New York: Greenwood Press, 1990).
8. See Ball, Chapter 2, "The Watergate Scandal Unfolds," 21–38.
9. See Arthur M. Schlesinger Jr., *The Imperial Presidency* (New York: Popular Library, 1973).
10. See Raoul Berger, *Executive Privilege: A Constitutional Myth* (New York: New American Library, 1974), 254–255. Also see Bob Woodward and Scott Armstrong, *The Brethren: Inside the Supreme Court* (New York: Avon Books, 1979), 363.
11. Alan Westin and Leon Friedman, *United States v. Nixon* (New York: Chelsea House Publishers, 1974), 528–529.
12. Bernard Schwartz, *A History of the Supreme Court* (New York: Oxford University Press, 1993), 314.
13. Westin and Friedman, xvi.
14. David M. O'Brien, *Storm Center: The Supreme Court in American Politics,* 3rd ed. (New York: W. W. Norton, 1993), 280–285.
15. Ball, 136.
16. *Washington Post,* March 5, 2004, A12. Excerpts from Blackmun's posthumously published papers.
17. Ball, 144–146.
18. From Woodward and Armstrong, 412. The most complete coverage of the internal discussions in the Court on *U.S. v. Nixon* can be found here, 337–412.
19. As quoted by Ball, 150.

INDEX